Physics 3U
WorkBook

D0904586

Contents

Introduction to Physics 30

We all are involved in physics and have been since we were born. The story of physics not only includes our personal experiences but also our history as shown in the development of ideas and inventions. To better understand our place in our world, history, and future an understanding physics is critical.

Physics is more than just solving problems; it is more than just getting a calculated answer. It involves a logical approach to challenges and a careful examination of the world around us. The language of mathematics is necessary to fully communicate an understanding of physics.

There are hundreds of practice questions in this book. It's important to do as many as possible. The general format within each chapter will be as follows:

> Introduction
> Summary notes
> Problems
> Extensions
> Review
> Review Assignments

- Equations in boxes are found on the data sheet in located in Appendix B at the back of the workbook.
- Access to the Physics 30 Webpage will be useful for some problems. This will be indicated by the QR code shown to the right: You may access the link directly using your smartphone and a QR reader. Just open up the app and aim your smartphone's camera at the pattern and you will be automatically taken to the Physics 30 web page.
- A stopwatch will be needed for the analysis of some videos. Many mp3 players and cellphones include stopwatch programs.

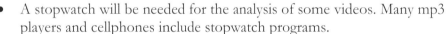

www.kophysics.com/Physics30WE

Abbreviations used in this resource include the following.

c.	circa - approximately	vs.	versus
e.g.	exempli gratia - for example	a.k.a.	also known as
i.e.	id est - that is (a restatement)	∴	Therefore
N.B.	nota bene - note well (important)	~	Approximately. There is uncertainty in every measurement taken. This symbol is a reminder, for certain questions, that no measured quantity is perfect. Your answer may differ slightly but should be approximately the stated value.
a	Unit for annum – year		

N.B., i.e., and e.g. are not the same. Don't use i.e., when you are giving an example.

The following QR Code means that extra help for that question may be found on the Physics 30 website. Simply use your smartphone and a QR reader.

www.kophysics.com/Physics30WB

4.5a

Studying Physics

Solving physics problems requires practice. Here are a few suggestions to help you get the most out of your physics course and this *Physics 30 Workbook*.

Problem solving

When solving problems, draw diagrams and <u>show all work</u> to demonstrate your thought process. Showing work may involve:

- underlining key words.
- writing a list of the given numbers and what is required.
- identifying appropriate formula.

Organizing the problem in a logical fashion is important to better communicate an understanding of the solution.

When solving problems in physics, use the following steps:

i.	List the given and required information
ii.	Write down the formula(e)
iii.	Isolate the desired variable
iv.	Substitute the variables with numbers including the units
v.	Solve for the answer
vi.	Write the answer in a sentence (including significant digits and appropriate units)

Help

Ask questions as needed. When asking about a question always <u>bring some work</u> to show your instructor what you've tried.

Homework

Complete all the questions assigned by your instructor. If a homework question is taking more than 15 minutes, leave it alone and go back to it later. If it is still problematic, ask your teacher, peer or tutor for help.

Reviewing

Reviewing problems you've already done (homework or class examples) is valuable for long term memory of a concept. This should not be just a matter of looking at the work; cover the solution with a blank piece of paper and <u>redo the entire solution</u>. A quick look at your original solution is always available if needed.

Interested in a Student Solution Manual? Check the link below for more information.

www.kophysics.com/Physics30WB

Solutions Manual for

Physics 30 Workbook

Including helpful hints for problem solving

1 Introduction

Introduction

Physics relies on measurement and the mathematical treatment of the measurements. This chapter reviews concepts from Physics 20 that are important for success in Physics 30.

1.1 Summary Notes — Measurement

Most measurements in Physics can be made in terms of the following fundamental quantities:

Dimension	Fundamental (base) unit	Symbol
length	metre	m
mass	kilogram	kg
time	second	s

Units that are made up of more than one fundamental unit are called derived units (e.g., N or J).

Every measurement has some uncertainty. It is impossible to have a perfect measurement. The quality of a measurement must be communicated. This can be done using the idea of significant digits.

Significant Digit Rules

	Rule	Example
i.	All counting numbers are exact.	1 chair or 25 people
ii.	All measured quantities have some degree of uncertainty.	1.26 cm – 6 is estimated
iii.	All non-zero digits are significant.	234 m – three sig. digs.
iv.	All zeros between non-zero digits are significant.	1.002 m – four sig. digs.
v.	All trailing zeros are significant.	3.000 mm – four sig. digs.
vi.	Leading zeros (in numbers less than 1) are not significant.	0.000 35 kg – two sig. digs.

Accuracy

There are many ways of comparing two values. One way, commonly used in physics, is the % difference calculation. This calculation can identify how far off a measured value is from an "accepted" value.

$$\% \text{ difference} = \left| \frac{\text{accepted value} - \text{measured value}}{\text{accepted value}} \right| \times 100 \%$$

Examples

1. State the number of significant digits in each of the following:

    a. 8 people   NA   40 000 m   5
    b. 0.00433 s   3   0.003 040 h   4

2. Convert 20 km/h to m/s using unit analysis.

    $$v = \frac{20 \text{ km}}{h} \times \frac{1000 \text{ m}}{1 \text{ km}} \times \frac{1 h}{3600 s} = 5.\bar{5} \text{ m/s}$$

    The conversion is 5.6 m/s.

Problems

1. Ruler A is a centimetre ruler and ruler B is a millimetre ruler. Use rulers A and B to determine the length of the rectangle to the correct precision. A tolerance of ± half the smallest scale division is allowed on analogue devices. Place your answers in the blanks provided. After the measurement state the number of significant digits. [Appendix A]

    A   centimetre ruler

    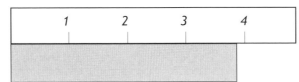

    _____ cm

    _____ sig. digs.

    B   millimetre ruler

    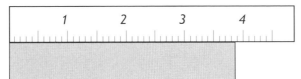

    _____ cm

    _____ sig. digs.

2. State the number of significant digits in each of the following: [Appendix A]

    a. 200 000 m   c. 0.030 060 h
    b. 0.00403 s   d. 12 chairs

3. Round each of the following measurements to 3 digits. [Appendix A]

a. 0.004 095 0 d _____   e. 18 521 000 km _____

b. 7.245 001 cm _____   f. 84 300.2 cm^2 _____

c. 5.0045 g _____   g. 0.000 408 50 g _____

d. 86 520 km _____   h. 2.9979 x 10^8 m/s _____

4. Complete the following chart. [Appendix A]

	Scientific Notation	Standard Notation
a.		4 900 000 000 000 mm
b.	2.34 x 10^7 L	
c.	3.56 x 10^{-5} cm	
d.		0.000 000 95 m

5. Convert the given measurements to the indicated units. [Appendix A]

a.	430 cm	m
b.	1.40 m	cm
c.	800 mm	m
d.	4.100 kg	g
e.	76 g	kg

f.	0.335 kg	g
g.	0.650 L	mL
h.	55.0 mL	L
i.	2.00 minutes	s
j.	0.557 s	ms

6. Perform the following operations using your calculator and round to the appropriate number of significant digits. [Answers in Appendix A]

a. (2.3 x 10^4) (5.6 x 10^{-6}) _____

b. $\dfrac{2.9 \times 10^{-6}}{4.7 \times 10^{-3}}$ _____

Intro 1.1.1

7. Carry out the following conversions using the factor-label (i.e., unit analysis) method.
   a. Convert 2.0 years to seconds. (The metric symbol for year is "a".) [6.3 x 10^7 s]

   b. Convert 85 km/h to m/s. [24 m/s]

1.2 Summary Notes — Graphical Analysis

Graphing experimental data uses different rules than the graphs you have drawn in math classes.

Intro 1.2.1

Graphs are powerful for presenting information and analyzing data. Typically the slope of a graph or the graph's intercepts is used as a type of average. There are many different types of averages (e.g., mean, mode, median, weighted averages). One method of obtaining a weighted average uses graphical analysis. The average obtained using graphical analysis should be better than the arithmetic average for a couple of reasons:

- All measurements contain some random error (it's impossible to have a perfect measurement). Some numbers will be lower than they really should be and others will be higher. Drawing a best fit line accounts for this and reduces the effect.

- Consistent errors can be reduced. If a measurement is consistently off, the graph will correct the problem - never force a best fit line to go through zero even though it theoretically should.

Graphical analysis includes

> i. Finding an appropriate formula that contains your manipulated and responding variables.
> ii. Relating your equation to that of a straight line in the form: $y = mx + b$ using the following steps:
>
> - Isolate the responding variable
> - Set the manipulated variable outside a set of brackets.
> - Everything left in the brackets comprises the slope of the line.
> - The y-intercept is represented by the term added or subtracted from the manipulated.

Curve Straightening

It is often useful to change a curved graph into a linear one. A linear graph may supply information that is not as apparent in a non-linear graph. We shall now explore techniques for changing a non-linear graph into a linear graph.

You must **memorize** the following general equations, their relationships, and corresponding graph shape.

Line shape	Equation	Relationship	Graph
linear	$y = mx + b$	directly proportional	
parabolic (around the y-axis)	$y = x^2$	proportional to the square	
parabolic (around the x-axis)	$y = \sqrt{x}$	proportional to the square root	
hyperbolic	$y = \dfrac{1}{x}$ or $y = \dfrac{1}{x^2}$	inversely proportional	

Procedure for making a curved line straight:

- Isolate the responding variable.
- Recognize what is happening to the manipulated variable (e.g., is it squared or inversed)
- Modify (square it or inverse it) the manipulated variable and place the modified numbers in a new column.
- The modified variables are then re-plotted to give the linear graph.

Example

1. A pendulum is allowed to swing and the period of its swing is determined. The length of the pendulum is then manipulated and its period is again determined. The length is manipulated 8 times and the period changes each time.
   a. Identify the equation that relates the length of a pendulum to the period of its swing.
   b. Sketch the shape of the graph obtained if the period of the pendulum's swing was graphed as a function of its length.
   c. Identify what must be plotted on the y-axis and the x-axis in order to obtain a straight line.
   d. Show how the slope of the line is to be used to determine the acceleration due to gravity.

a) $T = 2\pi\sqrt{\dfrac{\ell}{g}}$

b)

c)

$\text{Slope} = \dfrac{2\pi}{\sqrt{g}}$

$\therefore g = \left[\dfrac{2\pi}{\text{Slope}}\right]^2$

or

$\text{Slope} = \dfrac{4\pi^2}{g}$

$g = \dfrac{4\pi^2}{\text{Slope}}$

Problems

1. For each of the equations below x is the manipulated variable and y is the responding variable. Place each in slope-intercept form by isolating the responding variable. Complete the chart by identifying the slope and the y-intercept. The first one is done as an example.

	Equation	Slope-intercept form	Slope	y-intercept
a.	$H = 2y + x$	$y = \dfrac{-1}{2}x + \dfrac{H}{2}$	$\dfrac{-1}{2}$	$\dfrac{H}{2}$
b.	$y = 5 + knx$			
c.	$x = 2ay$			
d.	$A = 2By + 4B^2x$			

2. A spring is secured to the ceiling and different weights are suspended by it. The amount each weight stretches the spring is measured and recorded.

Weight of Suspended Object (N)	Total extension (m)	Constant (N/m)
4.80	0.079	
12.00	0.141	
18.00	0.209	
24.20	0.238	
26.00	0.294	

a. Use Hooke's Law (F = kx) to calculate the spring constant (k) for each trial. Place the answers in the last column.

b. Determine the average (mean) for the spring constant from the data in the last column. [84 N/m]

c. Plot the data.

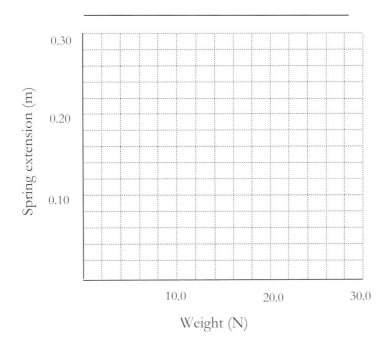

d. Use the graph to determine the spring constant. [~100 N/m]
e. Discuss why the spring constant obtained from the graph should be better than the arithmetic mean. [Appendix A]

3. Use your formula sheet to identify examples of the different types of relationships. State their manipulated and responding variables.

Relationship	Example	Manipulated variable	Responding variable	Graph
Squared $y = x^2$				
Square root $y = \sqrt{x}$				
Inverse $y = \dfrac{1}{x}$				
Inverse square $y = \dfrac{1}{x^2}$				

4. You are given the task to investigate the relationship between x and y in the formula $y = x^2$.
   a. Complete the chart to the right.

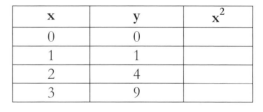

x	y	x^2
0	0	
1	1	
2	4	
3	9	

   b. Use the data below to construct the graph of

   i. <u>y as a function of x</u>

   ii. <u>y as a function of x^2</u>

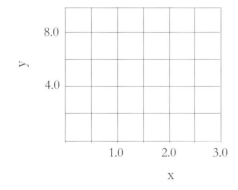

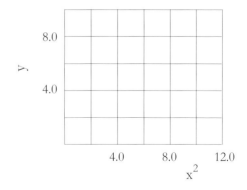

   c. Identify the shape of each graph. [Appendix A]

   d. Determine the slope of the y as a function of x^2 graph. [1]

5. Complete the chart below (refer to curves on page 5).

	Formula	Curve	Linear	Slope	y-intercept
a.	$a = \dfrac{1}{b}$	a vs b			
b.	$m = \dfrac{PW}{n^2} + L$	m vs n			
c.	$H = 50DB^2$	H vs B			
d.	$E_k = \dfrac{1}{2}mv^2$	E_k vs v			
e.	$T = 2\pi\sqrt{\dfrac{m}{k}}$	T vs m			

The volume (V) of a gas will change as a function of the pressure (P) exerted on it as described by the Ideal Gas Law:

$$V = \frac{nRT}{P}$$

6. In an experiment to determine the value of the constant R, the pressure (P) of a gas is varied at constant temperature (T) and the volume (V) changes. The following data is collected.

   n = 1.00 mol   T = 300 K

Pressure (kPa)	Volume (L)	
124	20.1	
139	17.9	
156	16.0	
176	14.2	
209	11.9	

   a. Plot the variables that would give you a straight line.

   b. Determine the slope of the line. [~2.6 x 10^3 L•kPa]
   c. Use the graph to determine the value of the constant R. [~8.6 L•kPa/mol•K]

1.3 Summary Notes — Kinematics

Kinematics is the mathematical study of motion. Motion requires the use of vector quantities.

- Vectors have both magnitude and direction.
- Scalars only have magnitude.
- Direction may be defined as + or −.

Position is the distance and direction away from a reference point.

Displacement is a vector that describes an object's change in position.

Velocity is a vector that describes an object's change in position during time.

$$\vec{v}_{ave} = \frac{\Delta \vec{d}}{\Delta t} = \frac{\vec{d}}{t}$$

Where:

$\vec{v}_{ave}$ is average velocity (m/s)

$\vec{d}$ is displacement (m)

t is measured time interval (s)

Uniform motion is when the velocity of an object remains constant.

Non-uniform motion is when the velocity of an object is not constant (changes).

Instantaneous velocity is the velocity of an object at a point in time during its motion (uniform or non-uniform).

Acceleration is a vector that describes an object's change in velocity over time. Uniform accelerated motion can be determined using:

$$\vec{a} = \frac{\Delta \vec{v}}{\Delta t} = \frac{\vec{v}_f - \vec{v}_i}{t}$$

$$\vec{d} = \left(\frac{\vec{v}_f + \vec{v}_i}{2} \right) t$$

$$\vec{d} = \vec{v}_i t + \tfrac{1}{2} \vec{a} t^2$$

$$\vec{v}_f^2 = \vec{v}_i^2 + 2\vec{a}\vec{d}$$

Where:

$\vec{a}$ is acceleration (m/s^2)

$\vec{v}_f$ is final (second) velocity (m/s)

$\vec{v}_i$ is initial (first) velocity (m/s)

Δt is change in time (the time it takes to change velocity) (s)

$\vec{v}_{ave}$ is average velocity (m/s)

$\vec{d}$ is displacement (m)

Examples

1. The first controlled, powered airplane flight was by Orville Wright on December 17, 1903 in Kittyhawk North Carolina. Their airplane, called the Flyer, was airborne for 12 s and travelled a distance of 37 m. Calculate the Flyer's average speed.

    $t = 12 s$ $\quad\quad v = \dfrac{d}{t}$

    $d = 37 m$

    $v = ?$ $\quad\quad v = \dfrac{37 m}{12 s}$

    $\quad\quad\quad\quad\quad v = 3.08\overline{3} m/s$

    The Flyer's average speed was 3.1 m/s.

2. A ball is dropped and hits the floor at a speed of 4.1 m/s. The ball compresses and then reforms to spring upwards from the floor at 3.8 m/s. The time from the ball's first contact to when it left contact with the floor was 0.11 s. Determine the ball's acceleration while it is in contact with the floor.

    $v_i = 4.1 m/s$ $\quad v_f = 3.8 m/s$ $\quad\quad a = \dfrac{v_f - v_i}{t}$

    contact $\quad\quad$ bounce $\quad a = ?$ $\quad\quad a = \dfrac{3.8 m/s - (-4.1 m/s)}{0.11 s}$

    $t = 0.11 s$ $\quad\quad\quad\quad\quad\quad\quad a = 71.8\overline{1} m/s^2$

    The magnitude of the ball's bounce was 72 m/s^2, upwards.

Problems

1. The Burji Khalifa in Dubai became the tallest building in the world, 828 m, on 4 January 2010. Calculate the speed of its elevators if they can rise 387 m without stopping in a time of 22.4 s. [17.3 m/s]

2. The first airplane flight from Calgary to Edmonton, a distance of 302 km, was by Katherine Stinson on July 9, 1919 flying at a an average speed of 144 km/h to make Canada's first airmail delivery. Determine how long her flight took to the nearest hour. [2 h]

3.   Sketch the graph shape of a displacement as a function of time graph and a velocity as a function of time graph for an object moving uniformly. [Appendix A]

4.   Two objects are in motion as shown below. Identify the object that is slowing down as indicated by its velocity (v) and acceleration (a) vectors. [Appendix A]

5.   A race car travelling north accelerates uniformly from 40.0 m/s to 85.0 m/s over a 3.0 s time period. Calculate the car's acceleration. [15 m/s², north]

6.   A ball is dropped from a bridge and takes 4.0 s to reach the water directly below. Calculate the elevation of the bridge above the water in metres (neglect air resistance). [78 m]

7.   A ball is travelling at 9.0 m/s to the north when it collides with a window. Determine the ball's change in velocity if it
     a.   breaks the window and continues to travel to the north at 4.0 m/s. [5.0 m/s, south]
     b.   bounces off the window and travels south at 4.0 m/s. [13.0 m/s, south]

1.4 Summary Notes — Dynamics

Dynamics is the study of forces.

A **force** may be defined as a push or a pull.

Forces are vector quantities; therefore direction is an important part of any force.

A force can change the velocity of a mass.

While forces can appear in a variety of forms, they can all be classified as one of four fundamental types:

- gravitational
- electromagnetic
- weak nuclear
- strong nuclear

Newton summarized his studies on forces into three laws.

Newton's First Law of Motion

An object continues in a state of rest, or uniform motion in a straight line, unless acted upon by an unbalanced force.

This first law is often called the law of **inertia**. Inertia is the resistance to change in the motion of an object.

When a force is exerted in the same direction an object is moving, the object **speeds up**.

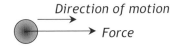

When a force is exerted in an opposite direction to which an object is moving, the object **slows down**.

Newton's Second Law of Motion

An unbalanced force causes an object to accelerate.

$$\vec{a} = \frac{\vec{F}_{Net}}{m}$$

Where:

$\vec{F}_{Net}$ is the net force in newtons (N)

$\vec{a}$ is acceleration (m/s^2)

m is mass (kg)

How to draw free-body diagrams

Free-body diagrams are necessary to communicate forces acting on an object.

> - Draw the object (or a simple shape representing the object) without any surrounding objects.
> - Use arrows to represent forces acting on the object. Label them.
> - The length of an arrow represents the relative magnitude of the force.
> - Do not draw a net force or acceleration arrow on the object.

Newton's Third Law of Motion

For every action (force) there is an equal and opposite reaction (force).

Forces always occur in pairs.

Mass & Weight

The terms mass and weight are often interchangeable in common usage but have more precise meanings in physics.

Mass may be defined as either the:
- amount of matter in an object.
- measure of inertia possessed by the object.

Weight may be defined as:
- the force due to gravity acting on an object.
- how much you feel you weigh, or how much you feel gravity pulling on you. This may be called apparent weight.

Gravitational field strength is the gravitational force exerted on each kilogram of mass.

Examples

1. Bullets start with a speed of zero and obtain a maximum speed of 745 m/s as they travel through a rifle barrel that is 1.1 m long. Determine the magnitude of the average force acting on an 11.3 g bullet in the rifle's barrel.

$m = 11.3 \times 10^{-3} kg$

$v_i = 0$

$v_f = 745 m/s$

$d = 1.1 m$

$F = ?$

$v_f^2 = \overset{0}{v_i^2} + 2ad$

$a = \dfrac{v_f^2}{2d}$

$a = \dfrac{(745 m/s)^2}{(2 \cdot 1.1 m)}$

$a = 252284.1 m/s^2$

$a = \dfrac{F_{net}}{m}$

$F_{net} = ma$

$\quad = 1.13 \times 10^{-2} kg \times 2.52 \times 10^{5} m/s^2$

$F_{net} = 2850.8 N$

The magnitude of the average force is 2.9 x 10³ N.

2. A horizontal 100 N force is applied to a 10.0 kg object on a level surface. The force of friction between the object and the surface is 20.0 N. Determine the magnitude of the object's acceleration.

$F_{app} = 100N$

$m = 10kg$

$F_f = 20N$

$a = ?$

$F_{app} > F_f$

$F_{net} = F_{app} - F_f$

$F_{net} = 100N - 20N$

$F_{net} = 80N$

$F_{net} = ma$

$a = \frac{F_{net}}{m}$

$= \frac{80N}{10kg}$

$a = 8.0 m/s^2$

The magnitude of the object's acceleration is 8.0 m/s².

Problems

1. Determine the net force acting upon a 1000 kg rocket accelerating at 5.0 m/s² directly upwards. [5.0 kN, upwards]

2. A ball started from rest and acquired a speed of 12 m/s when a force is applied for a distance of 50 cm. If the ball has a mass of 1.0 kg, determine the magnitude of the force applied. [0.14 kN] (See example #1 page 15)

3. Free-body diagrams (FBD) are necessary to communicate an understanding of the forces acting on an object and are a typical first step for solving force questions. A free-body diagram identifies the forces acting on an object, shows their direction, and indicates their relative magnitudes. Complete the free-body diagrams below: [Appendix A]

Force due to gravity F_g
Force of friction F_f

Normal force F_N
Applied force F_{app}

a. A block is stationary on a horizontal surface.	b. A block is being pulled at a constant velocity to the right against a force due to friction.
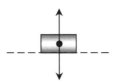	

4. A block of wood on a horizontal surface may have two horizontal forces, F_1 and F_2, acting on it. Either force may pull to the left or right. (The normal force and force due to gravity are equal and opposite and may be ignored for this exercise.)

Complete the chart below by providing the missing force values, direction (left or right), and use vector arrows to draw the two forces, F_1 and F_2 on the diagram. [Appendix A]

Description of motion	Net force (N)	F_1 (N)	F_2 (N)	Diagram
a. Stationary		10 left		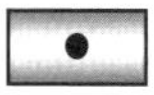
b. Moving to the right at a constant velocity		5 left		
c. Accelerating to the left	25 left		10 left	
d. Accelerating to the left		25 _____	20 right	

5. A certain sled has a weight of 52 N. A horizontal force of 18 N is required to pull the sled across a level cement sidewalk at constant speed. Determine the coefficient of friction between the sidewalk and the metal runners of the sled. [0.35]

6. A sled having a weight of 702 N is placed on packed snow. Determine the magnitude of the force necessary to slide the sled across the level snow at a constant speed. The coefficient of friction is 0.012 for the sled runners on packed snow. [8.4 N]

7   Use a ruler to draw a free-body diagram for each of the following situations. Use T for the
     tension force in the elevator cable and F_g for the force due to gravity. [Appendix A]

a. An elevator is stationary at the third floor of a high-rise.	b. An elevator passes the fourth floor at a constant velocity.
c. An elevator accelerates downwards from rest.	d. An elevator accelerates upwards from rest.

8.   A 60.0 kg man is standing on a scale calibrated in newtons inside an elevator. Determine the
     apparent weight of the man as shown by the scale as the elevator is accelerating
     a. upwards at 1.30 m/s². [667 N]
     b. downwards at a rate of 2.10 m/s². [463 N]

1.5 Summary Notes — 2D Vectors

An angle given in degrees must include a reference. While there are many ways of referencing a direction on a surface, in this book the following will be used:

Cardinal (Cartesian) References

Cardinal points are the four main points of the compass: north, south, east, and west.

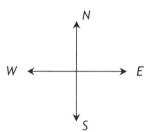

The vector may be referenced to one of the nearest axis for a cardinal reference.

Due east, north, etc. means directly east, north, etc.

Bearing (Navigators) Reference

This is the system used for all navigation on or near the Earth's surface; by airplanes or by orienteers, and many others. In the bearing system the reference is north (0°). From north, move clockwise.

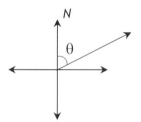

An angle reference may be stated in different ways. For example, the following three directions are equivalent:

bearing 120°   30° S of E   E30°S

These three statements all mean the same thing and are commonly used directional references when working with a map.

- The solution to vector addition may involve calculations or drawing a scale diagram.
- Adding vectors requires that they be lined up tail to tip.

Vector Components

It is possible to regard a single vector as the resultant of two vectors: one acting horizontal (x) and the other vertical (y). Vector resolution is the process of determining these two components.

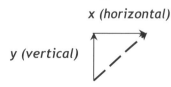

x (horizontal)

y (vertical)

Examples

1. John walks 40.0 m east then 100.0 m south. Determine his
    a. distance travelled.
    b. displacement relative to his starting point.

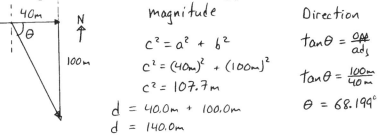

magnitude

$$c^2 = a^2 + b^2$$
$$c^2 = (40m)^2 + (100m)^2$$
$$c^2 = 107.7m$$
$$d = 40.0m + 100.0m$$
$$d = 140.0m$$

Direction

$$\tan\theta = \frac{opp}{adj}$$
$$\tan\theta = \frac{100m}{40m}$$
$$\theta = 68.199°$$

a. John travelled a distance of 140.0 m.
b. John's displacement relative to his starting point is 108 m, 68.2° S of E.

2. A cyclist leaves her home and rides 3.0 km due south. She then turns on a bearing of 110° and rides 5.50 km. From this location she heads 40° E of N for 2.9 km, and turns once more and rides for 4.5 km on a heading of 20° N of E. Determine the biker's displacement relative to her home.

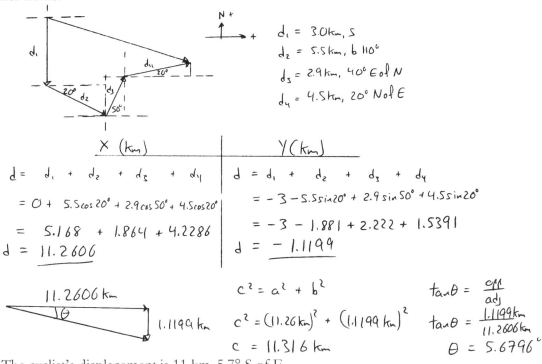

$d_1 = 3.0km, S$
$d_2 = 5.5km, b\ 110°$
$d_3 = 2.9km, 40° E of N$
$d_4 = 4.5km, 20° N of E$

X (km)	Y (km)
$d = d_1 + d_2 + d_3 + d_4$	$d = d_1 + d_2 + d_3 + d_4$
$= 0 + 5.5\cos 20° + 2.9\cos 50° + 4.5\cos 20°$	$= -3 - 5.5\sin 20° + 2.9\sin 50° + 4.5\sin 20°$
$= 5.168 + 1.864 + 4.2286$	$= -3 - 1.881 + 2.222 + 1.5391$
$d = 11.2606$	$d = -1.1199$

$$c^2 = a^2 + b^2$$
$$c^2 = (11.26km)^2 + (1.1199\ km)^2$$
$$c = 11.316\ km$$

$$\tan\theta = \frac{opp}{adj}$$
$$\tan\theta = \frac{1.1199km}{11.2606km}$$
$$\theta = 5.6796°$$

The cyclist's displacement is 11 km, 5.7° S of E.

Problems

1. Use trigonometric ratios and the Pythagorean Theorem to solve for θ or the identified variable "x" for the following right triangles. Place your answer in the blank at the right of the question. [Appendix A]

   a.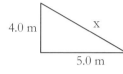

   _____

   b.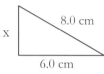

   _____

   c.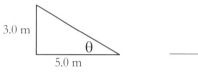

   _____

   d.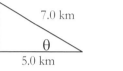

   _____

2. Use a protractor and ruler to neatly draw the indicated vectors on each grid. Make each vector 3 cm long. [Appendix A]

   a. N70°E (70° E of N)
   b. 30° S of E

   c. bearing 240° (30° S of W)

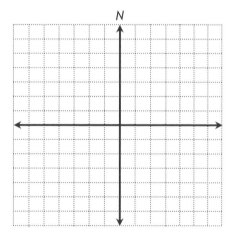

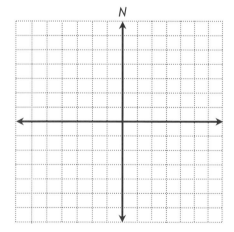

3.	Complete the chart by stating the direction of the vectors A, B, and C. [Appendix A]

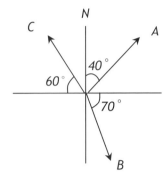

Vector	Bearing	Cardinal reference	Cardinal reference
A			
B			
C			

4.	Dave walks the following route from the rotunda in his school: 20 m due south and then 30 m east through the cafeteria to his physics class. Calculate the displacement of the physics class relative to the rotunda. [36 m, 56° E of S]

5.	Two scientists pull on a particle accelerator. One pulls with a force of 600 N due south while the second pulls with a force of 900 N due east. Determine the net force. [1.08 kN, 33.7° S of E]

6. Three forces are pulling on a mass as shown to the right. They must be arranged head-to-tail in order to correctly add them. List the preferred order, if any, of addition. [Appendix A]

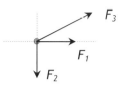

7. Makiya walks 3.0 km from her house to school as shown on the diagram below. Determine her displacement along the
   a. x-component. [2.3 km, east]
   b. y-component. [1.9 km, north]

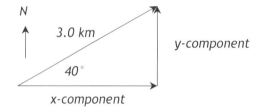

8. By applying a force of 72 N along the handle of a lawnmower, a student can push it across a level lawn. Determine the horizontal component of this force when the handle is held at an angle of 60° relative to the horizontal. [36 N]

9. Free-body diagrams (FBD) are necessary to communicate an understanding of the forces acting on an object and are a typical first step for solving force questions. A free-body diagram identifies the forces, direction, and relative magnitudes on an object. Label the vector arrows on each free-body diagram below with the appropriate forces: [Appendix A]

Force due to gravity	F_g	Normal force	F_N
Force of friction	F_f	Applied force	F_{app}

a. A block is sliding down a frictionless incline.	b. An applied force causes a block to remain stationary on a frictionless incline.

10. Determine the acceleration of a 34.0 kg block along a frictionless inclined plane with a 35° slope (i.e., gradient). [5.6 m/s² down]

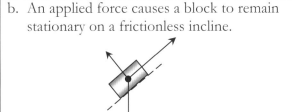

11. Use components to determine the resultant displacement when a horse trots 80.0 m due west stops at a watering hole for a drink and then gallops 120 m, 40.0° S of W. [188 m, 24.2° S of W]

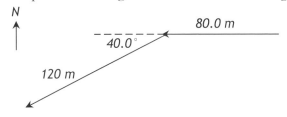

12. Three forces are acting on an object: $F_1 = 25.0$ N, $30°$ E of N; $F_2 = 40.0$ N, bearing $140°$; $F_3 = 30.0$ N, due west Determine the net force acting on the object. [12.2 N, $47.6°$ S of E]

13. A marble rolling along a table at 18 cm/s rolls off the edge. The table is 80.0 cm high. Calculate the distance the marble lands from the edge of the table (distance along the floor). [7.3 cm]

14. A castaway stands on a cliff over the ocean and throws a message in a bottle with a horizontal speed of 8.0 m/s. The bottle hits the water 15.0 m from the base of the cliff.
    a. Using arrows draw the components of the bottle's velocity for three different positions (i. ii, and iii) as it travels to the water on the diagram below. [Appendix A]
    b. Name the shape of the trajectory. [Appendix A]
    c. Using arrows, draw free-body diagrams for the same three positions you used in part a.
    d. Determine the height of the cliff. [17 m]

    a. velocity components   c. free-body diagrams

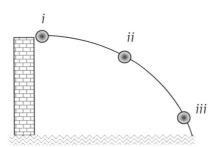   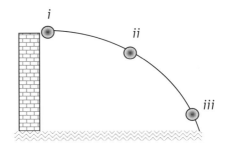

15. A projectile is fired at an angle of 53.0° relative to the horizontal with a speed of 20.0 m/s. Ignoring air resistance, calculate the
    a. time the projectile is in the air. [3.26 s]
    b. projectile's range (horizontal distance travelled). [39.2 m]

1.6 Summary Notes — Work & Energy

Work may be defined as

   i.   the product of the force applied on an object and the object's displacement.

$$W = Fd$$

   ii.   a change in energy.

$$W = \Delta E$$

Where:

   W is work in joules (J)
   F is force (N)
   d is the displacement of the object (m)
   E is energy in joules (J)

Energy may be defined as the ability to do work.

Work and energy are scalar quantities.

A **system** is a defined collection of objects.

When work is done on a system, the type of energy in the system changes.

When objects (i.e., mass) can neither enter nor leave a system it is called a **closed system**.

If no external forces are exerted and no mass or energy (e.g., heat due to friction) is lost or added, the system is an **isolated system**.

Work is equal to the area under a force-displacement graph.

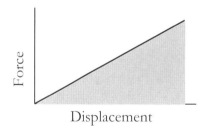

Kinetic energy is defined as the energy of motion. Mathematically it is given as:

$$E_k = \tfrac{1}{2}mv^2$$

Where:

E_k is kinetic energy (J)

m is mass (kg)

v is the velocity or speed relative to a reference point (m/s)

Net work changes an object's kinetic energy: $W_{net} = \Delta E_k$

Potential energy is stored energy. It is capable (or has the potential) of doing work. Energy can be stored in many ways; e.g., springs, heights or chemical bonds.

Gravitational Potential Energy

A mass at a height (relative vertical position) has gravitational potential energy that can be determined by:

$$E_p = mgh$$

Where:

E_p is gravitational potential energy (J)

g is the gravitational field strength (N/kg) e.g., 9.81 N/kg at the Earth's surface.

m is mass (kg)

h is the height above a reference point (m)

Law of Conservation of Energy

Energy can neither be created nor destroyed. It can only change its form (e.g., light energy to heat energy).

In an isolated system, the energy is always conserved, though it may change its form. This may be expressed mathematically as

$$\sum E_{before} = \sum E_{after}$$

Σ is a Greek letter indicating a sum.

Total mechanical energy is the sum of the kinetic and potential energy and should remain constant in a frictionless system.

$$E_{Total} = E_k + E_p$$

If energy is converted to heat (H), the total mechanical energy is not constant.

$$E_{tot} = E_k + E_p + H$$

For any question that asks you to **explain** energy transformations ensure you do the following.

- State that energy is conserved (Law of Conservation of Energy).
- List the different types of energies involved.
- Describe the transformations of one type of energy into another.
- State that heat energy is produced as described in the second law of thermodynamics (unless an idealized frictionless system is used).

Problems

1. Andrew applies a 10 N force to push a 20 kg toolbox horizontally along a level surface at a constant velocity for a distance of 2.0 m.
    a. Draw a free-body diagram of the situation. [Appendix A]
    b. Determine the work done by Andrew on the toolbox. [20 J]

2. Fill in the blanks. Olga is pushing a 50 kg crate along a level floor at a constant velocity by applying a 200 N force. Since the crate is moving at a constant velocity, the magnitude of the force due to friction must be _____ and the net work done on the crate is _____. [Appendix A]

3. Work is done against gravity in lifting a 50.0 kg box a vertical distance of 10.0 m at a constant velocity. Calculate the amount of work done against gravity on the box. [4.91 kJ]

4.   Determine the kinetic energy of a 3.0 kg rock falling at 2.0 m/s. [6.0 J]

5.   A 5.0 kg book is placed on a shelf 1.2 m high. Determine the gravitational potential energy stored in the book relative to the ground. [59 J]

6.   A ball has 20 J of gravitational potential energy as it is held above the ground. Ignoring any friction effects, determine the amount of kinetic energy the ball has just as it is to hit the ground after being dropped. Explain. [Appendix A]

7.   A ball is dropped from a height of 1.00 m and accelerates until it hits the floor. Complete the chart below assuming no energy loss due to air resistance. [Appendix A]

Height (m)	Kinetic energy (J)	Gravitational Potential energy (J)	Total Mechanical energy (J)
1.00	0		10
0.75		7.5	
0.50	5.0		
0.25		2.5	
0			

8.   A pendulum is released from a height of 50 cm. Determine the greatest speed of the pendulum if its bob has a mass of 2.0 kg. [3.1 m/s]

Part of what is called the Second Law of Thermodynamics is that it is impossible for any energy transformation be 100 % efficient - energy is always lost to heat. The efficiency of an energy transformation may be calculated using:

$$\% \ Efficiency = \frac{E_{out}}{E_{in}} \times 100\%$$

Where:

E_{in} is the energy the system starts with.

E_{out} is the energy remaining in the system: $E_{out} = E_{in} -$ Energy lost as heat

9. It is impossible for any energy transformation to be 100 % efficient but a bicycle is the most energy efficient method of human transportation. A 60 kg cyclist uses 486 kJ to cycle 5.0 km. Determine the efficiency of the ride if 24 kJ of this energy is converted to heat due to friction in the gears, tires, and air resistance. [95 %]

10. A pendulum is released with an initial gravitational potential energy of 10 J and swings back and forth. Assume frictional losses result in the pendulum losing 20 % of its energy each complete swing.
    a. Complete the chart below. [Appendix A]

Number of complete swings	Gravitational potential energy (J)
0	10
1	
2	
3	

    b. Determine the amount of heat energy produced by the pendulum during the 3 complete swings. [4.9 J]

1.7 Summary Notes — Uniform Circular Motion

Uniform circular motion is a special case of two-dimensional motion where the object constantly changes direction in such a way that a force and therefore, acceleration, always acts at a right angle to the velocity.

The force causing the circular motion may result from a number of sources such as gravity, tension, friction, or electrostatic attraction.

A **Centripetal force** is a force that causes an object's motion to deviate from linear motion to circular motion. Centripetal means "centre-seeking".

Centripetal acceleration (a_c) and centripetal force (F_c) are always directed to the centre (perpendicular to the direction of motion).

The **tangential velocity** is the velocity of an object tangent to its circular path.

Centripetal acceleration, force and tangential velocity may be calculated using the following:

$$a_c = \frac{v^2}{r} = \frac{4\pi^2 r}{T^2}$$

$$v = \frac{2\pi r}{T}$$

Where:

a_c is centripetal acceleration and is always directed inwards (m/s^2)

v is tangential velocity (m/s)
r is radius of curvature (m)
T is the period (s)
m is mass (kg)

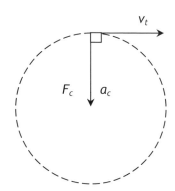

Example

1. A 250 g mass is attached to a 1.00 m length of string. The string completes a horizontal circle in 0.42 s. Calculate the
   a. speed of the mass.
   b. force acting on the mass.

$$m = 0.25 \text{ kg} \quad v = \frac{2\pi r}{T} \qquad a_c = \frac{v^2}{r} \qquad f = ma_c$$

$$r = 1.00 \text{ m}$$
$$v = \frac{2\pi (1\text{m})}{0.42\text{s}} \qquad = \frac{(14.95\text{m/s})^2}{1.0\text{m}} \qquad 0.25\text{kg} \times 223.5\text{m/s}^2$$
$$T = 0.42 \text{s} \qquad\qquad\qquad\qquad\qquad\qquad f = 55.88\text{N}$$
$$v = ? \qquad v = 14.95 \text{ m/s} \quad a_c = 223.5\text{m/s}^2$$
$$a_c = ?$$

   a. The mass' speed is 15 m/s.
   b. The force acting on the mass is 56 N towards the centre of the circle.

Problems

1. Velocity and force vectors are drawn on a ball in the diagrams below. Match the diagram with one of the descriptions of motion (i, ii, or iii). [Appendix A]

    a.   b.   c.

      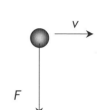

    i.   circular motion
    ii.   decreasing velocity
    iii. increasing velocity

2. A rubber stopper is tied to a 1.0 m long string and is whirled around in a horizontal circle at a constant speed. Determine the stopper's speed if it completes one cycle in a time of 0.91 s. [6.9 m/s]

3. A car turns a circular curve with a speed of 20 m/s. If the radius of the curve is 100 m, calculate the centripetal acceleration of the car. [4.0 m/s^2 towards the centre]

4. A 50 g mass is swung in a circle on the end of a 90 cm long string at a speed of 5.9 m/s. Calculate the magnitude of the centripetal force acting on the mass. [1.9 N]

1.8 Summary Notes — Waves

Energy may be transferred by the motion of particles or by waves.
Waves occur when a medium (substance) vibrates.

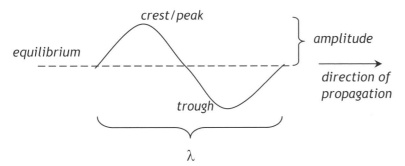

The universal wave equation and the period-frequency relationship work for all types of waves and are given by:

$$v = f\lambda$$

$$T = \frac{1}{f}$$

Where:

v is the speed of the wave

f is the frequency of the wave (cps or Hz)

λ is the wavelength of the wave (λ is the Greek letter "lambda")

T is the period of the wave.

- The colour of a light wave is usually associated with its frequency or wavelength.
- **Monochromatic** light is a beam of light containing a single frequency (or wavelength).

Example

1. Light from a blue laser diode has a period of 2.23 x 10^{-15} s. Determine the laser light's
   a. frequency.
   b. wavelength.

$$T = 2.23 \cdot 10^{-15} s$$
$$f = ?$$
$$v = ?$$

$$f = \frac{1}{T}$$
$$f = \frac{1}{2.23 \cdot 10^{-15} s}$$
$$f = 4.4843 \cdot 10^{14} Hz$$

$$v = \lambda f$$
$$\lambda = \frac{v}{f}$$
$$= \frac{3 \times 10^8 m/s}{4.4843 \times 10^{14} Hz}$$
$$\lambda = 6.69 \times 10^{-7} m$$

   a. The light from the diode has a frequency of 4.48 x 10^{14} Hz.
   b. The light from the diode has a wavelength of 669 nm.

Problems

1. A tourist shouts across a canyon. The sound wave she creates travels at 340 m/s across the canyon and reflects off the opposite rock wall. She hears the echo 1.01 s after she shouts. Calculate the width of the canyon. [172 m]

2. A tuning fork is struck and produces a frequency of 256 Hz. Determine the wavelength of the sound wave produced if the speed of sound is 343 m/s. [1.34 m]

1.9 Review Assignment

1. Convert 25 m/s to km/h.

2. Round each of the following measurements to 3 digits.

   a. 0.003 094 5 d _____
   b. 4.245 002 cm _____
   c. 3.0045 g _____
   d. 87 449 km _____
   e. 14 521 000 m _____
   f. 56 300.2 m^2 _____
   g. 0.000 309 50 g _____
   h. 2.9979 x 10^8 m/s _____

3. A student placed a mass on a horizontal air table and applied a force, causing it to accelerate. The experiment was repeated numerous times manipulating the mass and keeping the applied force constant.

Mass (kg)	Acceleration (m/s^2)
1.0	11.9
1.5	8.2
2.0	6.0
2.5	4.9
3.0	4.1

   a. Plot an appropriate graph of the data.
   b. Identify the relationship between mass and acceleration as shown by the graph.

4. Complete the chart below. For each question consider m to be the responding variable and n the manipulated variable.

	Equation	Slope-intercept form	Curve	Linear	Slope	y-intercept
a.	$m = A(n - B)$					
b.	$mn = B$					
c.	$m^2 = \dfrac{A}{2\pi^2}\,n$					
d.	$m + 4 = n^2 - 6$					
e.	$\dfrac{1}{m} = \dfrac{1}{n} + \dfrac{1}{B}$					

5. A racquetball is moving towards a player at 3.0 m/s. It is hit so it changes its direction giving it a speed of 5.0 m/s, opposite of its original direction. Calculate the ball's acceleration during contact if the ball was in contact with the racquet for 0.60 s.

6. Canada's Motor Torpedo Boats (MTB) patrolled the English Channel during World War II. A MTB could start from rest and accelerate to 50 m/s in a time of 8.0 s over a distance of 200 m. Determine the magnitude of the unbalanced force propelling the boat forward if it has a mass of 5.5×10^4 kg when fully loaded.

7. Determine the weight, in newtons, of a 60.21 kg student on the Earth's surface.

8. When a car is in a major head on collision and comes to a sudden stop, object such as books placed in the back window area may become lethal projectiles. They can kill or injure the occupants even though they are wearing their seat belts and have air bags to protect them. Explain why this is so using Newton's laws of motion.

9. Joe Student walks the following route from the rotunda in his school: 20 m due south and then 30 m east through the cafeteria to his physics class. Determine the displacement of the physics class relative to the rotunda.

10. Four forces are acting on a 12.0 kg object: F_1 = 2.20 N, 23° E of N; F_2 = 4.00 N, bearing 160°; F_3 = 3.00 N, bearing 270°; and F_4 = 2.00 N, 15° N of W. Determine the net force acting on the object.

11. A projectile is fired at an angle of 53° with the horizontal. The speed of the projectile is 20.0 m/s. Ignoring air resistance, calculate the
    a. time the projectile is in the air.
    b. projectile's range (horizontal distance travelled).

12. A 22.0 g mass is tied to a 1.12 m long string and caused to move in a horizontal circle once every 0.93 s. Determine the kinetic energy of the mass.

13. An alpha particle is a subatomic particle often produced during radioactive decay. Determine the kinetic energy of an alpha particle, having a mass of 6.65 x 10^{-27} kg and a speed of 4.24 x 10^5 m/s.

14. Calculate the speed of an electron in a television tube if its kinetic energy is equal to 9.5 x 10^{-18} J. The mass of an electron is 9.11 x 10^{-31} kg.

2 Momentum

Introduction

Many of the fundamental laws of nature are conservation laws. While many aspects of motion are not conserved, momentum is a quantity of motion that is conserved.

2.1 Summary Notes — Momentum

Momentum is the product of an object's mass and velocity.

$$\vec{p} = m\vec{v}$$

Where:

$\vec{p}$ is momentum (kg·m/s) or N·s
m is mass (kg)
$\vec{v}$ is the velocity (m/s)

Momentum is a vector quantity and therefore has magnitude and direction. The direction is in the same direction as the velocity of the object.

Notes:

_____

_____

_____

_____

_____

_____

_____

Example

1.   A golfer putts a 45.7 g golf ball at velocity of 1.50 m/s, west along a level green. Determine the ball's momentum.

$$m = 45.7g \qquad p = mv$$

$$v = 1.5 m/s \qquad p = 0.0457 kg * 1.5 m/s$$

$$p = ? \qquad p = 0.06855 kg\,m/s$$

The golf ball's momentum is 0.0686 kg•m/s, west.

Problems

1.) A 1905 kg truck has a velocity of 30.6 m/s to the north. Determine the truck's momentum. [5.83 x 10^4 kg•m/s, north]

$p = mv$

$p = 1905 kg \times 30.6 m/s [N]$

$p = 5.83 \times 10^4 \dfrac{kg \cdot m}{s} [N]$

2.) Determine the momentum of an electron (9.11 x 10^{-31} kg) travelling at 4.51 x 10^7 m/s to the north. [4.11 x 10^{-23} kg•m/s, north]

$p = mv$

$p = (9.11 \times 10^{-31} kg)(4.51 \times 10^7 m/s)$

$p = 4.11 \times 10^{-23} \dfrac{kg \cdot m}{s} [N]$

3.) A 540 g toy truck moving west has a kinetic energy of 0.327 J. Determine its momentum. [0.594 kg•m/s, west]

① $E_k = \frac{1}{2} mv^2 \quad \therefore v = \sqrt{\dfrac{2E_k}{m}}$

$v = \sqrt{\dfrac{2(0.327 J)}{0.540 kg}} = 1.100... m/s [W]$

$p = mv = 0.540 kg \times 1.100... m/s [W]$

$p = 0.594 \dfrac{kg \cdot m}{s} [W]$

4.) A 20 g ball is dropped from a height of 10 m. Determine its momentum when it is half-way to the ground. [0.20 kg•m/s, downwards]

$\delta E = E_p \quad \Delta E = E_p + E_k.$

$\therefore E_p = E_k$

$E_p = mgh$

$E_p = (0.020 kg)(9.81 m/s)(5m) = 0.981 J.$

$\therefore E_k = 0.981 J = \frac{1}{2} mv^2$

$\therefore v = \sqrt{\dfrac{2E_k}{m}}$

$v = \sqrt{\dfrac{2(0.981 J)}{0.020 kg}}$

$v = 9.9045... m/s [downwards]$

$p = mv$

$p = 0.020 kg \times 9.9045... m/s$

$p = 0.1980... \dfrac{kg \cdot m}{s}$

$\therefore p = 0.20 \dfrac{kg \cdot m}{s} [downward]$

5. The displacement of a 1300 kg car over time was recorded and graphed as shown as it travelled at a constant velocity towards the west. Use the graph to determine the car's momentum. [~1.0 x 10³ kg•m/s, west]

Position as a function of Time

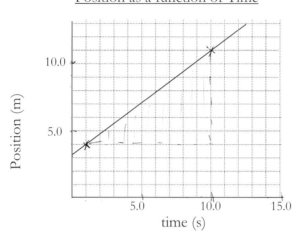

Position (m)

time (s)

$$\text{slope} = \frac{rise}{run} = \frac{\Delta d}{t} \quad \therefore \text{slope} = v$$

$$\therefore \frac{y_2 - y_1}{x_2 - x_1} = v$$

$$v = \frac{(11.0_m - 4.0_m)}{(10.0s - 1.0s)} = \frac{7.0m}{9.0s} = 0.\overline{77}... \, m/s$$

$$p = mv = 1300kg \times 0.\overline{77} \, m/s \, [West]$$

$$p = 1.0 \times 10^3 \, \frac{kg \cdot m}{s} \, [West]$$

6. Use the graph of momentum as a function of speed to determine the object's mass. [~1.08 x 10³ kg]

Momentum as a function of Speed

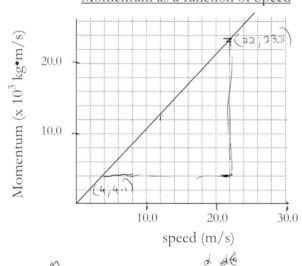

Momentum (x 10³ kg•m/s)

speed (m/s)

$$p = mv \quad \therefore \quad m = P/v.$$

$$\therefore \frac{rise}{run} = \frac{p}{v} = \frac{y_1 - y_2}{x_1 - x_2}$$

$$= \frac{23.8 - 4.1}{22 - 4}$$

$$= \frac{19\,700 \, \frac{kg \cdot m}{s}}{18 \, m/s}$$

$$= 1.09 \times 10^3 \, kg$$

7. A 0.25 kg mass is attached to a 1.00 m length of string. The string completes a horizontal circle in 0.420 s. Calculate the
   a. speed of the mass. [15.0 m/s]
   b. magnitude of its momentum. [3.7 kg•m/s]

a) $v = \frac{d}{t} = \frac{...}{0.420s} =$

8. Determine the magnitude of the maximum momentum of a 200 g pendulum released from a vertical height of 8.0 cm. [0.25 kg•m/s]

$mgh = \frac{1}{2}mv$ $(0.200 kg)(9.81 m/s^2)(0.08 m) = \frac{1}{2}(0.200 kg)(v)$

$2(0.15696 J) = 0.2 kg(v)$ ∴ $v = 1.5696$ m/s.

$\dfrac{0.31392 J}{0.2 kg} = v$ $P = mv$ $P =$

$P = (0.200 kg)(1.5696 m/s)$

Use the information below to answer question 9.

Since a Cessna-172 is a small airplane (750 kg) it may be easily blown off course by a strong cross wind.

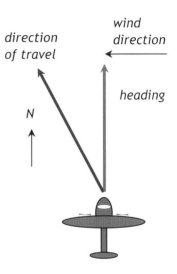

9. An airplane is travelling at 27.8 m/s due north in calm air when an east wind of 11.2 m/s begins. This blows the airplane off course as shown in the diagram. Determine the plane's momentum relative to the ground as it is being blown off course. [2.25 x 10^4 kg•m/s, 21.9° W of N]

10. A person standing on a cliff over the ocean throws a message in a bottle horizontally off a cliff as shown in the diagrams below. [Appendix A]
    a. Using arrows draw the components of the bottle's velocity for three different positions (i. ii, and iii) on the way to the water on the diagram below.
    b. Using arrows draw momentum components for the same three positions you used in part a.

a. velocity components

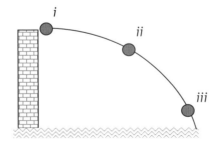

b. momentum components

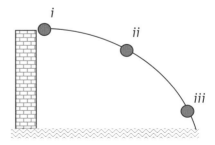

2.2 Summary Notes — Impulse

Impulse may be defined as a change in momentum (Δp). A force is required for this to occur.

Impulse is also a vector quantity in the same direction as the force applied.

$$\vec{F}t = m\Delta\vec{v}$$ $$\vec{F}t = \Delta\vec{p}$$

Where:

$\vec{F}$ is force (N)
t is time (s)
$\Delta\vec{p}$ is change in momentum or impulse (N·s)

Impulse may be determined from a graph of net force and time.

The area under the graph is impulse

Net Force (N)

time (s)

☐ Notes:

_____

_____

_____

_____

_____

_____

_____

_____

_____

_____

_____

_____

_____

_____

Examples

1. Show how Ft = mΔv is related to Newton's second law of motion.

$F = ma$ — Newton's 2nd law

$a = \dfrac{v_f - v_i}{t}$ $\therefore F = \dfrac{m\Delta v}{t}$

$\therefore F = \dfrac{m(v_f - v_i)}{t}$ $Ft = m\Delta v$

2. High jumpers land on a soft mat to avoid injury. Use physics terminology and formulae to describe how the soft mat works to prevent injuries.

   The soft mat allows the jumper to slow down gradually thus reducing the forces acting on the jumper as shown by the equation Ft = mΔv. This equation shows that as the time of impact increases the force of impact decreases.

3. A 50.0 N force is applied on a 4.00 kg object for 15.0 s, causing it to speed up. Determine the magnitude of the
    a. change in velocity of the object.
    b. impulse.

$F = 50N$

$m = 4.0 kg$

$t = 15s$

$\Delta p = ?$

$\Delta v = ?$

a) $Ft = m\Delta v$

$\Delta v = \dfrac{Ft}{m}$

$= \dfrac{50N \times 15s}{4 kg}$

$\Delta v = 187.5 m/s$

b) $p = mv$

$\Delta p = m\Delta v$

$\Delta p = 4 kg \times 187.5 m/s$

$\Delta p = 750 N \cdot s$

or

$\Delta p = Ft$

$= 50N \times 15s$

$\Delta p = 750 N \cdot s$

    a. The change in velocity is 188 m/s.
    b. The impulse on the ball is 750 N•s.

Problems

1. A ball has a momentum of 2.0 kg·m/s north before it is hit. Determine the impulse acting on the ball while it is being hit if its momentum after being hit is 5.0 kg·m/s to the
    a. north. [3.0 N•s, north]
    b. south. [7.0 N•s, south]

2. Momentum and impulse may be represented using bar graphs as shown below. Determine the impulse for each situation. [+1.0 N•s, -7.0 N•s, +6.0 N•s]

    a.
    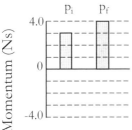

    b.
    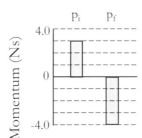

    c.
    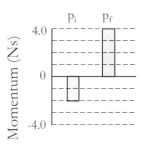

A 40.0 g bullet hits a block of wood, travels through the wood and exits the opposite side as shown in the diagram.

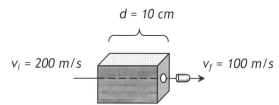

3. Determine the impulse on the bullet while it travels through the block. [4.00 N•s, left]

4. Fill in the blank. Since impulse is a vector, an object travelling to the north while slowing down must have an impulse directed to the _____. [Appendix A]

5. A 42.0 g racquetball is moving east at 14.0 m/s when it is struck by a racquet giving it a velocity of 22.0 m/s east. Determine the impulse given to the ball. [0.336 N•s, east]

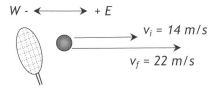

6. A 42.0 g racquetball is moving east at 14.0 m/s when it is struck by a racquet giving it a velocity of 22.0 m/s to the west. Determine the impulse given to the ball. [1.51 N•s, west]

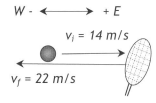

7. A three-wood is used to hit a golf ball from the tee box on a par three at a local golf course. The club is in contact with the ball for 0.0050 s and exerts a force of 500 N on the ball as it slices the ball into the bushes. Determine the magnitude of the impulse on the ball. [2.5 N•s]

Use the information below to answer question 8.

Native Americans first used the atlatl, or throwing stick, about 8000 years ago. It consists of a light spear or arrow placed on a notch of an arm's length stick. An atlatl extends the arm's motion, allowing for the throwing force to be applied for a longer time resulting in a greater speed and distance. The atlatl could send a small spear accurately up to 40 m.

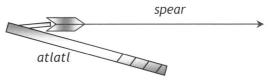

8. A hunter uses an atlatl in a throwing motion by starting it from rest behind his head and extending it in front of his body before the arrow is released. A force of 7.0 N acts on a 75 g arrow mass for 0.31 s during the throwing motion. Determine the magnitude of the arrow's
   a. impulse. [2.2 N•s]
   b. change in velocity. [29 m/s]

9. A 1400 kg car travelling at 18.0 m/s collides with a brick wall. The car rebounds from the wall with a speed of 2.10 m/s. The car is in contact with the wall for a time of 0.900 s. Determine the force the
   a. wall applies on the car. [-31.3 kN]
   b. car applies on the wall. [31.3 kN]

10. Two identical cars are travelling at the same velocity. The first car gradually slows to a stop while the second car accidentally collides with a strong concrete wall that doesn't break. Compare (i.e., smaller, the same, or larger) the
    a. impulse of the two cars. [Appendix A]
    b. stopping force of the two cars. [Appendix A]

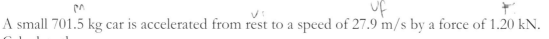

11. A small 701.5 kg car is accelerated from rest to a speed of 27.9 m/s by a force of 1.20 kN. Calculate the
    a. change in momentum (impulse) produced by the force. [19.6 kN•s]
    b. time the force acted on the car. [16.3 s]

12. A pole-vaulter lands on soft foam mats. Use physics terminology and formulae to explain why landing on a soft surface is less likely to produce injury than landing on a hard surface. [Appendix A]

Use the information below to answer question 13.

A typical automobile air bag is activated during a collision if the car is travelling faster than 20 km/h. The sudden deceleration during a collision triggers the decomposition of sodium azide to produce nitrogen gas. The gas inflates the air bag in less than 40 ms. The air bag then takes about 2.0 s to fully deflate while the occupant is in contact with the bag.

13. Use physics terminology and formulae to describe how an air bag works to reduce or prevent injuries. [Appendix A]

14. Impulse can be determined using a graph of net force versus time. The impulse will be the area between the graph and the x-axis. In the graph below area A is 100 N•s and area B is 60 N•s. Determine the total impulse. [+40 N•s]

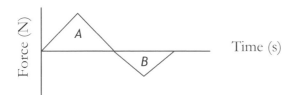

Use the information below to answer question 15.

An 1100 kg car crashes into a concrete retaining wall and comes to a stop. The car's bumper is made to crush during a crash as a safety feature to protect the occupants. The net force on the car's bumper is plotted as a function of the time it takes for the car to come to a stop.

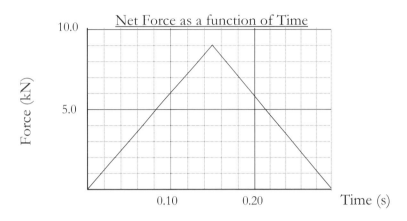

15. Determine the
    a. impulse on the car during the collision. [~1.35 kN•s]
    b. car's speed before contact. [~1.23 m/s]

16. An experiment is performed where a car is accelerated from rest to a speed of 30 m/s. The time required to get to reach 30 m/s is manipulated and the force is the responding variable. [Appendix A]
    a. Identify the equation that relates the net force as a function of time.
    b. Sketch the shape of the graph obtained if force is graphed as a function of time.
    c. Draw the line and label the axis on the supplied graph to identify what must be plotted on the y-axis and the x-axis in order to obtain a straight line.
    d. Show how the slope of the line is to be used to determine the car's mass.

17. A 7.82 g ball is dropped on a hard table surface and rebounds. The same ball is then dropped on a soft cardboard surface and rebounds as shown on the video clip. [Appendix A]

Ball 2.21

a. Watch the video and make measurements to complete the table below. (Show one sample calculation for each column.)

	Initial height (m)	Final height (m)	Downwards contact velocity* (m/s)	Upwards contact velocity** (m/s)	Δv (m/s)	Impulse (N•s)
Hard surface	1.00					
Soft surface	1.00					

* The maximum downwards speed as the ball contacts the floor.
** The speed of the ball after the bounce as it leaves the floor on the way back up.

b. Compare the impulse of an object colliding with a hard surface with the impulse of an object colliding with a soft surface.

2.3 Summary Notes — Conservation of Linear Momentum

☐ Notes:

_____

_____

_____

_____

_____

_____

_____

_____

_____

_____

_____

_____

_____

_____

_____

_____

_____

_____

_____

A **system** is defined as a collection of objects.

An **isolated system** does not interact with anything outside the system (no external forces are exerted and no energy is gained or lost).

The sum of a **conserved** quantity does not change in an isolated system. The amount of momentum within an isolated system is conserved.

The Law of Conservation of Momentum:

The total momentum within a system is constant. Momentum is conserved when objects within a system interact. An interaction is typically a collision or explosion.

$$\sum \vec{p} = \sum \vec{p}\,' \qquad\qquad \Delta \vec{p} = 0$$

Not all quantities of motion are conserved; velocity, force and acceleration are not conserved. Since momentum is conserved, it is useful when objects within an isolated system collide.

Always use momentum to solve collision questions. An exception may be made if a percent of the kinetic energy conserved given.

To solve conservation of momentum questions:

> i.   Draw momentum vectors diagrams for each object before and after the collision.
> ii. Determine the momentum of each object where possible.
> iii. Label the direction of each momentum vector using -, + signs.
> iv. Add up all the known momenta according to the law of conservation of momentum.
> v.   Solve for the unknown.

Examples

1. A 150 g puck travels to the right at 20 cm/s and collides with a stationary 200 g puck on an air table. After the collision the 150 g puck is moving right with a velocity a quarter of its original velocity. Determine the velocity of the 200 g puck after the collision.

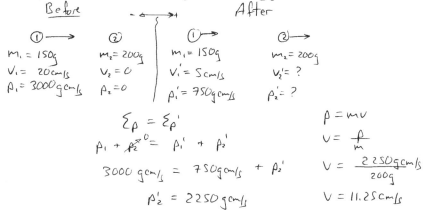

Before ·←——→· After

① →	②	① →	② →
$m_1 = 150g$	$m_2 = 200g$	$m_1 = 150g$	$m_2 = 200g$
$V_1 = 20 cm/s$	$V_2 = 0$	$V_1' = 5 cm/s$	$V_2' = ?$
$P_1 = 3000 g cm/s$	$P_2 = 0$	$P_1' = 750 g cm/s$	$P_2' = ?$

$$\Sigma p = \Sigma p'$$
$$P_1 + P_2^{\,0} = P_1' + P_2'$$
$$3000 \ gcm/s = 750 \ gcm/s + P_2'$$
$$P_2' = 2250 \ gcm/s$$

$$P = mv$$
$$V = \frac{P}{m}$$
$$V = \frac{2250 gcm/s}{200g}$$
$$V = 11.25 cm/s$$

The puck's velocity is 11 cm/s, to the right.

2. A 10 g firecracker explodes into two pieces; a 7.0 g piece moves at 25 m/s east. Determine the velocity of the second piece.

Before   w ·←——→· E   After

○	←①	② →
$m = 10g$	$m_1 = 3g$	$m_2 = 7g$
$V = 0$	$V_1' = ?$	$V_2' = 25 m/s$
$P = 0$	$P_1' = ?$	$P_2' = 175 g m/s$

$$\Sigma p = \Sigma p'$$
$$P = P_1' + P_2'$$
$$0 = P_1' + 175 g m/s$$
$$P_1' = -175 g m/s$$

$$P = mv$$
$$V = \frac{P}{m}$$
$$V = \frac{-175 g m/s}{3g}$$
$$V = 58.3 \ m/s$$

The velocity of the second piece after the collision is 58 m/s, to the west.

Problems

1. Two identical air pucks collide head-on and stick together. Their momenta before the collision are described in the diagram below. Determine the momentum of the combined air pucks after the collision. [4.0 kg•m/s, left]

16.0 kg•m/s ——→   *20.0 kg•m/s* ←——

2. An 80 kg rugby player running at 2.0 m/s north collides with a 50 kg player running at 2.6 m/s, south. Determine the resulting velocity if they hold on to each other. [0.23 m/s, north]

3. A curler slides a 20 kg curling rock 4.0 m/s north that is caught by a stationary 65 kg player. If frictional losses are ignored, determine the
   a. velocity of the player immediately after catching the rock. [0.94 m/s, north]
   b. impulse of
      i. the 65 kg player. [61 N•s, north]
      ii. rock. [61 N•s, south]

4.   Two objects, A and B, are on a head on collision course. Object A's mass is 2.0 g and it is travelling at 12.0 m/s to the right. Object B's mass is 4.0 g and it is travelling at 3.0 m/s to the left. After the collision object A is travelling to the right at 1.5 m/s. Determine the velocity of object B after the collision. [2.3 m/s to the right]

5.   Alison throws a 0.30 kg ball due east at 4.7 m/s. It collides head on with a 0.35 kg ball thrown by Anna at 5.1 m/s, due west. After the collision the 0.30 kg ball is travelling 1.9 m/s, due west. Determine the
     a.   velocity of the 0.35 kg ball after the collision. [0.56 m/s to the east]
     b.   impulse of each ball during the collision. [2.0 N•s, west; 2.0 N•s, east]

6. A car was travelling north when it collided head-on with a truck travelling south. Each vehicle was travelling at 50 km/h before the collision and stuck together after the collision. The mass of the car is half that of the truck. Determine the velocity of the vehicles immediately after the collision. [17 km/h, S]

7. A small car was travelling north when it collided head-on with a truck travelling south. Each vehicle was travelling at 50 km/h before the collision and stuck together after the collision. The mass of the car is half that of the truck. Identify the vehicle that experienced the larger
    a. force. [Appendix A]
    b. impulse. [Appendix A]
    c. acceleration. [Appendix A]

8. Pachelbel fires a 150 kg cannon ball at 110 m/s from his stationary 8000 kg cannon. Calculate the recoil velocity (i.e., backwards speed) of the cannon. [2.06 m/s]

9.	A 1000 kg car travelling to the north at an unknown speed and a 2000 kg truck is travelling at 80.0 km/h to the south, collide head on and stop at impact. Determine the car's speed before impact. [160 km/h]

10.	Two carts on an air track collide together. The mass of cart 1 is 300 g and the mass of cart 2 is 600 g. Cart 1 is moving to the right at a speed of 20.0 cm/s while cart two is moving to the left at a speed of 15 cm/s. After the collision cart 2 is moving at 2.0 cm/s to the left. Determine the velocity of cart 1 after the collision. [6.0 cm/s to the left]

11. By the 16th century cannons were commonly used in warfare. A 1200 kg cannon is placed on a 12.0 m tall tower as shown in the diagram. It fires a 72.0 kg cannon ball that lands 81.3 m away from the base of the tower. The cannon is not restrained and moves backwards off the tower according to Newton's third law. Calculate the distance the cannon lands from the base of the tower. [4.88 m]

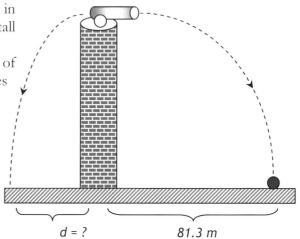

d = ?   81.3 m

2.4 Summary Notes — Two Dimensional Collisions

Momentum is a vector quantity. Since momentum must be conserved, the momenta in each dimension must also be conserved:

$$\Sigma p_x = \Sigma p_x' \qquad \Sigma p_y = \Sigma p_y'$$

☐ Notes:

_____

_____

_____

_____

_____

_____

_____

_____

_____

_____

_____

Examples

1. A 3.0 kg ball is moving directly south with a velocity of 3.0 m/s when it collides with a 5.0 kg ball moving due west at 3.2 m/s. Calculate their final velocity if they stick together upon impact.

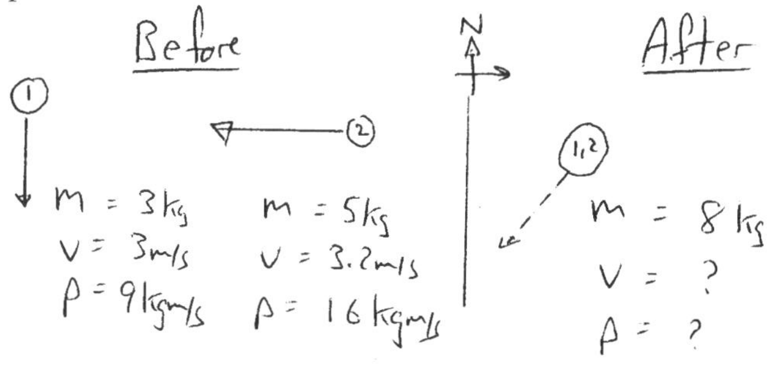

<u>Before</u>   N↑   <u>After</u>

① ↓ ◁———②

m = 3kg   m = 5kg
v = 3m/s   v = 3.2m/s
p = 9kgm/s p = 16 kgm/s

(1,2)
m = 8 kg
v = ?
p = ?

$\tan\theta = \dfrac{opp}{adj}$

$= \dfrac{9\,kgm/s}{16\,kgm/s}$

$\theta = 29.36°$

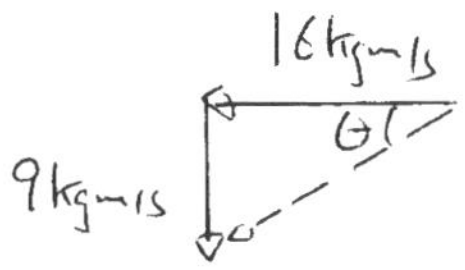

16kgm/s
θ
9kgm/s

$c^2 = a^2 + b^2$

$= (9\,kgm/s)^2 + (16\,kgm/s)^2$

$c = 18.358\ kgm/s$

$p = mv$

$v = \dfrac{p}{m}$

$= \dfrac{18.358\,kgm/s}{8kg}$

$v = 2.295\,m/s$

The velocity after the collision is 2.3 m/s, 29° S of W.

2. A 12.0 kg ball is moving due east at 5.0 m/s when it collides with a stationary 8.0 kg ball. After this collision the 12.0 kg ball is moving with a velocity of 4.5 m/s, 20° S of E. Determine the velocity of the 8.0 kg ball after the collision.

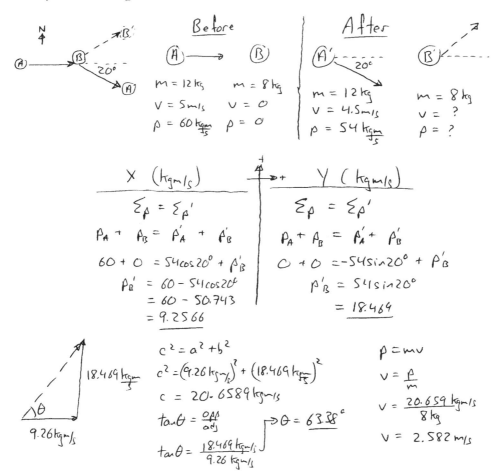

$$X \ (kgm/s)$$

$$\Sigma p = \Sigma p'$$

$$P_A + P_B = P'_A + P'_B$$

$$60 + 0 = 54\cos 20° + P'_B$$

$$P'_B = 60 - 54\cos 20°$$

$$= 60 - 50.743$$

$$= 9.2566$$

$$Y \ (kgm/s)$$

$$\Sigma p = \Sigma p'$$

$$P_A + P_B = P'_A + P'_B$$

$$0 + 0 = -54\sin 20° + P'_B$$

$$P'_B = 54\sin 20°$$

$$= 18.464$$

$$c^2 = a^2 + b^2$$

$$c^2 = \left(9.26 \, kg\text{-}m/s\right)^2 + \left(18.464 \, kg\text{-}m/s\right)^2$$

$$c = 20.6589 \, kgm/s$$

$$\tan \theta = \frac{opp}{adj}$$

$$\tan \theta = \frac{18.464 \, kgm/s}{9.26 \, kgm/s}$$

$$\theta = 63.88°$$

$$p = mv$$

$$v = \frac{p}{m}$$

$$v = \frac{20.659 \, kgm/s}{8 \, kg}$$

$$v = 2.582 \, m/s$$

The final velocity of the ball is 2.6 m/s, 63° N of E.

Problems

1. Two identical air pucks collide at right angles and stick together. Their momenta before the collision are described in the diagram. Determine the momentum of the combined air pucks after the collision. [25.6 kg•m/s, 38.7° S of E]

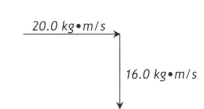

20.0 kg•m/s

16.0 kg•m/s

2. A 1500 kg car travels north at 25.0 m/s when it collides with a 2200 kg SUV travelling east at 15.0 m/s. They stick together upon impact. Determine the velocity of the vehicles immediately after the collision. [13.5 m/s, 41.3° E of N]

3. A 3.0 g magnetic ball is moving due south when it collides with a 5.0 g magnetic ball moving due west. They collide and stick together, travelling at a velocity of 4.0 cm/s, 36° S of W. Calculate the velocity of the
   a. 3.0 g ball. [6.3 cm/s, south]
   b. 5.0 g ball. [5.2 cm/s, west]

Cue balls on coin operated billiard tables are either larger than the numbered balls or are magnetic. This allows them to be returned for play in the event they are accidentally pocketed (i.e., scratched).

4. A 0.17 kg cue ball is moving at 4.0 m/s when it strikes a 0.16 kg stationary numbered ball (object ball). After the collision, the cue ball moves 60° to the left of its original direction while the object ball moves 30° to the right of the cue ball's original path. Determine the speed of the
    a. cue ball after the collision. [2.0 m/s]
    b. object ball after the collision. [3.7 m/s]

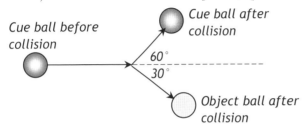

5. A 20.0 kg curling rock is moving due east when it collides with a stationary curling rock of equal mass. After the collision, the first rock is travelling at 1.50 m/s, 47.0° north of east, and the other is travelling 1.71 m/s 40.0° S of E. Determine the velocity of the first rock before the collision. [2.33 m/s, east]

6. A 10.0 kg ball is moving due east at 5.0 m/s when it collides with a stationary 8.0 kg ball. After this collision the 10.0 kg ball is moving with a velocity of 3.5 m/s, 20° S of E. Determine the velocity of the 8.0 kg ball after the collision. [2.6 m/s, 35° N of E]

7. Two students etch a grid on the surface of an ice rink. One student slides a 12 kg mass to the east at 9.0 m/s. It collides with a stationary 10 kg mass. After the collision the 12 kg mass moves with a velocity of 5.2 m/s, 25° S of E. Determine the velocity of the 10 kg mass after the collision. [5.8 m/s, 27° N of E]

8. A 150 g puck on an air table is moving east at 5.0 m/s when it collides with a 120 g puck moving at 4.0 m/s north. After the collision the 150 g puck travels at a velocity of 3.2 m/s 25° N of E. Determine the velocity of the 120 g puck after the collision. [3.5 m/s, 41° N of E]

2.5 Summary Notes — Energy & Momentum Conservation

Notes:

_____

_____

_____

_____

_____

_____

_____

_____

_____

_____

_____

_____

_____

_____

_____

_____

_____

_____

_____

_____

_____

_____

Momentum is conserved in all collisions. A collision may be defined as elastic or inelastic.

Elastic collisions occur when kinetic energy is conserved. The total **kinetic energy** before the collision must equal the total kinetic energy after.

Only subatomic collisions come close to being perfectly elastic.

Some common types of elastic collisions:

- **Stop and go**: An object collides with another object of equal mass head-on. The first object stops and the second object gains the velocity the first object had.

- **In and out**: Two identical objects collide head-on. They both rebound with equal and opposite velocities.

- **One in, two out**: An object in a glancing collision strikes a stationary object. The two objects are moving at right angles to each other after the collision if the objects have identical mass and the collision is elastic.

Inelastic collisions occur when kinetic energy is not conserved.

- Breaking, crumpling or bending during a collision are empirical evidence of inelasticity.

- A collision is totally inelastic if it loses as much kinetic energy as possible. This does not necessarily mean the objects lose all their kinetic energy.

- Whenever two objects collide and stick together the collision is completely inelastic.

Example

1. On an icy winter day in Edmonton a 2000 kg truck slams on its brakes but unfortunately slides at a speed of 5.00 m/s into a 1400 kg stationary car waiting at a stop sign. Upon collision their bumpers lock together and they both slide into the intersection.
   a. Determine the speed of both vehicles after the collision.
   b. Show that the collision was inelastic.

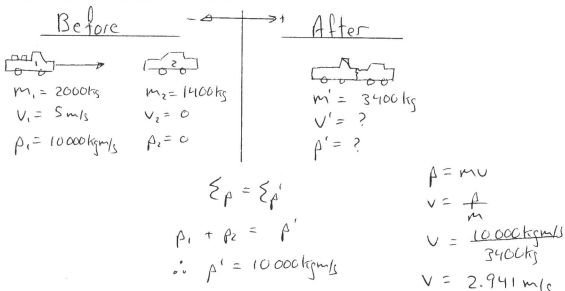

$$\Sigma_p = \Sigma_{p'}$$

$$p_1 + p_2 = p'$$

$$\therefore p' = 10\,000 \text{ kgm/s}$$

$$p = mv$$
$$v = \frac{p}{m}$$
$$v = \frac{10\,000 \text{ kgm/s}}{3400 \text{ kg}}$$
$$v = 2.941 \text{ m/s}$$

   a. The vehicles' speed after the collision is 2.9 m/s.

If the collision is elastic the total kinetic energy before the collision will equal the total kinetic energy after the collision.

$$E_k = \tfrac{1}{2}mv^2$$
$$= \tfrac{1}{2}(2000 \text{ kg})(5 \text{ m/s})^2$$
$$E_k = 25\,000 \text{ J}$$

$$E_h = \tfrac{1}{2}mv^2$$
$$= \tfrac{1}{2}(3400 \text{ kg})(2.941 \text{ m/s})^2$$
$$E_h = 14704.1 \text{ J}$$

$$\% \text{ lost} = \frac{E_{k \, lost}}{E_{k \, initial}} \times 100\%$$
$$= \frac{10296 \text{ J}}{25000 \text{ J}}$$
$$\% \text{ lost} = 41.18\%$$

$$E_k \, lost = 25\,000 \text{ J} - 14704.1 \text{ J}$$
$$E_k \, lost = 10296 \text{ J}$$

   b. The kinetic energy after the collision is less than the total kinetic energy before the collision (41 % of the kinetic energy was lost). Therefore, the collision is inelastic. Since the two vehicles stuck together the collision is totally (completely) inelastic.

Problems

1. Mass A is moving with a kinetic energy of 160 J when it collides with mass B having a kinetic energy of 160 J.
    a. Determine the total amount of kinetic energy after the collision if the collision is completely elastic. [320 J]
    b. Assume the collision is perfectly elastic and mass A has 180 J of kinetic energy after the collision. Determine the amount of kinetic energy possessed by mass B after the collision. [140 J]
    c. Assume the collision is inelastic and mass A has 130 J of kinetic energy after the collision. Determine the amount of kinetic energy possessed by mass B after the collision if 40 J of heat energy is released during the collision. [150 J]

Use the information below to answer question 2.

While momentum is always conserved during a collision kinetic energy is only conserved during elastic collisions. Therefore the kinetic energy can be used to solve collision questions only if the collision is elastic or a percent of the kinetic energy conserved is known.

2. A 1200 kg car travelling at 20 m/s collides with a stationary 1400 kg car. The two cars lock together. Determine the speed of the vehicles immediately after the collision if 53.9 % of the initial kinetic energy is converted to heat and sound during the collision. [9.2 m/s]

3. Must all the kinetic energy be lost in a collision for the collision to be considered completely inelastic? Explain. [Appendix A]

4. A 2300 kg truck slams on its brakes on an icy winter day in Calgary but continues to slide at a speed of 3.50 m/s into a 1700 kg stationary car at a stop sign. Upon collision the car slides forward into the intersection at a speed of 2.5 m/s.
    a. Determine the speed of the truck after the collision. [1.7 m/s]
    b. Show that the collision was inelastic. [Appendix A]

5. Two masses collide head-on and come to a stop. Explain what has happened in terms of
    a. each mass' original momentum. [Appendix A]
    b. the elasticity of the collision. [Appendix A]

6. Two identical 350 g toy cars with magnets on their ends are used to compress a spring at the bottom of a frictionless incline. Car 1 is moving with a speed of 0.25 m/s before rolling down the incline and connecting and sticking to car 2 that is initially at rest.
   a. Determine the velocity of the cars after they collide. [0.87 m/s to the right]
   b. Show that the collision is not elastic. [Appendix A]
   c. If the toy cars come to a stop by compressing the spring a distance of 1.50 cm, determine the spring's constant. [2.3 x 10^3 N/m]

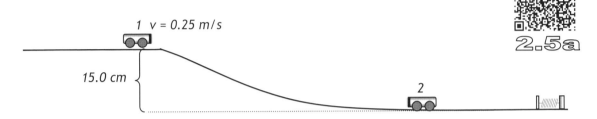

7. A student sets up a collision experiment with two masses on a horizontal air track as shown in the diagram. The mass of A is 100 g and B is 200 g.

Each spring has a constant of 20 N/m. Spring 1 was initially compressed 5.00 cm to start mass A moving.
    a. Determine the speed of mass A as it leaves spring 1. [0.71 m/s]
    b. If A has a velocity of 20 cm/s to the right after it collides with B, determine the velocity of mass B. [0.25 m/s to the right]
    c. Determine the maximum compression of spring 2 when mass B collides with it. [2.5 cm]

8. A 25.0 g arrow is shot into a 1.00 kg block of Styrofoam. The Styrofoam absorbs the impact of the arrow and slides into a spring (140 N/m) compressing it 5.30 cm as shown in the diagram. As the Styrofoam and arrow compress the spring, 60 % of the energy is dissipated as heat. Calculate the speed of the arrow before it hits the Styrofoam [40 m/s]

2.5b

You and your lab partner will investigate the collision between two pucks on an air table. The data and some of the lab write-up are provided below.

Purpose:
To test the law of conservation of momentum (i.e., is the momentum before the collision equal to the momentum after the collision?)

Experimental Design:
Two air pucks will be collided on an air table. Their total momentum before will be compared to their total momentum afterwards.

Prediction:
The total momentum before the collision should be equal to the total momentum after the collision.

Analysis:
Carefully draw lines showing the path of the pucks before and after the collision and a reference line for measuring angles as shown below. (The diagram is not drawn to scale.)

She then measures the angles and distances between 5 or 6 sparks for each puck, before and after. She then calculates the speed of puck 1 before the collision and after the collision as shown below. As her partner it is your job to complete the analysis.

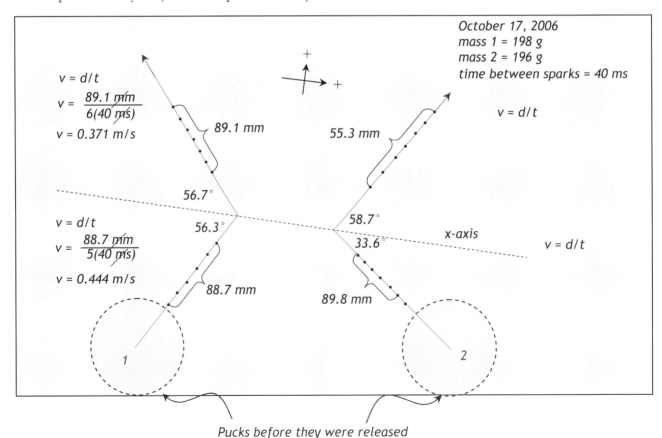

Pucks before they were released

---

9   It is your job to complete the work of your lab partner.
   a.   Use the data from the spark sheet to complete the following table.

Puck	Speed before (m/s)	Speed after (m/s)	Momentum before (g•m/s)	Momentum after (g•m/s)
1	0.444	0.371	87.91	73.46
2				

   b.   Use the direction of each puck relative to the reference line to determine the
        components of the mass' momentum, before and after the collision. Place
        your results in the chart below.

Collision 2.51

x (g•m/s)   y (g•m/s)

P_1 + P_2 = p'_1 + p'_2 P_1 + P_2 = p'_1 + p'_2

+87.9cos56.3°   -73.5cos56.7°   87.91sin56.3°   +73.46sin56.7° +

+48.78   -40.33   +73.14   61.40

Evaluation:
   c.   The momentum in the x-dimension before the collision should be equal to the
        momentum in the x-dimension after the collision. Calculate their percent difference.
        Repeat the same procedure for the y-dimension. [31.0 % in x, and 18.0 % in y]

   d.   Use the kinetic energy before and after to determine if the collision was elastic. [inelastic]

2.6 Extensions

1. 300 mL of liquid A is added to 70 mL of liquid B resulting in a total volume of 366 mL. Assuming no chemical reaction or spilling has occurred; explain if this contradicts the law of conservation of mass. [Appendix A]

2. Tjecrd Visser is at a par 3 at the Neerlandia Golf Classic when he uses a 7-iron to slice a 45.9 g golf ball off a high tee. The ball initially travels horizontal relative to the ground and hits a sand trap 120 m from where it was hit. The tee box is 6.00 m higher than the sand trap. Determine the

    a. impulse given to the ball when it was hit by Tjecrd's 7-iron. [4.98 N•s]
    b. ball's momentum immediately after it left contact with the club. [4.98 kg•m/s]

    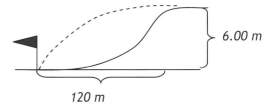

    c. momentum of the golf ball as it contacted the sand. [5.00 kg•m/s, 5.71 ° relative to the horizontal]

3. Two men, each having a mass of 100 kg, stand on a stationary 200 kg cart. The cart is able to roll along an east-west track with negligible friction. The system is initially at rest. The first man jumps off to the east with a speed of 5.0 m/s relative to the cart. After he has jumped the second man jumps off to the west at 5.0 m/s relative to the cart. Determine the velocity of the cart after both men have jumped. [0.83 m/s]

4. A 100 g mass moving at 2.0 m/s collides head on with a stationary 100 g mass. Determine the speed of each mass after the collision if they do not stick together and the collision is perfectly elastic. [The first mass = 0 m/s, the second mass is 2.0 m/s.]

5. Two identical objects collide in a direct one-dimensional elastic collision. The first object is travelling at east 2.0 m/s when it collides with the second object at rest. Determine the velocities of both objects after the collision. [0; 2.0 m/s, east]

6. Two objects collide elastically, in a head-on, one-dimensional collision. The first object is travelling at 2.0 m/s when it collides with the second object that was at rest. The mass of the moving object is twice the mass of the stationary object. Determine the speeds of both objects after the collision. [0.67 m/s, 2.7 m/s]

2.7 Review

1. A 4.0 kg wagon travelling at 1.2 m/s has a momentum magnitude of
   a. 2.0 kg•m/s
   b. 4.8 kg•m/s
   c. 3.3 kg•m/s
   d. 6.2 kg•m/s

2. A bat strikes a 300 g baseball travelling at 40 m/s. The ball is in contact with the bat for 20 ms and leaves the bat in the opposite direction with a speed of 80 m/s. The average force exerted by the bat on the ball is
   a. 0.60 kN
   b. 1.8 kN
   c. 1.2 kN
   d. 2.0 kN

3. An object moves with a certain undetermined speed. If the object's mass is doubled and its speed is halved, by what factor will its momentum change?
   a. Zero. It does not change
   b. 0.5
   c. 2
   d. 4

4. Determine the recoil velocity on an unrestrained 4.0 kg rifle after it shoots a 20 g bullet with a muzzle velocity of 200 m/s.
   a. 0.25 m/s
   b. 1.0 m/s
   c. 2.0 m/s
   d. 4.0 m/s

5. In inelastic collisions,
   a. kinetic energy and momentum are both conserved.
   b. kinetic energy and impulse are both conserved.
   c. only kinetic energy is conserved.
   d. only momentum is conserved.

6. A 1200 kg car passes traffic light at a velocity of 10.2 m/s to the north and accelerates at a rate of 2.45 m/s^2. Calculate the car's momentum after 4.21 s. [2.46 x 10^4 kg•m/s, north]

7. Explain why a stretchy cord is used rather than a non-stretchy cord when bungee jumping. [Appendix A]

8. Use words from the list below to fill in the blanks to correctly complete each sentence. [Appendix A]

     momentum   conserved
     impulse   inertia

 a. The product of an object's mass and its velocity may be called _____.
 b. The tendency for an object to continue in its motion is called _____.
 c. The law of conservation of _____ states that the _____ before an interaction is equal to the _____ after the collision in a closed system.
 d. _____ is defined as a change in momentum.

9. Determine the magnitude of the maximum momentum of a 400 g pendulum released from a vertical height of 18.0 cm. [0.752 kg•m/s]

10. Explain how it is possible for an object to obtain a larger impulse from a smaller force than it does from a larger force. [Appendix A]

11. A 50.0 g ball moving at a velocity of 1.45 m/s E collides with a 25.0 g stationary ball. After the collision the first ball is still moving 0.271 m/s E. Determine the velocity of the second ball. [2.36 m/s, E]

12. Using your air hockey table at home you propel a 400 g toy truck west at a velocity of 1.8 m/s and it collides with a 200 g toy car moving south at a velocity of 1.1 m/s. These two vehicles have magnets attached to the front bumpers and stick together upon collision. Determine their velocity after collision. [1.25 m/s, 17° S of W]

Top view

13. You forget to poke a potato with a fork before cooking it in a microwave and it explodes into three equal mass pieces. One piece moved east at 10.0 m/s. The second moves 12.0 m/s 40.0° S of E. Determine the velocity of the third piece. [20.7 m/s, 21.9° N of W]

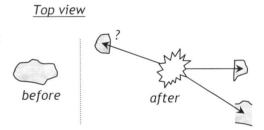

before   *after*

2.8 Review Assignment

1. Determine the momentum of an 82 kg linebacker running south at 5.2 km/h.

2. A 200 g ball is dropped from a height of 80 cm. Calculate its momentum as it makes contact with the floor.

3. Modern vehicles have bumpers designed to crush upon impacted. Many older vehicles had hard metal bumpers that were designed not to crush upon impact. Use physics terminology and formulae to describe how a modern bumper works to reduce or prevent injuries to occupants of the vehicle.

4. Momentum and impulse may be represented using bar graphs as shown below. Draw the
    missing bar graph representing impulse for each situation.

a.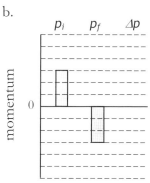

b.

c.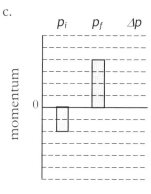

5. Two children throw identical balls with the same velocity towards a house. The first ball hits a
    wall and bounces directly back at half of its contact speed. The second ball hits a window,
    breaks it and continues through at half of its contact speed. Did the two balls experience the
    same impulse? Explain.

6. The position of a 2100 kg truck over time was recorded and graphed as shown as it travelled at
    a constant velocity to the west. Use the graph to determine the car's momentum.

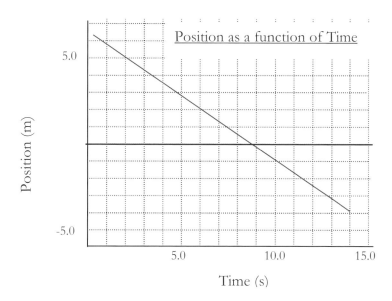

7. A 170 g puck travels to the right at 20 cm/s and collides with a stationary 150 g puck on an air
    table. After the collision the 170 g puck is moving left with 10 cm/s. Determine the velocity of
    the 150 g puck after the collision.

8. A 1400 kg car moving at 20 m/s crashes into a solid barrier and comes to a complete stop. The car's crumple zone compresses a distance of 0.20 m during the collision.
    a. Calculate the impulse acting on the car.
    b. Calculate the magnitude of the stopping force acting on the car.
    c. Determine the number of "g" forces acting on an occupant in the car.
    d. A physics textbook is sitting on the rear window ledge of the car. Use physics concepts and terminology to describe what would happen to the text during the crash.

9. A study by Streff and Geller had people race a go-kart around a track. It was found that when the drivers wore a seatbelt they drove faster than when they did not wear a seatbelt. A similar study regarding wearing bicycle helmets found that wearing a helmet resulted in higher risk riding. A compensation for using safety equipment by modifying other behaviours to the level of risk an individual is comfortable with seemed to occur. The study of risk compensation calls into question the effectiveness of many laws such as mandatory seat belt laws. Discuss the pros and cons of laws mandating the use of safety equipment. Use your own experience and analyze your thoughts on risk compensation.

10. When force is plotted on the y-axis of a graph and time is plotted on the x-axis, the area between the graph and the x-axis may be interpreted as _____.

11. Rowing is an Olympic sport and may be analyzed using the science of biomechanics. Part of the analysis is a net force versus time graph showing the two main stages of rowing as shown below.

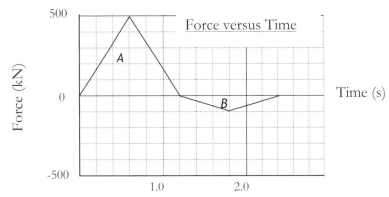

    a. Identify the section of the graph (A or B) that you would want to reduce or eliminate to improve the overall speed of the boat.
    b. Use the graph to determine the net impulse.

12. A car carrying a driver and passenger of equal mass crashes. The driver had an airbag while the passenger did not. The net force that varies with time for the driver and for the passenger are graphed and presented below.

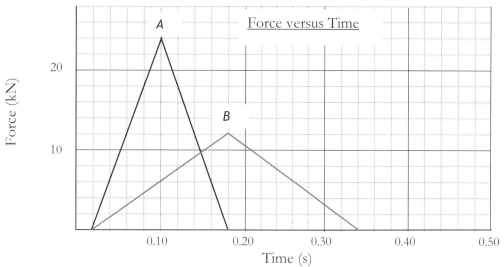

a. Identify the graph (A or B) that represents what happens to the
   i. driver.
   ii. passenger.
b. Use the graph to determine the impulse on the passenger.
c. Use the graph to determine the impulse on the driver.
d. Should the driver and passenger (they have identical mass) have equal impulses? Explain.
e. Use the graph to explain why having an airbag can be safer during a car crash.

13. Block A, shown below, starts from rest and slides 8.0 m down a frictionless ramp. It then crosses a 4.0 m horizontal surface where the coefficient of kinetic friction is 0.20. At the 4.0 m mark it collides with ball B on the end of a string. After the collision block A continues to move with a velocity of 3.0 m/s to the right. Block A has a mass of 5.0 kg and ball B has a mass of 2.5 kg. (The diagram is not drawn to scale.)

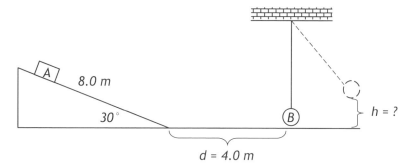

Determine the maximum possible height (h) ball B could swing after the collision.

14. A gas canister is rolling due west at 0.954 m/s along a floor when it explodes into three pieces of equal mass. The first piece moves at 3.6 m/s, 20° N of W. The second travels at 5.8 m/s 62° S of W. Calculate the velocity of the third piece.

3 Electrostatics

Introduction

The idea that matter is made of positive and negative particles (e.g., protons and electrons) allows for powerful explanations of electrical phenomena. Knowledge of electrostatic phenomena allows for a better understanding of our world and modern technology.

3.1 Summary Notes — Static Electricity

Electrostatics is the study of electrical charges that are not in motion.

The fundamental and empirical electrical interaction: opposite charges attract and like charges repel.

Conservation of Charge is a fundamental law in physics. Charge must always be conserved.

Neutral matter contains no net charge; the amount of positive charge is equal to the amount of negative charge.

An **electrical ground** is a source of charge.

Grounding is the process of connecting a charged object to the Earth. This allows excess charge to leave an object. Grounding will neutralize a charged object.

Conductors (e.g., metals) allow charge to flow.

Insulators (e.g., wood and plastic) are substances that do not allow charge to flow well.

Only electrons flow in solid conductors. Positive charges may flow in solutions or in a vacuum.

☐ Notes:

_____

_____

_____

_____

_____

_____

_____

_____

_____

_____

_____

_____

_____

_____

Notes:

_____

_____

_____

_____

_____

_____

_____

_____

_____

_____

_____

_____

_____

_____

_____

_____

A **charge separation** can be **induced** when a charged object is brought close to a neutral object.

Since unlike charges attract, a charge separation is induced when the electrons in the neutral sphere move towards the positively charged ruler. The attractive forces are larger than the repulsive force because of the difference in distance. A net attractive force results.

There are three ways to transfer charge:

Friction

Different substances have different affinity for electrons. By rubbing two different objects together, the substance with the greater affinity for electrons will take electrons away from the other. One object ends up being negative; the other gets an equal but opposite charge.

Conduction

When two objects with different charges are brought into contact, electrons will flow from the more negative object to the other until a charge balance is obtained. Both objects then have the same charge.

Induction

When charging by induction the object that gets charged will have a charge opposite to that of the charging object. Charging by induction involves the following steps:

Induction 3.1.1

   i. Bring a charged object **close** (but not touching) to a neutral object that you wish to charge.

  ii. Ground the neutral object.

 iii. Remove the ground.

 iv. Remove the charged object.

When explaining electrostatic phenomena:

- Use diagrams with + and − to represent excess charge.
- Used labelled arrows to indicate forces.
- Differentiate between explanation (theoretical) and description (empirical).
- Use the law of conservation of charge.

Examples

1. Object A is positively charged and is brought into contact with a neutral object B, then separated as shown in the diagram below. Draw the charge distribution on the two objects after contact and separation. Explain.

    Due to the fact that like charges repel, excess charge moves as far away as possible. When the two objects are in contact this results in the charge being evenly distributed on the two objects.

2. Pith is a substance from plants used for many electrostatic demonstrations because it is light and holds a charge well. Describe the process of charging a pith ball by induction and explain how it works.

Description	Explanation
Positively charged pith ball A is far away from the neutral pith ball B. Pith Ball B is grounded.	The charged pith ball, A, is too far away from B to affect the charges in B.
Pith ball A is brought close to pith ball B.	Pith ball A's positive charge attracts electrons from the ground causing B to become negatively charged.
The ground is disconnected and then A is removed.	Pith ball B has a negative charge.

Problems

1. Val comes inside on a cold winter day in Red Deer and removes her toque. She notices that her hair is charged with static electricity. If the toque has a positive charge, identify the charge her hair must have. Explain. [Appendix A]

Positive

2. When two substances are rubbed together they may transfer charge with one becoming negative and the other becoming positive. The relative tendency for a substance to gain electrons or lose electrons can be rated in an electrostatic series (aka triboelectric series) and may be used to predict electrostatic phenomena. [Appendix A]

   a. Use the provided electrostatic series to determine what combination of substances is most likely to produce the greatest charge separation.

   b. A small brick of Styrofoam is rubbed against glass. The Styrofoam is then brought into contact with a neutral electroscope. Describe the electroscope's behaviour when the glass is then brought near to the electroscope.

rabbit fur	**very positive**
glass	↑
human hair	
silk	
aluminium	
steel	**neutral**
amber	
hard rubber	
copper	
Styrofoam	↓
Scotch tape	
Teflon	**very negative**

3. The sign shown to the right is posted by a propane refill tank. Explain the reasoning behind the third warning. [Appendix A]

4. Two identically shaped objects (one is a conductor the other is an insulator) are touched on their left side by a negatively charged object. Their charge distribution is as shown in the diagram.

    Explain why the charge on the conductor is spread out evenly on its surface while it is localized where it was touched on the insulator. [Appendix A]

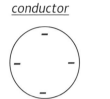

conductor   *insulator*

5. Object A is negatively charged and is brought into contact with a neutral object B, then separated as shown in the diagram below. Draw the charge distribution on the two objects after contact and separation. [Appendix A]

A   *B*   contact   *A*   *B*

6. A negatively charged pith ball on a string is brought close to a negatively charged ruler. Draw the free-body diagram for the pith ball. [Appendix A]

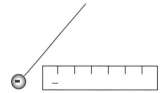

7. A positively charged ruler is brought close to a neutral pith ball and the pith ball is attracted to the ruler. Explain how the neutral pith ball could be attracted to a charged ruler. [Appendix A]

    The electrons is the pith ball are attracted to the positively charged ruler, causing the electrons to pull the pith ball closer.

8. Pith ball A is charged positively and its interaction with charge B is shown below (pith balls A and B do not touch). Pith ball B is then placed near pith pall C and the interaction shown in the diagram occurs.
   a. Identify the charge (positive, negative or neutral) on pith ball C. [Appendix A]
   b. Draw a free-body diagram for each charged sphere below. [Appendix A]

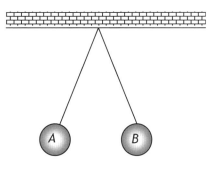 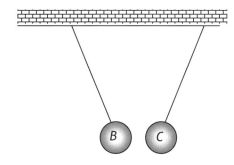

9. A child's balloon is rubbed on her hair to charge it and then placed in contact with a neutral ceiling. The balloon does not fall but remains in contact with the ceiling. [Appendix A]
   a. Draw a free-body diagram of the forces acting on the balloon.
   b. Explain how the charged balloon is electrostatically attracted to the neutral ceiling.

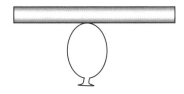

10. Use labelled diagrams to describe how to negatively charge an electroscope through induction. [Appendix A]

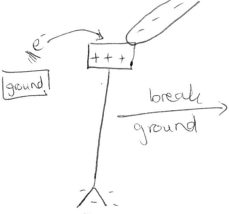 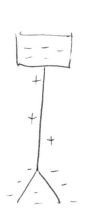

3.2 Summary Notes — Coulomb's Law

Coulomb's law describes the electrostatic force between two charged objects:

$$F_e = \frac{kq_1q_2}{r^2}$$

☐ Notes:

Where:

F_e is electrostatic force (N)

k is Coulomb's constant (8.99×10^9 N•m^2/C^2)

q is charge in coulombs (C)

r is the distance separating the two charges (m)

A **point charge** or point source may be a small positive or negative charge.

Coulomb determined the constant (k) much like Cavendish determined the gravitational constant (G) using a torsion balance.

Two equally charged masses were placed close. By measuring the amount of twist when the charges repelled each other the force could be measured and the constant could be determined:

- Manipulated the charge (q)
- The separation distance (r) responded
- The force and constant (k) could be determined.

Coulomb's Torsion balance

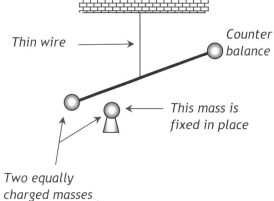

Thin wire →

Counter balance

This mass is fixed in place

Two equally charged masses

The relationship between the electrostatic force and distance is an inverse squared relationship as is Newton's universal law of gravitation. This relationship may be shown graphically:

F

r

Examples

1. Calculate the magnitude of the electric force between two point charges of +4.00 μC and +3.00 μC when they are 45.0 cm apart.

    $r = 0.45\ m$ $F = \dfrac{kq_1q_2}{r^2}$

    $q_1 = 4.0\ \mu C$

    $q_2 = 3.0\ \mu C$ $F = \dfrac{k\ 4\cdot10^{-6}C * 3\cdot10^{-6}C}{(4.5*10^{-2}m)^2}$

    $F = 53.27\ N$

    The magnitude of the repulsive force is 53.3 N.

2. Two point charges produce an electrostatic force of attraction of 5.5 mN. Determine the electrostatic force produced if the charge on both objects is doubled and the distance between them is tripled.

    $F_a = 5.5*10^{-3}N$

    $F_a = \dfrac{kq_1q_2}{r^2}$ $\therefore\ F_B = \dfrac{4}{9}F_A$

    $F_b = \dfrac{k\ 2q_1\ 2q_2}{(3r)^2}$ $F_B = \dfrac{4}{9}[5.5*10^{-3}N]$

    $F_b = \dfrac{4}{9}\left[\dfrac{kq_1q_2}{r^2}\right]$ $F_B = 2.\bar{4}*10^{-3}N$

    The electrostatic force of attraction is 2.4 x 10⁻³ N.

3. Three point charges, A, B, and C, are arranged in a line as shown.

    a. Determine the net electrostatic force acting on charge B.
    b. The charge on object C is negative. Identify the sign of the charge (+ or -) on object
        i. A.
        ii. B.

    $F_{net} = F_{BC} - F_{AB}$

    $= 5*10^{-3}N - 3*10^{-3}N$

    $F_{net} = 2.0*10^{-3}N$

    a. The net electrostatic force is 2.0 x 10⁻³ N to the right.
    b. The charge on object A is negative and positive on object B.

Problems

1. Calculate the electric force between two point charges of -4.00 μC and +3.00 μC when they are 3.50 cm apart. [88.1 N]

2. Determine the separation distance of two charged spheres, each having a net charge of -2.00 μC, so that the net force on them is 1.50 N. [15.5 cm]

3. Two equal point charges exert an electric force on each other of 0.0385 N when positioned 0.15 m apart. Determine the magnitude of the charge on each point. [3.1 x 10^{-7} C]

4. Two identical objects, one neutral and the other with a charge of +6.0 μC, are brought into contact and then separated to distance of 0.20 m.
    a. Is the force between the objects attractive or repulsive after contact? [Appendix A]
    b. Calculate the magnitude of the electrostatic force between the two charged objects. [2.0 N]

5. Two small identical spheres have different charges. One sphere has a charge of +6.00 μC while the other has a charge of -2.50 μC. If these two spheres are brought in contact and then removed to a distance of 25.0 cm, determine the
    a. charge on each sphere after contact. [1.75 μC]
    b. electrical force between them after they are separated by the 25.0 cm. [0.441 N]

6. Two small spheres, each having a mass of 3.00 x 10^{-8} kg, are placed 0.375 m apart. One sphere has a charge of -3.00 μC and is fixed in place. The other sphere has a charge of -4.50 μC and is to the right of the first charge and is free to move. Determine the initial acceleration of the free sphere due to the electrostatic forces. [2.88 x 10^7 m/s^2 to the right]

7. Two charged objects, one having a charge of -12.00 μC and the other +1.00 μC, are separated by 2.00 m. Identify the charge that exerts the stronger force of attraction on the other charge. Explain. [Appendix A]

The term electron is from the Greek word for amber. An electron is used as the elementary charge (the elementary charge is the smallest possible charge that can be isolated; e.g., the charge on an electron or proton: 1.60×10^{-19} C). The charge value of charged particles is often given in multiples of the elementary charge.

8.   Some common subatomic particles, along with their relative charge and mass, are organized in the table below. Determine the charge-to-mass ratio for each particle. Place your answers in the chart. [Appendix A]

Subatomic particle	Relative charge	Charge (C)	Rest Mass (kg)	Charge-to-mass ratio (C/kg)
electron (e⁻)	1⁻		9.11×10^{-31}	
proton (p⁺)	1⁺		1.67×10^{-27}	
neutron (n)	0		1.67×10^{-27}	
positron (e⁺)*	1⁺		9.11×10^{-31}	
alpha (α^{2+})**	2⁺		6.65×10^{-27}	

*A positron is the antimatter particle of an electron; it has identical rest mass and charge magnitude.
**An alpha particle is made from two protons and two neutrons.

9.   Use the chart from the previous question to determine which particle would provide the strongest electrostatic force when placed near a proton. [Appendix A]

10. An electron and a proton are separated by a distance of 5.29×10^{-11} m in a hydrogen atom.
   a. Determine the magnitude of the
      i. electrostatic attractive force acting between the two particles using Coulomb's Law. [8.22×10^{-8} N]
      ii. gravitational attractive force acting between the two particles using Newton's Universal Law of Gravitation: [3.63×10^{-47} N]

$$F_g = \frac{Gm_1 m_2}{r^2}$$

   b. How many times larger is the electrostatic force? [2.27×10^{39}]

11. Two charged objects, A and B, separated by 40 cm, exert a force of 4.0×10^{-6} N on each other. If the distance between A and B were doubled, determine the magnitude of the resulting electric force. [1.0×10^{-6} N]

12. Two point charges produce an electrostatic force of attraction of 5.5×10^{-3} N. Determine the magnitude of the electrostatic force produced if the charge on each object is doubled and the distance between them is tripled. [2.4×10^{-3} N]

13. Two point charges produce an electrostatic force of attraction of 3.5×10^{-6} N. Determine the magnitude of the electrostatic force produced if the charge on one object is doubled, the other is tripled and the charges are brought to halve their original distance. [8.4×10^{-5} N]

14. Two equally charged identical pith balls are placed near each other and the electrostatic repulsive force is measured. Their position is changed and the force is again measured. This is repeated for a number of trials. [Appendix A]
    a. Identify the formula that describes the information.

    b. Sketch a graph of the relationship.

    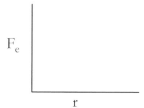

    c. Identify the graph's shape.

    d. Identify what must be plotted on the x-axis and y-axis to straighten the graph.

    e. Predict the identity for the slope of the straight line.

    f. Predict the identity for the intercept of the straight line.

15.   Three point charges, A, B, and C, are arranged in a line as shown.

A   B   C

$F_{AB} = 2.0 \times 10^{-3}$ N $F_{BC} = 5.0 \times 10^{-3}$ N

   a.   The charge on object C is positive. Determine the sign of the charge (+ or -) on object
         i.   A. [Appendix A]
         ii.   B. [Appendix A]
   b.   Determine the net electrostatic force acting on charge B. [3.0 x 10^{-3} N to the right]

16.   Three point charges, A, B, and C, are arranged in a line as shown.

          0.50 m   1.50 m
      A   B   C

   +20 μC -40 μC +80 μC

Determine the net electrostatic force acting on charge
   a.   B. [16 N, left]
   b.   C. [9.2 N, left]

17. The vector nature of electrostatic forces may be communicated using scale diagrams as shown below. (1 division = 1 newton)

a. Identify the nature of the charge, positive or negative, located at the origin of the grid. [Appendix A]

b. Use a ruler and protractor to draw the three force vectors head-to-tail and determine the resultant force. [~5.4 N, 22° N of E]

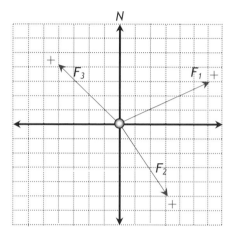

18. Three point charged objects are arranged in a right angle as shown in the diagram.
   a. The charge on object A is positive. Identify the sign of the charge (+ or -) on object
      i. B. [Appendix A]
      ii. C. [Appendix A]
   b. Determine the net electrostatic force acting on charge B. [5.4 x 10^{-3} N, 21.8° W of N]

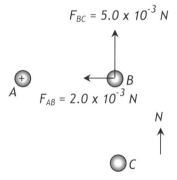

19. Three point charged objects of $\pm 30\ \mu C$ each are arranged in a right angle as shown. Calculate the initial net electric force on charge B. [3.6 kN, 63° E of N]

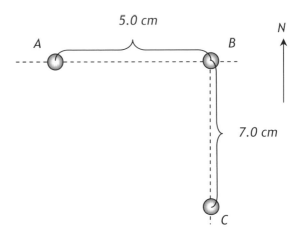

5.0 cm

A   B   N

7.0 cm

C

20. Three point charges, each having identical charges of $+2.0\ \mu C$, are aligned as shown in the diagram below. Determine the initial net force acting on charge B due to charges A and C. [10 N, 28° N of E]

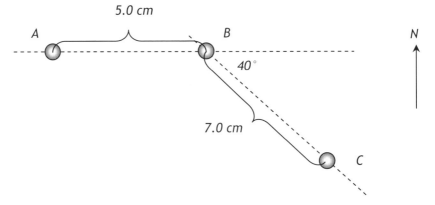

5.0 cm

A   B   N

40°

7.0 cm

C

3.3 Summary Notes   Electric Fields

A **force** may be defined as a push or pull.

Fields are the space around an object that can be influenced by that object. The effect produced is a force.

Fields may be scalar or vector, e.g.,

Scalar fields	Vector fields
temperature	gravitational
sound	electric
	magnetic

Vector fields include direction. **Scalar** fields have only magnitude.

Electric field is the force acting on a coulomb of charge. It is an attempt to explain the interaction of charges. A field is not a force, though it is related.

$$\vec{E} = \frac{\vec{F}_e}{q}$$

N.B., q represents the charge in the field experiencing a force - not the charge creating the field.

Where:
$\vec{E}$ is electric field (N/C or V/m)
$\vec{F}_e$ is electrostatic force (N)
q is the charge in the field (C)

_____

_____

_____

_____

_____

_____

_____

_____

_____

_____

_____

_____

_____

_____

_____

Elcotrio Ficld Dircotion

The direction of an electric field is defined as the direction a small positive charge (test charge) would move when placed in the field.

A **test charge** may be defined as an imaginary positive charge placed in the field.

To determine electric field direction we ask the question, "which way would this positive charge move?" The direction of movement is the direction of the field.

Electric Field Magnitude

The electric field from a point charge may be calculated using

$$\left|E\right| = \frac{kq_1}{r^2}$$

N.B., the q represents the charge producing the field.

Where:

$\left|E\right|$ is electric field (N/C)

k is Coulomb's constant

q is the charge producing the field (C)

r is the distance from the charge producing the field (m)

Point sources produce non-uniform radial (arranged in lines coming from a central point) fields.

Field patterns, indicating direction and magnitude, may be represented using field lines:

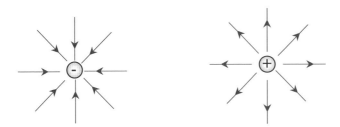

Examples

1. Determine the electric field 90.0 cm north of a -9.50 μC charged object.

$$r = 0.90m \qquad |E| = \frac{kq}{r^2}$$

$$q = -9.5 \mu C$$

$$|E| = ? \qquad = \frac{k(9.5 \times 10^{-6}C)}{(0.90m)^2}$$

$$|E| = 105438.3 N/c$$

The electric field is 1.05×10^5 N/C, south.

2. Two point charges are aligned as shown in the diagram below. Determine the net electric field at point P.

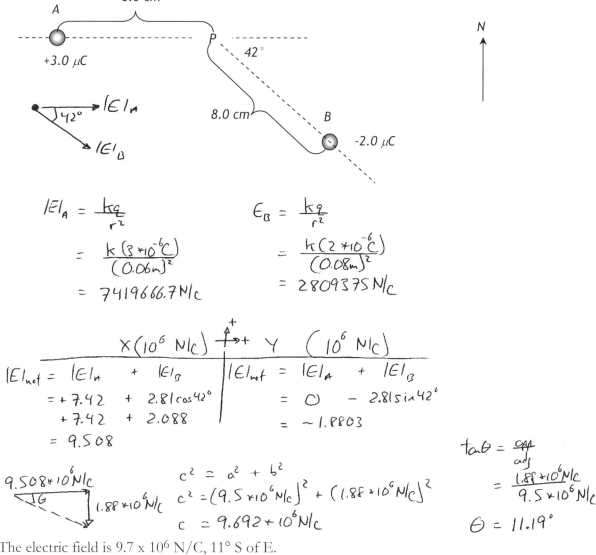

$$|E|_A = \frac{kq}{r^2}$$

$$= \frac{k(3 \times 10^{-6}C)}{(0.06m)^2}$$

$$= 7419666.7 N/c$$

$$E_B = \frac{kq}{r^2}$$

$$= \frac{k(2 \times 10^{-6}C)}{(0.08m)^2}$$

$$= 2809375 N/c$$

$$\underline{X (10^6 \text{ N/c}) \qquad\qquad Y \ (10^6 \text{ N/c})}$$

$$|E|_{net} = |E|_A + |E|_B \qquad\quad |E|_{net} = |E|_A + |E|_B$$

$$= +7.42 + 2.81\cos 42° \qquad = 0 - 2.81\sin 42°$$

$$+7.42 + 2.088 \qquad\qquad = -1.8803$$

$$= 9.508$$

$$c^2 = a^2 + b^2$$

$$c^2 = (9.5 \times 10^6 N/c)^2 + (1.88 \times 10^6 N/c)^2$$

$$c = 9.692 \times 10^6 N/c$$

$$\tan\theta = \frac{opp}{adj}$$

$$= \frac{1.88 \times 10^6 N/c}{9.5 \times 10^6 N/c}$$

$$\theta = 11.19°$$

The electric field is 9.7×10^6 N/C, 11° S of E.

Problems

1. Vector arrows can be used to represent electric fields at a point. The arrow length represents the relative magnitudes of the vectors and the field direction is indicated by the direction the arrow points. For each charge below draw an electric field vector at point P representing the electric field resulting from each individual charge. [Appendix A]

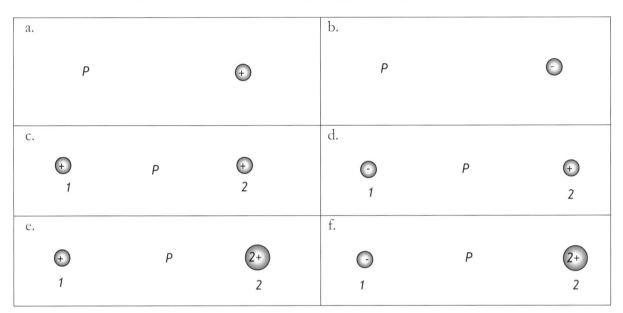

2. Determine the electric field strength 0.700 m south of a -8.50 μC charged object. (Include a diagram.) [1.56×10^5 N/C, north]

3. There is an electric field of 3.20×10^5 N/C at an unknown distance away from a +5.40 μC charged object. Determine the distance to the charged object producing the field. [38.9 cm]

4.   The electric field ($|E|$) near a charged object is measured at different distances (r). [Appendix A]
    a.   Identify the formula that describes the information.

    b.   Sketch a graph of the relationship.

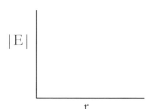

    c.   Identify the graph's shape.

    d.   Identify what must be plotted on the x-axis and y-axis to straighten the graph.

    e.   Predict the identity for the slope of the straight line.

    f.   Predict the identity for the intercept of the straight line.

5.   Two identical charges are placed close together and generate field lines as shown in the diagram.

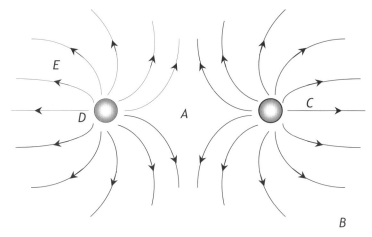

    a.   List the relative magnitudes of the electric fields at points A through E from smallest to largest. [Appendix A]
    b.   Identify the signs (+ or -) of the two charges. [Appendix A]

6. Clouds can build up large charges that are responsible for the production of lightning. Assume the cloud shown below is charged and the area of the ground beneath it is oppositely charge. A negatively charge dust particle between the cloud and ground is accelerated upwards by the electric field. Determine, and label, the
    a. charge (positive or negative) on the cloud and on the ground. [Appendix A]
    b. direction of the net electric field between the cloud and ground. [Appendix A]

ground

7. A +5.00 µC charged object is placed in an electric field of 2.20 x 10^4 N/C to the east. Determine the electric force acting on the charge. (Include a diagram.) [0.11 N, to the east]

8. An alpha particle is placed in a 5.64 x 10^4 N/C electric field. Determine the
    a. charge on the alpha particle. [3.20 x 10^{-19} C]
    b. initial electrostatic force acting on the alpha particle. [1.80 x 10^{-14} N]
    c. magnitude of the initial acceleration for alpha particle. [2.71 x 10^{12} m/s^2]

9.   A negative charge of 2.6 μC experiences an electric force of 0.043 N, acting to the right. Determine the electric field at that point. [1.7 x 10^4 N/C to the left]

10.   An electric field of 1.20 x 10^4 N/C to the north exerts force of 0.034 N on a positively charged particle. Determine the
      a.   direction the charged particle will accelerate. (Include a diagram.) [Appendix A]
      b.   charge on the particle. [2.83 x 10^{-6} C]

Use the information below to answer question 11.

Two point charges are placed as shown in the diagram below. At point P the magnitude of the electric field due to charge A is 8.00 x 10^6 N/C. The magnitude of the electric field due to charge B at point P is 6.00 x 10^6 N/C.

11.   Determine the net electric field at point P if charge A is negative and B is
      a.   also negative. [2.00 x 10^6 N/C to the left]
      b.   positive. [14.00 x 10^6 N/C to the left]

12. Determine the electric field strength at point P in the following situation where charge A is -4.00 µC and charge B is -3.00 µC. [6.89 x 10^6 N/C to the left]

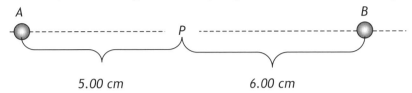

13. Draw vector arrows representing the electric field at point P as a result of each of the two charges for each given situation. The arrow length should represent the relative magnitudes of the vectors. [Appendix A]

a.	b.
P +1 +2	P -1 +2
c.	d.
P + 1 + 2	P + 1 - 2
e.	f.
P + 1 2+ 2	P 2- 1 + 2

14   Two positive point charges are placed as shown in the diagram. At point P the magnitude of the electric field due to charge A is 8.0 x 10^6 N/C. The magnitude of the electric field due to charge B at point P is 6.0 x 10^6 N/C. Determine the net electric field at point P. [1.0 x 10^7 N/C, 53° E of N]

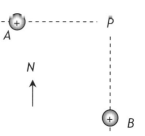

15.   Determine the electric field strength at point P in the following situation if charge A is -4.00 µC and charge B is +3.00 µC. [1.80 x 10^7 N/C, 36.9° N of W]

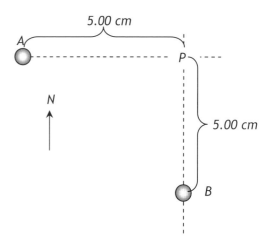

16. Determine the electric field strength at point P in the following situations if charge A is -4.00 μC and charge B is +3.00 μC. [1.12 x 10^7 N/C, 19.8° N of E]

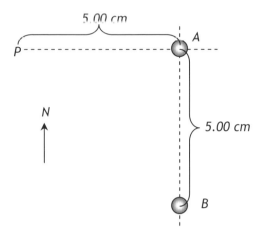

17. Determine the electric field strength at point P in the following situation if charge A is -4.00 μC and charge B is +3.00 μC. [3.44×10^6 N/C, 3.41° S of W]

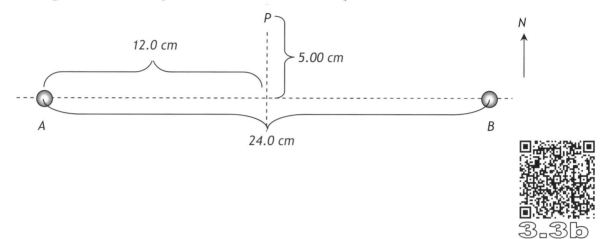

3.4 Summary Notes — Parallel Plates

□ Notes:

The behaviour of charged particles may be controlled using charged metal plates to generate uniform electric fields. A battery may be used to charge the plates as shown in the diagram below.

Since the electric field between the plates is uniform, charged particles between the plates will experience a uniform electric force.

Potential difference (V) is the electrical potential energy per unit charge and is often expressed as voltage.

$$\Delta V = \frac{\Delta E}{q}$$

$$|E| = \frac{V}{d}$$

N.B., For charged plates only

Where:

    V is potential difference in units of volts (V)

    ΔE is potential energy (J)

    q is charge inside the electric field (C)

    $|E|$ is electric field (N/C or V/m)

    d is the distance between charged plates (m)

Current is the rate of flow of electric charge. A potential difference is required to cause current.

$$I = \frac{q}{t}$$

Where:

    I is current in C/s or A (amperes)

    q is charge in coulombs (C)

    t is time in seconds (s)

N.B., Current can be considered to be the flow of electrons. Often current is considered to be the flow of positive charge and may be called conventional current. An ammeter may be used to measure current.

Ampere (amps) is the fundamental unit of current. It is the measure of electric charge that passes a point in one second of time.

As the potential difference (voltage) increases the amount of electrons that flow (current) will also increase.

The amount of current through a conductor depends on the potential difference and the resistance of the conductor.

Electrical potential difference is the change in potential difference experienced by a charge as it moves from one location to another inside an electric field. $\Delta V = V_f - V_i$

Potential Energy
- A change in **electrical potential energy** is caused by an electric force acting over a distance parallel to an electric field.
- A change in **gravitational potential energy** is caused by a gravitational force acting over a distance parallel to a gravitational field.

The **electron volt** (eV) is a unit of energy used in modern physics. It is defined as the amount of energy gained by an electron as it passes through a potential difference of 1 V.

$\therefore 1 \text{ eV} = 1.60 \times 10^{-19} \text{ J}$

Examples

1. Calculate the electric field strength between two parallel plates that are 5.00 cm apart if the potential difference between the plates is 18.0 V.

$d = 5 \text{cm}$ $|E| = \dfrac{V}{d}$

$V = 18V$

$|E| = ?$ $= \dfrac{18V}{0.05m}$

$|E| = 360 \, V/_m$

The electric field strength is 360 V/m.

2. Determine the maximum speed an alpha particle obtains if it moves from rest across a potential difference of 250 V.

$V_i = 0$ $Vq = \frac{1}{2}mv^2$

$V = 250V$

$V = \dfrac{\Delta E}{q}$ $v = \sqrt{\dfrac{2Vq}{m}}$

$E_k = \frac{1}{2}mv^2$ $v = \sqrt{\dfrac{2(250V)(3.2 \times 10^{-19} C)}{6.64 \times 10^{-27} kg}}$

$v = 155230 \, m/_s$

The alpha particle reaches a speed of 1.55×10^5 m/s.

Problems

1. A 12.0 V battery is connected to two parallel metal plates that are 0.0600 m apart. Calculate the electric field strength between the two parallel plates. [200 V/m]

2. Determine the electrical potential difference between two parallel plates, 2.00×10^{-3} m apart, containing an electric field of 50.0 V/m. [0.100 V]

3. The potential difference between two parallel plates is 18.0 V. Determine the separation distance if the uniform electric field between the plates is 80.0 V/m. [0.225 m]

4. An electric field of 3000 V/cm may cause the air to ionize and allow electrons to jump from one surface to another causing a spark. An electrostatic charge is produced on a student walking across a rugged floor. He reaches for a doorknob. Assuming an electric field of 3000 V/cm, determine the electrical potential difference required between the finger and doorknob to produce a spark when they are separated by 1.2 cm. [3.6 kV]

5.   A battery is attached to two parallel metal plates and the plates are separated by 4.00 mm to produce an electric field of 600 V/m. Determine the electric field strength if the plates are moved to a separation distance of 3.00 mm. [800 V/m]

6.   1.78 C of charge flows past a certain point between two parallel plates in a time of 6.53 s. Calculate the value of the current crossing the plates. [0.273 A]

7. 2.8×10^{16} electrons flow through the gap between two parallel plates in a time of 0.80 s. Determine the current. [5.6 mA]

8.   Complete the following energy conversions. [Appendix A]

	Energy (J)	Energy (eV)
a.	1.68×10^{-18}	
b.	5.42×10^{-19}	
c.		5.50

9. A proton enters a uniform electric field between two parallel plates in the two situations described below. [Appendix A]

   i. The proton increases speed.

   ii. The proton decreases speed.

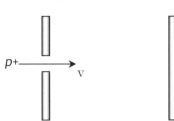
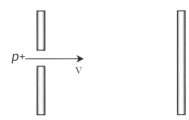

   For each situation
   a. label the plates as positive and/or negative.
   b. draw a battery attached to the plates that would result in the correct charges.
   c. draw arrows between the charged plates to represent the electric field direction.

10. An alpha particle gains 1.60×10^{-15} J of kinetic energy as it passes through an electric field. Determine the potential difference causing its acceleration. [5.00 kV]

11. Determine the maximum speed an alpha particle could obtain if it moves from rest through a potential difference of 8.40 kV. [8.99×10^5 m/s]

12. Determine the maximum speed a proton obtains if it moves from rest through a potential difference of 5000 V. [9.79×10^5 m/s]

13. Determine the voltage between parallel plates needed to accelerate an electron to a kinetic energy of 5000 eV. [Appendix A]

14. An electron starts from rest and accelerates across two charged parallel plates to obtain a kinetic energy of 600 eV. Determine the
    a. potential difference between the plates. [Appendix A]
    b. electrical potential energy the electron initially possessed. [Appendix A]
    c. maximum speed of the electron. [1.45×10^7 m/s]

15. A proton starts from rest and accelerates across a potential difference of 200 V between two charged plates that are 20 cm apart. Determine the
    a. maximum speed of the proton. [1.96×10^5 m/s]
    b. magnitude of the proton's acceleration. [9.6×10^{10} m/s^2]
    c. time the proton requires to cross the plates. [2.0×10^{-6} s]
    d. current. [7.8×10^{-14} A]

16. An electron starts from rest and crosses the region between two parallel plates having a potential difference of 600 V. Determine the kinetic energy increase, in eV, of the electron. [600 eV]

17. When using the eV as a unit of energy, an electron will gain 1 eV of kinetic energy for every V of potential difference crossed. An electron is inside two charged parallel plates. The potential difference between the plates is 300 V. Determine the amount of work done on the electron if it moves

   a. all the way from the negative plate to the positive plate. [300 eV]

   b. half the way from the negative to the positive plate. [150 eV]

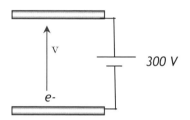

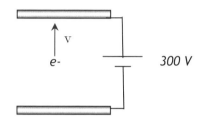

18. An electron is placed between two parallel plates having a potential difference of 100 V. Determine the potential difference the electron crosses if it is initially placed
   a. at the negative plate. [100 V]
   b. halfway between the plates. [50 V]

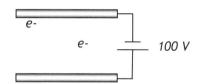

19. To measure the speed of an electron it must be directed through charged parallel plates so that it will slow down. The potential difference between the plates is adjusted so that the electron comes to a stop by the time it reaches the far plate. This potential difference is then called the stopping voltage. [Appendix A]
   a. Label the plates as positive and/or negative so that the electron will slow.
   b. Draw a battery attached to the plates that would result in the correct charges.
   c. Draw arrows to represent the electric field between the charged plates.

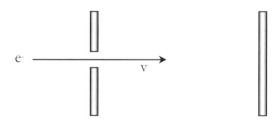

20. Determine the stopping voltage for an electron travelling at 6.50 x 10⁶ m/s. [120 V]

21. Determine the stopping voltage for an electron travelling at 3.52 x 10⁷ m/s. [3.53 kV]

22. Determine the voltage between parallel plates that would be required to stop an electron with a kinetic energy of 500 eV. [Appendix A]

23. A neutron having a kinetic energy of 3.6 MeV strikes a proton and transfers all its kinetic energy to the proton. Determine the voltage between parallel plates that would be required to stop the proton. [Appendix A]

24. Fill in the blanks to complete the sentence. A change in electrical potential energy is caused by an electric _____ acting over a distance _____to an electric field. [Appendix A]

25. An electron has a kinetic energy of 12.0 eV when it enters the through a hole in a negative plate. Determine the electrical potential energy between the plates if the electron's kinetic energy when colliding with the positive plate is 19.0 eV. [7.0 eV]

26. An electron is accelerated from rest across a potential difference between two parallel plates separated by 4.0 cm as shown in the diagram below. Use the law of conservation of energy to complete the chart. [Appendix A]

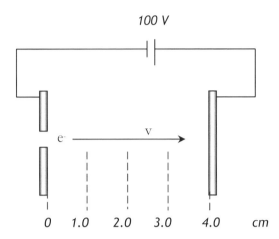

Distance travelled (cm)	Kinetic energy (eV)	Electrical potential energy (eV)
0.0		
1.0		
2.0		
3.0		
4.0		

27. An electron travelling with a kinetic energy of 30 eV enters through a hole in a positive plate. It slows down as it travels from the positive plate to the negative plate. It has a kinetic energy of 20 eV when it collides with the negative plate. Determine the electrical potential difference between the charged plates. [10 V]

28. An electron travelling at 5.0×10^5 m/s enters through a hole in a positive plate and collides with the negative plate at 1.0×10^5 m/s. Determine the electrical potential difference between the charged plates. [0.68 V]

29. A positron having a kinetic energy of 1.14×10^{-15} J enters an electric field. The positron is accelerated to a kinetic energy of 5.50×10^{-15} J. Determine the
    a. amount of work done on the positron. [4.36×10^{-15} J]
    b. potential difference required to cause the positron to accelerate. [27.3 kV]

30. A neutron is a subatomic particle found inside the nucleus of an atom. A neutron travelling at a uniform speed of 4.5×10^3 m/s enters an electric field of 250 N/C between two charged plates, separated by 10.0 cm, encased in a vacuum. Determine the speed of the particle when it reaches the far plate if it entered through a hole in the negative plate. [Appendix A]

31. Two different subatomic particles (A and B) pass through a uniform field as shown in the diagram to the right. Fill in the blanks to properly complete the sentences.

    The sign of the charge on particle A is _____ and _____ on particle B. Each charge acts as a projectile as it travels through the uniform _____ field. The direction of the electric field is from plate number _____ to plate number _____. The shape of the motion of the particles as they travel through the field is _____. [Appendix A]

32. An electron moving horizontally at 2.50×10^6 m/s enters a 150 N/C electric field exactly halfway between two horizontal parallel plates and follows a parabolic path as shown in the diagram. Determine the vertical displacement of the electron as it travels between the plates. [4.13 cm]

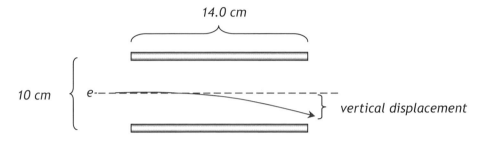

33. An electron enters an electric field between two horizontal parallel plates with a speed of 4.00×10^6 m/s, as shown in the diagram. The electric field between the plates is 175 V/m. Determine the distance the electron travels into the plates before coming to a stop. [0.26 m]

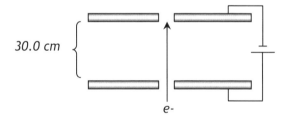

A particle accelerator is used to accelerate charged particles with a mass "m" and a charge "q" by having them cross a potential difference "V." [Appendix A]

34. An equation relating a particle's speed (v) to the potential difference (V) is
    a. $v = \sqrt{\dfrac{2Vm}{q}}$ b. $v = \sqrt{\dfrac{2Vq}{m}}$

    c. $v = \sqrt{\dfrac{Vq}{2m}}$ d. $v = \sqrt{\dfrac{m}{2Vq}}$

35. Identify the graph that correctly shows the relationship between the ion's speed (v) and the potential difference (V).

    a.

    b.
    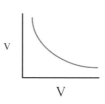

    c.
    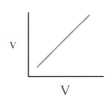

    d.
    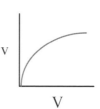

36. A straight line graph would be obtained if "v" was graphed on the y - axis and
    a. V on the x - axis   b. $\dfrac{1}{B}$ on the x - axis

    c. V^2 on the x - axis   d. $\sqrt{V}$ on the x - axis

37. The slope of the graph of the straight line from question 36 is
    a. $\sqrt{\dfrac{2q}{m}}$ b. $\sqrt{\dfrac{2m}{q}}$

    c. $\sqrt{\dfrac{qm}{2}}$ d. $\sqrt{\dfrac{q}{2m}}$

38. A straight line could also be obtained by plotting
    a. v versus the inverse of V   b. v^2 versus the inverse of V
    c. v^2 versus V   d. v versus V^2

3.5 Summary Notes — Charged Droplets in Fields

☐ Notes:

_____

_____

_____

_____

_____

_____

_____

_____

_____

_____

When charged masses such as drops of oil or water are place in electric fields, the gravitational effects cannot be ignored as they are with atomic and subatomic masses.

Millikan used charged oil drops inside charged parallel plates to determine the elementary charge – the charge on an electron. The charge on any object is always an integer multiple of the elementary charge.

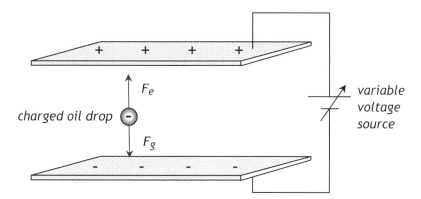

Example

1. A 2.50 x 10⁻¹³ kg oil drop accelerates upward at a rate of 2.80 m/s² when placed between two horizontal parallel plates that are 0.34 m apart. The potential difference between the two plates is 890 V.

$$m = 2.5 \times 10^{-13} kg$$

    a. Draw a free-body diagram of the oil drop.
    b. Determine the magnitude of the charge on the oil drop.
    c. Determine the number of excess electrons.

$m = 2.5 \times 10^{-13} kg$ ↑F_e

$q = ?$

$V = 890 V$

$d = 0.34 m$ ↓F_g

$F_e > F_g$

$F_{net} = F_e - F_g$

$F_e = F_{net} + F_g$

$F_e = 7 \times 10^{-13} N + 2.45 \times 10^{-12} N$

$F_e = 3.1524 \times 10^{-12} N$

$F_g = mg$

$= 2.5 \times 10^{-13} kg \times 9.81 N/kg$

$F_g = 2.4525 \times 10^{-12} N$

$F_{net} = ma$

$= 2.5 \times 10^{-13} kg \times 2.8 m/s^2$

$F_{net} = 7.0 \times 10^{-13} N$

$|E| = \frac{V}{d}$ $|E| = \frac{F_e}{q}$

$\therefore \frac{F_e}{q} = \frac{V}{d}$

$q = \frac{F_e d}{V}$

$q = \frac{3.15 \times 10^{-12} N \times 0.34 m}{890 V}$

$q = 1.204 \times 10^{-15} C$

$\#e^- = \frac{1.20 \times 10^{-13} C}{1.60 \times 10^{-19} C/e^-}$

$= 750000 \ electrons$

    b. The magnitude of the charge on the drop is 1.20 x 10⁻¹³ C.
    c. There are 7.50 x 10⁵ excess electrons.

Problems

1. Free-body diagrams (FBD) are necessary to communicate an understanding of the different forces acting on an object and are a typical first step for solving force questions. Draw a free-body diagram for each of the following situations. [Appendix A]

a. A ball is dropped from rest and falls to the ground (ignore air resistance).	b. A ball was thrown upwards and is still travelling to the top of its trajectory (ignore air resistance).
c. A small charged oil drop travels upwards at a constant velocity inside an electric field between two parallel plates.	d. A small charged oil drop accelerates upwards inside an electric field between two parallel plates.
e. A small charged oil drop accelerates downwards at a rate of 5.0 m/s² inside an electric field between two parallel plates.	f. A small charged oil drop accelerates downwards inside an electric field between two parallel plates at a rate of 12.0 m/s².

2. A negatively charged oil drop accelerates upwards in the electric field between two horizontally charged plates. Identify the direction of the electric field between the plates. [Appendix A]

3.   Determine the number of excess electrons on a pith ball that has a net charge of –2.0 μC. $[1.3 \times 10^{13}]$

Use the following information to answer question 4.

A simplified version of Millikan's experiment involves adjusting the potential difference between two parallel plates and observing the motion a charged oil drop inside the uniform electric field. The forces acting on the drop may be analyzed to determine the charge on the drop.

4.   A 4.84×10^{-14} kg oil drop is suspended between two horizontal parallel plates where the electric field strength is 1.10×10^4 N/C. Determine the magnitude of the charge on the oil drop. $[4.32 \times 10^{-17}$ C]

5.   An oil drop weighs 3.84×10^{-15} N and is suspended between two horizontal parallel plates where the electric field strength is 1.20×10^4 N/C. Determine the magnitude of the charge on the oil drop. $[3.20 \times 10^{-19}$ C]

6. A 4.0×10^{-16} kg oil drop between two horizontal charged plates is moving upwards with a constant speed of 2.50 m/s in an electric field of 22.0 kV/m. Determine the magnitude of the charge on the oil drop. [1.8×10^{-19} C]

7. A 5.50×10^{-16} kg oil drop accelerates upward at a rate of 2.80 m/s^2 when placed between two horizontal parallel plates that are 3.40 m apart. The potential difference between the two plates is 790 V. Determine the magnitude of the charge on the oil drop. [2.98×10^{-17} C]

8. A 1.50×10^{-14} kg oil drop accelerates downwards at a rate of 1.80 m/s^2 when placed between two horizontal parallel plates that are 9.40 cm apart. The potential difference between the two plates is 980 V. Determine the magnitude of the charge on the oil drop. [1.15×10^{-17} C]

9. A computer program is used to simulate a charged oil drop experiment. Multiple trials are performed on the same 6.1×10^{-16} kg oil drop where the potential difference is manipulated and the value of the upward acceleration responds. The separation between the charged plates is 6.0 cm. The data collected from the computer simulation is provided in the table below.

Potential difference (V)	Upward acceleration (m/s^2)
400	7.9
420	8.9
440	9.8
460	11.2
480	11.6

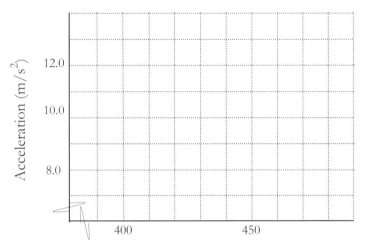

Potential Difference (V)

a. Plot the data showing the relationship between the acceleration and the potential difference.
b. Use your graph to determine the charge on the oil drop. [~1.7×10^{-18} C]
c. Determine the number of excess charges on the oil drop. [11]

10. Thomas Edison became convinced that electrical charge is quantized when he used Millikan and Fletcher's oil drop apparatus. He had previously thought that charge could be any continuous variable. Define quantized [Appendix A]

Use the information below to answer question 11.

A free-body diagram is a necessary part of the solution for oil drop problems. Four free-body diagrams for an oil drop are drawn below. [Appendix A]

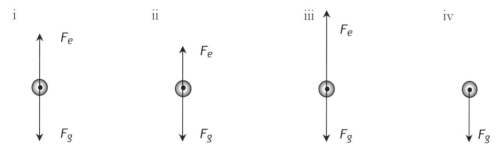

11. Considering only the vertical dimension, identify the free-body diagram(s) that best describes an oil drop that is
    a. moving at a constant velocity.
    b. accelerating upwards.
    c. accelerating downwards.

12. A 5.80×10^{-9} kg oil droplet having a charge magnitude of 5.40×10^{-14} C enters the electric field between two horizontally charged plates that are 8.00 cm apart, as shown in the diagram. The oil drop passes through the plates undeflected at a uniform speed of 10.0 cm/s. (Ignore the effects of the nonuniform electric field at the ends of the plates.)

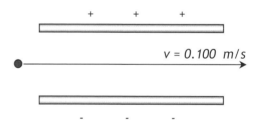

   a. Draw electric field lines between the plates in the diagram. [Appendix A]
   b. Identify the sign of the charge on the oil drop. [Appendix A]
   c. Determine the potential difference between the two plates. [84.3 kV]

13. A charged oil drop is sent in through the uniform electric field between two parallel plates as shown in the diagram below. The potential difference is adjusted so that the charged particle just contacts the upper right side of the positive plate. (Ignore the effects of the non-uniform electric field at the ends of the plates.) Determine the charge on the particle. [1.4 x 10^{-8} C]

Mass of oil drop: 5.0 x 10^{-5} kg
Initial velocity of particle: 0.70 m/s, directly to the right
Electric field between plates: 120 kV/m

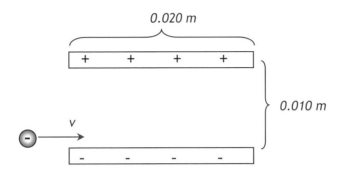

14. A 1.20 x 10⁻⁶ kg particle having a charge of -0.500 μC is travelling horizontally at 5.00 m/s when it enters the region between two charged plates as shown in the diagram. The particle strikes the top plate at its extreme right end. Determine the potential difference between the plates. (Ignore the effects of the nonuniform electric field at the ends of the plates.) [10.3 V]

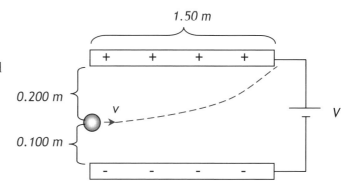

Paint may be applied to a surface using electrostatic principles. This process was invented by Ransburg in 1938. Negatively charged paint particles are sprayed at low speed to a charged surface which attracts the charged particles. This method of painting has the advantage of wasting much less paint than conventional painting methods. [Appendix A]

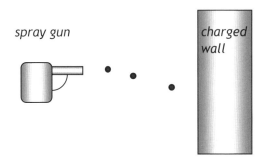

15.   A 2.30×10^{-10} kg negatively charged paint droplet of 9.25×10^{-14} C is travelling towards the wall where it enters the wall's uniform electric field of 4.50×10^{4} N/C shown below.
  a.   Draw the forces (i.e., free-body diagram) acting on the charged particle below.
  b.   Identify the charge (positive, negative or neutral) on the wall's surface.
  c.   Determine the net force acting on the particle. [4.74 nN, 28.5° down from the horizontal]

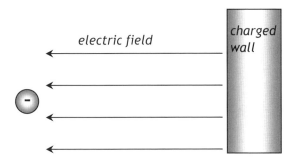

16. A 4.70 × 10⁻³ kg pith ball, having a charge magnitude of 2.40 μC, is suspended on a 90.0 cm long string between two oppositely charged parallel plates as shown in the diagram. The pith ball is 2.00 cm from its original vertical position before the plates were charged. [Appendix A]

a. Identify the sign of the charge on the pith ball.
b. Use arrows to draw the electric field direction between the two charged plates on the diagram.
c. Draw a free-body diagram for the pith ball.
d. Determine the magnitude of the electric field between the plates. [381 N/C]
e. Determine the potential difference between the two charged plates. [11.4 V]

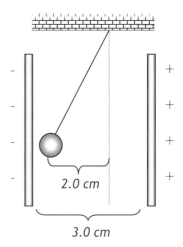

3.6 Extensions

1. List 4 factors that can help keep you safe from lightning. [Appendix A]

2. A water molecule can be assume to be dipolar with two half charges on each hydrogen atom separated by a distance of 0.40 nm. Determine the electrostatic force between the hydrogen atoms. [3.6×10^{-10} N]

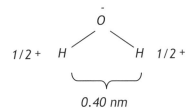

3. Three point-charges, each having identical charges of $+3.0\ \mu C$, are aligned as shown in the diagram below. Determine the initial net force acting on charge C due to charges A and B. [32 N, 40° S of E]

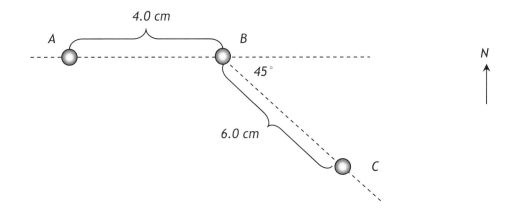

4. A negatively charged water droplet that has a radius 0.020 mm remains stationary in the air. If the electric field of the Earth is 100 N/C, determine the number of excess electrons on the water droplet. Ignore any buoyancy effect due to the air. [2.1×10^{7}]

5. A 2.00×10^{-5} kg oil drop, having a charge of 4.00×10^{-10} C, is accelerated upwards through parallel plates as shown to the right. As it exits the top plate the battery is turned off and the oil drop continues upwards with only gravity exerting a force on it. Determine the maximum height (h) the drop rises above the top plate. [2.15 m]

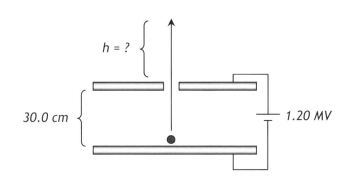

Use the information below to answer question 6.

Coulomb's law may also be written as follows, where Coulomb's constant is shown in its more fundamental form:

$$F_e = \frac{q_1 q_2}{4 \pi \varepsilon_o r^2}$$

Where:

F_e is the electrostatic force (N)

ε_o is permittivity (no units) (A vacuum has the lowest permittivity.)

q is charge (C)

r is distance separating the two charges (m)

6.　　Relate Coulomb's constant to the above equation. [Appendix A]

3.7 Review

Use the diagram below to answer question 1.

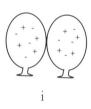　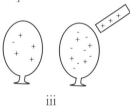　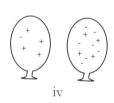

　　　i　　　　　　　　　　ii　　　　　　　　　　iii　　　　　　　　　　iv

1.　　The process described in steps 1 to 4 would be charging by
　　a.　friction
　　b.　magnetism
　　c.　conduction
　　d.　induction

2.　　Three small objects are used in an electrostatics demonstration. Object x has a charge of -1.00 nC while object y and z are initially neutral. Object x is brought into contact with object y and then separated. Object y is then brought into contact with object z and they are separated. The charge on object z is
　　a.　+0.25 nC
　　b.　-0.25 nC
　　c.　+0.50 nC
　　d.　-0.50 nC

3.　　The process of grounding
　　a.　keeps all charged objects positive
　　b.　does not follow the law of electric charge
　　c.　allows excess charge to move from one location to another
　　d.　stops electrons from moving onto an electroscope

4. The maximum speed of an electron in a cathode ray tube that is accelerated from rest through a potential difference of 4.00 kV is
    a. 1.41×10^{15} m/s
    b. 3.75×10^{7} m/s
    c. 1.41×10^{12} m/s
    d. 1.19×10^{5} m/s

5. Uniform electric fields
    a. do not follow the inverse square law
    b. break the law of electric charge
    c. always keep charges stationary
    d. allow one type of charge to flow in two directions

6. Dr. Brouwer demonstrates an interesting physics phenomena to his students: He takes a plastic comb and runs it through his dry hair. He then places it near an empty metal pop can that is lying on its side on a level table. The can accelerates towards the comb. Dr. Brouwer can move the pop can and back and forth across the table without touching it since it seems to be attracted to the comb. Explain. [Appendix A]

7. Although Coulomb is typically given credit for establishing the inverse square law for electrostatics, Scottish doctor John Robinson had previously explored the mathematical relationship in 1769.
    a. Calculate the magnitude of the electric force between two point charges of $+8.00\ \mu C$ and $+3.00\ \mu C$ when they are 3.50 cm apart. [176 N]
    b. Sketch the graph of the relationship between force and distance separating two charged particles. [Appendix A]

8. When calculating electrostatic forces between charged masses, when may the gravitational force of attraction be ignored because it is too small to be significant, and when must it be considered? [Appendix A]

9. Two charges, -5.00 μC and -6.00 μC, exert a force of repulsion of 0.0491 N on each other. Determine their separation distance. [2.34 m]

10. Two point charges produce an electrostatic force of attraction of 3.5×10^{-3} N. Determine the electrostatic force produced if the charge on both objects is tripled and the distance between them is doubled. [7.9×10^{-3} N]

11. Three point charges are arranged in a line as shown.

    a. force acting on sphere B. [20 N, West]
    b. field acting at sphere B. [1.0×10^{6} N/C, West]

12. Two +20 µC charges are placed as in the diagram. Determine the net electric field strength at point P. [1.0 x 10^5 N/C, 45° N of E]

A   50 cm

+20 µC

N

50 cm

B +20 µC

13. Determine the stopping voltage for an electron travelling at 5.52 x 10^7 m/s. [8.67 kV]

14. An alpha particle travelling at 5.0 x 10^5 m/s enters through a hole in a negative plate and collides with the positive plate at 1.0 x 10^5 m/s. Determine the potential difference between the charged plates. [2.5 kV]

15. A 5.60 x 10^{-16} kg oil drop accelerates upward at a rate of 3.80 m/s^2 when placed between two horizontal parallel plates that are 4.40 m apart. The potential difference between the two plates is 900 V. Determine the magnitude of the charge on the oil drop. [3.73 x 10^{-17} C]

3.8 Review Assignment

1. When pouring a flammable liquid from one metal container to another it is recommended that a conducting wire is attached between the two containers. Use electrostatic principles to explain the role of the conducting wire.

2. A stream of neutral soap bubbles is directed at a charged Van de Graaff dome. As the bubbles near the dome they can be observed to accelerate towards it. The first one hits the dome, breaks and splatters. The remaining bubbles are seen to stop, reverse and accelerate away.

   Explain the observations. Organize your response into two columns: the description and the corresponding explanation. Be sure to include diagrams.

Bubbles 3.8.1

3. Determine the magnitude of the electric force between a +4.00 µC and a +6.00 µC charge separated by 4.00 m.

4. Two charged objects, A and B, exert a force of 3.0 x 10^{-6} N on each other. If the distance between A and B were tripled, determine the magnitude of the resulting electric force.

5. Two charges are separated by a distance of 1.0 m as shown in the diagram below. A third charge of +2.0 nC is to be placed in line with the two fixed charges so that the net electrostatic force acting on the third charge will be zero. Determine the location on the line where this third charge should be located.

-1.0 nC   +4.0 nC

6. Three point-charges, each having identical charges of +4.0 μC, are aligned as shown in the diagram below. Determine the initial net force acting on charge B due to charges A and C.

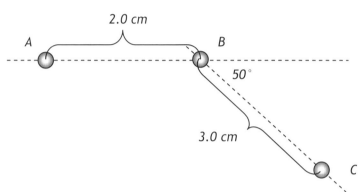

7. Determine the magnitude of an electric field 2.0 m away from a +5.00 μC charge.

8. Determine the electric field strength at point P in the following situations if charge A is +4.00 μC and charge B is -3.00 μC.

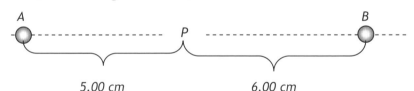

A

P

B

5.00 cm   6.00 cm

9. Determine the electric field at point P caused by the two charges separated by 4.00 m.

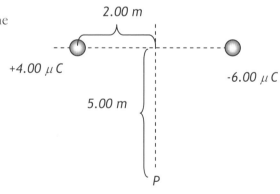

2.00 m

+4.00 μC

-6.00 μC

5.00 m

P

Ink jet printers work by sending a small drop of ink towards the media to be printed upon (e.g., paper). Ultra precise control over the ink drops is needed in order to effectively print. Each small ink drop travels past an electrode that gives it a charge. The charged ink drop passes through a uniform electric field generated by parallel plates.

If a gap in the printing is needed (e.g., a white space) the plates are charged so the ink drop will continue to travel directly through to the "gutter". When the ink drop is used to form part of a letter or a picture on the media, the plates are charged and the ink drop is forced to move upwards, past the gutter to the print media.

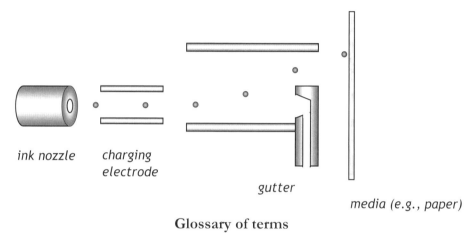

ink nozzle   charging electrode   gutter   media (e.g., paper)

Glossary of terms

Ink nozzle:	Produces a small drop of ink travelling at a constant velocity.
Charging electrode:	Charges each of the ink drops.
Deflection electrode:	Produces an electric field so that the drops will deflect.
Gutter:	Collects the unused ink.
Media:	The substance (e.g., paper) to be printed on.

10. Draw a free-body diagram for an oil droplet that travels to the
    a. gutter.
    b. paper.

11. A proton moving horizontally at 2.10 x 10^6 m/s enters a 200 N/C electric field exactly halfway between two horizontal parallel plates as shown in the diagram. Determine the vertical displacement of the proton as it travels between the plates.

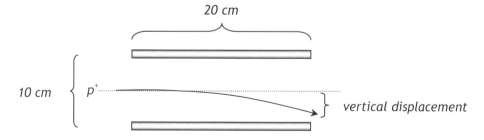

20 cm

10 cm p^+ vertical displacement

4 Magnetism

Introduction

Early experience with magnetism came from a form of iron ore called lodestone. It is now known that magnetic phenomena occur throughout the universe. Little of our modern technology would be possible without a thorough knowledge of magnetism and electromagnetism.

4.1 Summary Notes – Magnetism

Laws of Magnetic Poles:
- There are two types of poles; north and south.
- Like poles repel.
- Unlike poles attract.

Magnetic fields (B) are an attempt to explain the interaction of magnetic poles. It is the region where magnetic effects can be observed.

Magnetic field direction is defined as the direction the north end of a compass needle points (i.e., towards a south magnetic pole). The compass needle acts as a **test object** to test the direction of the field. The magnetic field lines can be drawn as shown:

magnetic field lines

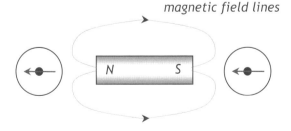

Notes:

_____

_____

_____

_____

_____

_____

_____

_____

_____

_____

Field 4.1.1

Examples

1. A small compass is placed next to a powerful bar magnet and the compass needle points at the magnet as shown below. Assume the dark end of the compass needle is its north pole.
    a. Label the polarity of the bar magnet.
    b. Is the magnetic force on the bar magnet stronger, weaker, or identical to the magnetic force on the compass needle.

    b. According to Newton's third law the forces should be equal in magnitude and opposite in direction.

2. Sketch the magnetic field lines, including direction, between the poles of a horseshoe magnet.

    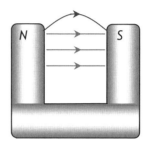

Problems

1. A small compass is placed next to a powerful bar magnet and the compass needle orientates itself to point at the magnet as shown in the diagram. Assume the dark end of the compass needle is its north pole. Label the polarity of the bar magnet. [Appendix A]

    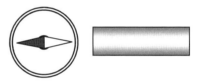

2. An arrow may be used to represent the north end of a compass needle. Draw a compass needle on the compass for each situation below. [Appendix A]

    a.
    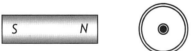

    b.

    c.

3. Determine the magnetic field direction at point P in the diagram below. [Appendix A]

       P

---

4. A bar magnet is placed under a piece of paper. Small iron filings are sprinkled on top of the paper and arrange themselves to show the bar's magnetic field pattern. Sketch the pattern of the iron fillings on the bar magnet below. [Appendix A]

5. Sketch the magnetic field lines in the area between the two bar magnets. [Appendix A]

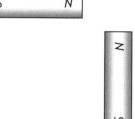

6. While electric fields and magnetic fields are different phenomena they have some common aspects. Use diagrams to compare the electric field produced by two point charge, one positive and one negative, with an analogous magnetic field situation. [Appendix A]

Electric Fields   **Magnetic Fields**

7. Field theory is used to explain gravitational, electrical, and magnetic phenomenon. List the source, direction (i.e., attraction or repulsions), and range for each type of field by completing the chart below. [Appendix A]

Field	Source/cause	Direction	Range
Gravitational	mass	attraction only	infinite
Electric			
Magnetic			

8. Identify what could be used as a test object for each of the fields listed. [Appendix A]

Field	Test object
Gravitational	Small mass
Electric	
Magnetic	

4.2 Summary Notes – Electromagnetism

☐ Notes:

_____

_____

_____

_____

_____

_____

Oersted discovered that a current through a wire produces a magnetic field **circling** the wire.

magnetic field (B)

electron flow

Magnetic field strength (B) is measured in units of tesla (T).

Magnetic field vectors must be described in three dimensions. Vector convention for arrows into or out of a page:

arrow directed into the page   X

arrow directed out of the page   •

Field 4.2.1

Hand Rules for relating magnetic field direction and current direction

First Left-Hand Rule for Straight Wires

- Thumb of the left hand points in the direction of electron flow.
- Fingers will circle the wire in the same direction as the magnetic field.

Second Left-Hand Rule for Coils

- Left hand grasps the coil.
- Fingers curl around the loops in the direction of electron flow.
- Thumb points in the direction of the North Pole of an imaginary bar magnet inside the coil.

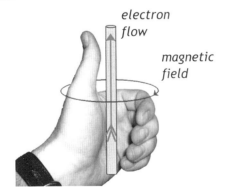

electron flow

magnetic field

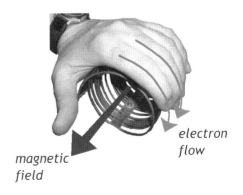

magnetic field

electron flow

N.B., Note the corresponding right hand rule for conventional current.

Examples

1. A horizontal wire's current (electron flow) is to the right as shown in the diagram below. Determine the direction of the magnetic field on a point that is directly beneath of the wire.

    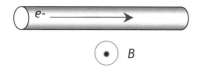

    (•) B

    Using a hand rule for electron flow, the magnetic field below the wire is directed out of the page. In the hand rule, the left hand represents the negative charge, the thumb represents the direction the electrons are moving, and the direction the fingers coil around the wire represents the direction of the magnetic field circling around the wire.

2. An iron bar inside current carrying coils of wire produces a strong electromagnet. On the diagram to the right,
    a. label the polarity of the electromagnet.
    b. draw the magnetic field lines outside the coil.

    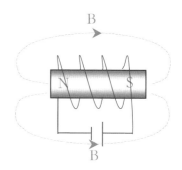

Problems

1. A current carrying wire produces a magnetic field (B) circling the wire as shown in the diagram. Use a hand rule to determine the direction of the electron flow through the wire. [Appendix A]

    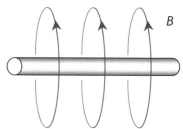

2. A current carrying wire (electrons flowing as shown) produces a magnetic field (B) circling the wire as shown in the diagram. Use a hand rule to determine the direction of the magnetic field circling around the wire. [Appendix A]

    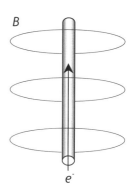

Use the information below to answer question 3.

One method for representing a three dimensional magnetic field on a two dimensional paper is by drawing vector arrows coming in and out of the pages as represented by using dots and Xs.

3.   A straight wire is orientated along the vertical and a battery is attached so that the electrons flow through the wire downwards to the ground. Two diagrams are given below to represent this situation: the first from the point of view of an observer on top, and second from the point of view of an observer looking at the apparatus from the side. For each diagram
a.   draw the magnetic field around the wire. [Appendix A]
b.   determine the magnetic field direction at a point just south of the wire. [Appendix A]

4.   The magnetic field circling a wire is three-dimensional but is often drawn two dimensionally with dots and Xs to represent the vectors coming into and out off the page. Determine the direction of the electron flow through each wire below that causes the indicated magnetic field. [Appendix A]

a.   Wire and 2-dimensional magnetic field   b.   Wire and 3-dimensional magnetic field

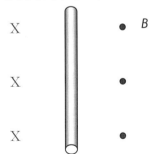

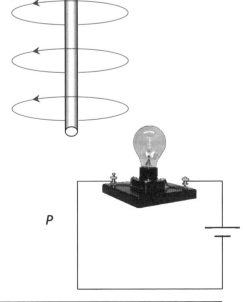

5.   Determine the direction of the magnetic field at point P beside the simple circuit shown. [Appendix A]

6. A wire is suspended vertically and a power supply is attached so that electrons flow through the wire, upwards from the ground. Determine the direction of the magnetic field on a point that is directly to the geographic south of the wire. [west]

7. An electromagnet is constructed using a soft iron core wrapped with insulated wire as shown in the diagrams. For each electromagnet [Appendix A]
   a. label the magnetic polarity of the iron core.
   b. draw the magnetic field lines around the electromagnet.

   i.
   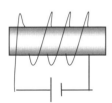

   ii.
   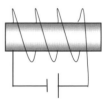

8. The electromagnet on the right has its poles as labelled. Draw in the battery (between terminals A and B) so that the magnet's polarity will be as shown in the diagram. [Appendix A]

   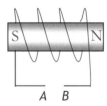

9. The diagram on the right shows a compass needle pointing towards an electromagnet. (The dark end of the compass needle is its north end.) Add a battery to the diagram (between terminals A and B) with the proper polarity which would cause the compass needle to point as indicated. [Appendix A]

   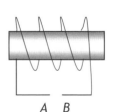

10. Two identical electromagnets are placed next to a compass as shown. Draw the needle on the compass pointing in the appropriate direction. [Appendix A]

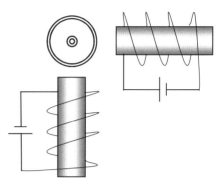

11. A coil is connected to a battery and a compass is set at various locations around and inside the coil as shown in the diagram below. [Appendix A]

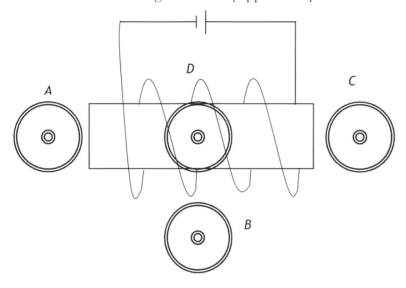

a. Use appropriate hand rules to predict the direction the compass needle (north end) will point for each location (i.e., left, right, up or down).

b. After recording your predictions confirm them by viewing the video showing an actual compass at each location. (The north end is red.) Complete the chart.

Location	Prediction	Observation
A		
B		
C		
D		

Coil 4.2.2

A current carrying wire has a magnetic field surrounding it which can be calculated using:

$$B = \frac{\mu_o}{2\pi}\left(\frac{I}{r}\right)$$

Where:
    B is the magnetic field strength in units of tesla (T)
    I current through the wire (A)
    r is the distance to the wire (m)
    μ_o is a constant (1.26×10^{-6} N/A^2)

12. Calculate the magnetic field strength in units of tesla (T) 5.00 cm away from a wire carrying a current of 1.20 A. [4.81×10^{-6} T]

Use the information below to answer question 13.

The unit of magnetic field strength is tesla (T).

Source	Magnetic field strength (T)
Surface of a neutron star	10^{13}
Highest sustained artificial magnet	45
MRI	1-4
NIB (rare earth) magnet	0.2 - 1.4
Bar magnet	0.09
Fridge magnet	0.06
Surface of the Earth	4.5×10^{-5}
Human brain	1.00×10^{-13}

13. Calculate the strength of a bar magnet relative to the Earth's magnetic field (calculate a ratio). [2.0×10^{3}]

14. Magnetic resonance imaging (MRI) requires strong magnetic fields so that they can interact with the magnetic field created by spinning hydrogen nuclei. Using the concepts of magnetic forces and fields explain why the following warning sign must be posted. [Appendix A]

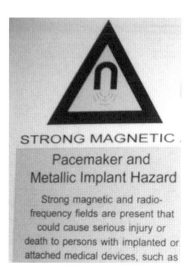

Use the information below to answer questions 15 & 16.

Moving charges create magnetic fields. Magnetic domains are collections of electrons within a substance that act as tiny bar magnets. These domains are responsible for a substance's magnetic properties.

Aligned domains   *Random domains*

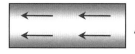 *Magnetic*    *Non magnetic*

15. Ferromagnetic substances such as iron, nickel and cobalt have a maximum temperature where their magnetic properties disappear called the Curie temperature. This occurs because of thermal agitation according to the kinetic molecular theory. Explain in terms of magnetic domains why a high temperature can cause magnetic properties to disappear. [Appendix A]

16. Iron combined with traces of carbon at high temperatures is used to make steel. Steel is much harder than pure iron and can be used to make permanent magnets. Soft iron works well for electromagnets where it is necessary to be able to turn the magnetic field on or off. Use the domain theory to explain how the addition of carbon creates a permanent magnet. [Appendix A]

4.3 Summary Notes – Moving Charges in Magnetic Fields

The magnetic field of a moving charged particle will interact with external magnetic fields to exert a force on the particle.

The velocity of the particle and the magnetic field must be perpendicular to each other to maximize the magnetic force produced.

Direction: Third left-hand Rule for Moving Charged Particles in Magnetic Fields:

- Left thumb points in the direction of electron flow.
- Fingers indicate the direction of permanent magnetic field (south).
- The palm shows the direction of the force produced through the interaction of the moving electrons and the magnetic field.

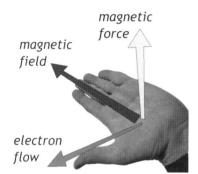

magnetic force

magnetic field

electron flow

The magnitude of the magnetic force on a moving charged particle is

$$F_m = qv_\perp B$$

Where:

    F_m is the force acting on the wire (N)

    B is the perpendicular magnetic field strength (T)

    q is the charge on the moving particle (C)

    $v_\perp$ is the speed of the particle perpendicular to the magnetic field (m/s)

□ Notes:

_____

_____

_____

_____

_____

_____

_____

_____

_____

_____

Examples

1. A proton is travelling due west when it enters a magnetic field that is towards the south. Determine the direction of the magnetic force on the proton.

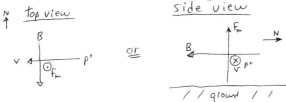

The beam is deflected upwards.

2. An electron is accelerated from rest across a potential difference of 20 000 V. It then enters a magnetic field of 60 mT that is perpendicular to the direction of the electron's path. Determine the electron's radius of curvature in the magnetic field.

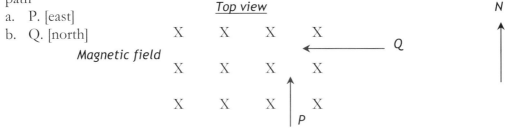

The electron's radius of curvature is 8.0 mm.

Problems

1. Electrons travel through a uniform magnetic field (represented by X) directed to the ground as shown below. An observer is looking downwards at the moving electrons (i.e., top view). Determine the directions of the magnetic force acting on the electron when it is travelling along path
   a. P. [east]
   b. Q. [north]

2. Electrons travel through a uniform magnetic field directed to the west as shown below. An observer is looking downwards at the moving electrons (i.e., top view). Determine the direction of the magnetic force acting on the electrons when it is travelling along path
   a. P. [down]
   b. Q. [no magnetic force]

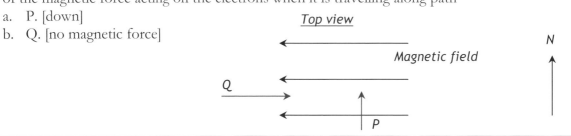

3. An electron approaches an electric field and a magnetic field as shown in the two diagrams below. Describe the direction of the electron's motion in each field. [Appendix A]

    a. _Electric field_

    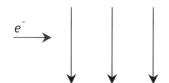

    b. _Magnetic field_

    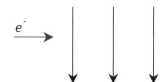

4. A beam of electrons is moving due east when it encounter a magnetic field directed to the geographic north. Determine the initial direction of the magnetic force acting on the electrons. [downward]

5. A beam of alpha particles is travelling south when it enter a magnetic field directed upwards from the ground. Determine the direction the beam is initially deflected due to the magnetic force acting on it. [west]

6. A beam of negatively charged chloride ions (Cl⁻) are moving due east when they encounter a magnetic field directed to the south. Determine the direction the beam is initially deflected due to the magnetic force acting on it. [upwards]

7. A beam of positively charged lithium ions (Li^+) are travelling vertically downwards towards the ground when they enter a magnetic field directed to the east. Determine the direction the beam is initially deflected due to the magnetic force acting on it. [south]

8. A beam of alpha particles is travelling north when it enters a magnetic field causing the beam to be deflected downwards to the ground. Identify the direction of the magnetic field. [east]

9. A beam of charged particles are travelling north when they enter a magnetic field directed upwards from the ground. The beam is deflected to the east due to the magnetic force. Identify the sign of the charge on the particle. [positive]

10. Three identical charge particles (a, b and c) enter a magnetic field (B) at the same speed as shown in the diagram. Identify the particle that would experience the greatest magnetic force. Explain your choice. [Appendix A]

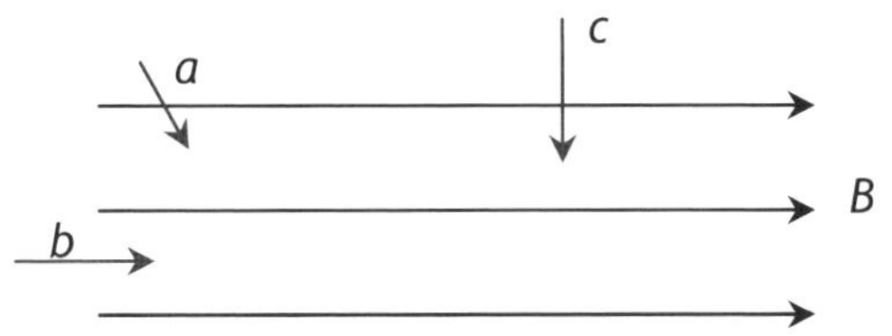

11. Fill in the blanks to properly complete the sentences.

    A charged particle travelling perpendicularly through a magnetic field will move in a _____ path because the magnetic force is directed _____ to the direction the particle moves. As a result the _____ force is a centripetal force. [Appendix A]

Use the information below to answer question 12.

The left-hand and right-hand rules used to relate magnetic force, magnetic field direction, and charge movement were developed by the English electrical engineer, Sir John Flemming (1849-1945). He also invented the vacuum diode as shown in the diagram. Early vacuum tube diodes were the basis for computers switches but have since been replaced by solid-state transistors that are much smaller, more reliable, and more energy efficient.

12. When a current is passed through the metal filament, electrons are ejected through a process called thermionic emission. These electrons accelerate through the vacuum towards the positively charged plate shown in the vacuum tube on the right.

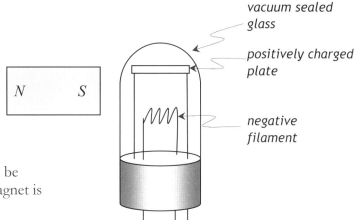

Describe how the electron's motion will be affected when the south end of a bar magnet is placed as shown. [Appendix A]

Use the information below to answer question 13.

Some artificial hearts pump the ions in blood using both electrical and magnetic fields as shown in the cross sectional diagram.

Positive ions are drawn to the negative plate while negative ions are drawn to the positive plate. The motion of the ions will then be perpendicular to the magnetic field which causes them to deflect along the length of the blood vessel.

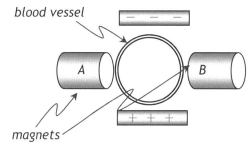

13. Identify the necessary magnetic polarity of A and B that would cause blood to flow out of the page in the diagram. Explain. [Appendix A]

14. The antiparticle of an electron is the positron. It has the same mass and charge as an electron but it is positive rather than negative. A beam of positrons, travelling north at 4.0×10^5 m/s, enters an upward magnetic field of 30 mT that is perpendicular to the direction of the beam. Determine the
    a. initial direction of the force acting on the positron. [east]
    b. magnitude of the force acting on the positron. [1.9×10^{-15} N]

15. Determine the magnetic field strength when an alpha particle travelling at 2.51×10^7 m/s experiences a magnetic force of 2.56×10^{-13} N. [0.0319 T]

16. During a solar storm the Sun ejects millions of tonnes of charged particles such as protons and electrons at high speeds. This solar wind causes the Earth's magnetic field to fluctuate and induce currents in terrestrial conductors (e.g., transmission lines, pipelines). These geomagnetically induced currents (GIC) can damage the conductors they flow through. The Earth's magnetic field protects us against normal solar wind but is often insufficient during solar storms.

    A proton that forms part of the solar wind is travelling at 600 km/s when it enters the Earth's magnetic field of 5.0×10^{-5} T. Determine the magnitude of the maximum possible deflecting force experienced by a proton. [4.8×10^{-18} N]

17. Fill in the blank. When the velocity of a charged particle is parallel to the magnetic field it is travelling through, the magnitude of the magnetic force on the particle is _____. [Appendix A]

A velocity selector is an electromagnetic device that will allow only ions with a certain velocity to pass through undeflected. This produces a beam of ions all with the same speed/energy. The velocity selector uses a magnetic field that is perpendicular to an electric field to produce opposing forces on the moving charged particles.

18.   A velocity selector is used to obtain a beam of lithium ions (Li^+) of uniform speed. Three possible paths for the lithium ions are shown in the diagram, each representing a different speed. Draw a free-body diagram for a lithium ion moving along path [Appendix A]
   a.   P.
   b.   D.
   c.   Q.

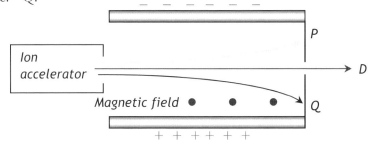

19.   A beam of singly ionized hydrogen ions is not deflected as it passes through a velocity selector having a magnetic field strength 1.8 x 10^{-3} T perpendicular to an electric field of 500 N/C.
   a.   Draw a free-body diagram of a hydrogen ion as it passes through the fields. [Appendix A]
   b.   Determine the speed of the ions. [2.8 x 10^5 m/s]

20.   A singly charged particle enters a 0.410 T magnetic field at 8.10 x 10^5 m/s. The velocity direction and the magnetic field direction are perpendicular to each other. Determine the particle's mass if it turns in a circle having a radius of 0.680 m as it travels through the magnetic field. [5.51 x 10^{-26} kg]

21. An alpha particle enters a 1.20 T magnetic field, causing it to turn with a radius of 2.34 cm. Determine the speed of the alpha particle as it enters the magnetic field. [1.35 x 10^6 m/s]

22. A proton is accelerated from rest across a potential difference of 6000 V. It then enters a magnetic field of 0.300 T that is perpendicular to the direction of its path. Calculate the proton's
    a. speed after crossing the potential difference. [1.07 x 10^6 m/s]
    b. radius of curvature in the magnetic field. [3.73 cm]

23. A beam of alpha particles is accelerated across a potential difference of 2500 V. They are then passed perpendicularly through a magnetic field and turn a circle with a radius of 9.10 cm. Determine the magnetic field strength. [0.112 T]

24. Electrons are accelerated across a potential difference and then passed perpendicularly through a 0.160 T magnetic field and turn a circle having a radius of 2.31 mm. Determine the potential difference the electrons cross before they enter the magnetic field. [12.0 kV]

25. Electrons are accelerated across an electric field. They then leave the electric field and enter a magnet field, causing them to turn in a circle. The path of the electrons is shown in the diagram below. Use labeled arrows to indicated the direction of the
    a. electric field.
    b. magnetic field.
    c. electric force acting on the electron.   [Appendix A]
    d. magnetic force acting on the electron.

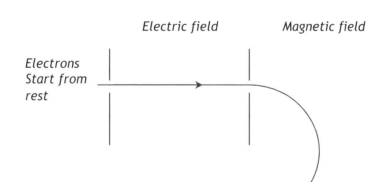

Use the information below to answer question 26.

Magnetic fields may be used to determine the mass of the ions and thus identify them. The mass spectrometer does this by first creating ions from a sample to be analyzed. These ions are then accelerated through an electric field in the accelerator. They then enter the magnetic field where the radius of their turn depends on their mass. They are detected using electronics or in the case of early mass spectrometers, photographic film.

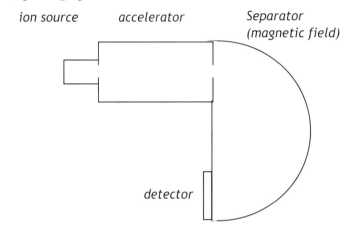

26. A beam of doubly ionized particles (i.e., twice the elementary charge) is accelerated across a potential difference of 2000 V in a mass spectrometer. They are then passed perpendicularly through a magnetic field of 0.085 T resulting in a radius of curvature of 12.5 cm. Calculate the mass of the unknown ion. [9.0 x 10^{-27} kg]

27. A simplified mass spectrometer may consist of three main parts: accelerator, velocity selector and separator. Label or identify the parts indicated on the mass spectrometer below. [Appendix A]

Section of mass spectrometer	Label/Identify the
Accelerator (uses an electric field)	i. charge on the particle ii. direction of the electric field
Velocity Selector (uses a magnetic field and electric field)	i. direction of the magnetic force ii. charge on the plates iii. direction of the magnetic field inside the wire loop iv. battery orientation to determine the direction of the current (electron flow) through the coil of wire that creates the magnetic field
Separator (uses a magnetic field)	i. direction of the magnetic force on the particle ii. direction of the magnetic field in the separator

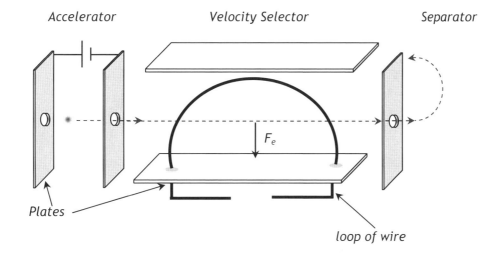

Accelerator   Velocity Selector   Separator

F_e

Plates

loop of wire

Natural uranium consists of the two isotopes, uranium-238 (99.29 %) and uranium-235 (0.71 %). The uranium-235 is used in atomic weapons and some nuclear power plants but must first be separated from the uranium-238 to produce enriched uranium (EU) or more pure uranium-235 called highly enriched uranium (HEU). International treaties govern the sale and production of HEU and some countries are barred from purchasing or producing it.

One of the early methods used to separate the isotopes of uranium was developed by Ernest Lawrence who invented of the cyclotron and won the 1939 Nobel Prize in Physics. The separation process is called Electromagnetic Isotope Separation but it was discontinued, as it was not as efficient as other methods. It was used, however, by Iraq in the 1990s because it is relatively easy to construct and international law restricts the sale of technology that could be used to enrich uranium by other more efficient methods. The apparatus is essentially a mass spectrometer:

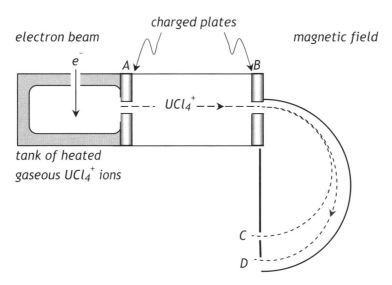

Process:
- Gaseous uranium tetrachloride (UCl_4) molecules are bombarded by electrons to produce positive ions (UCl_4^+).
- The ions are accelerated across the potential difference created by charged plates, A and B.
- The isotopes separate, following different trajectories as they turn through the magnetic field until they exit through the two openings, C and D.

28. Use the information above to complete the following: [Appendix A]
   a. Draw the electric field lines between the two charged plates, A and B.
   b. Identify the opening (C or D) that the U-235 isotope will most likely travel through.
   c. Identify the direction of the magnetic field causing the ions to move in a circle.

Rather than determining the mass of an ion, mass spectrometers may give a charge-to-mass ratio (q/m) which can be used to identify the ion. Various hydrocarbons, as listed in the table below, are ionized so they may be identified in a mass spectrometer.

Ion	Formula	q/m (x 10^6 C/kg)
Ethane	$C_2H_6^{2+}$	6.42
Propane	$C_3H_8^+$	2.18
Butane	$C_4H_{10}^{2+}$	3.31
Pentane	$C_5H_{12}^+$	1.34

29. A beam of hydrocarbon ions are accelerated across a potential difference of 1067 V and then passed perpendicularly through a magnetic field of 0.250 T. This results in a radius of curvature of 12.5 cm. Determine the identity of the ions using the provided chart and the ion's charge-to-mass ratio. [Appendix A]

30. Another type of mass spectrometer is call a time-of-flight (TOF) analyzer which uses the time for a charged particle to travel through a magnetic field to determine its mass. An unknown hydrocarbon ion required 9.415 x 10^{-6} s to travel through the 0.250 T magnetic field of a mass spectrometer with a radius of curvature of 14.1 cm. Since the magnetic field chamber is shaped as a "D" it only travels half way around the circle (i.e., 180°). Determine the
    a. speed of the ion through the magnetic field. [4.70 x 10^4 m/s]
    b. identity of the ion using its charge-to-mass ratio. [Appendix A]

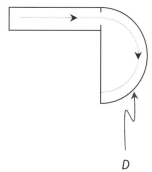

D

Use the information below to answer question 31.

Synchrotrons are particle accelerators that accelerate electrons in a circle using magnetic field to cause the electrons to follow a circular path and electric field to increase the electron's speed as they circle around. The Canadian Light Source Inc. (CLS) synchrotron in Saskatoon Saskatchewan has two circular paths that electrons may travel: a booster ring with a radius of 16.4 m to increase the electrons speed to 99.9999985 % the speed of light and a ring to store the fast electrons with a radius of 27.2 m.

According to Einstein's theory of special relativity as electrons approach the speed of light they become much more massive than electrons at rest. Electrons travelling at 99.9999985 % the speed of light through the storage ring have a relativistic mass of 6.79×10^{-27} kg.

31. Determine the strength of the magnetic field necessary to keep the 6.79×10^{-27} kg electrons moving through the storage ring in the CLS, assuming a uniform radius. [0.468 T]

Use the information below to answer questions 32 – 34.

Protons, all with the same constant velocity, are introduced into the magnetic field of a mass spectrometer. The strength of the magnetic field is varied and the resulting radii of the protons' path are measured. [Appendix A]

32. Identify the equation that correctly describes the radius of the proton's path through the magnetic field.

 a. $r = \dfrac{mB}{qv}$ b. $r = \dfrac{mv}{qB}$

 c. $r = \dfrac{qv}{mB}$ d. $r = \dfrac{qB}{mv}$

---

33. A straight line is obtained by modifying the manipulated variable. Identify the graph from the following choices that correctly shows the manipulation.

a.

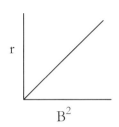

B^2

b.

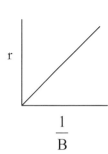

$\dfrac{1}{B}$

c.

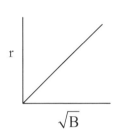

$\sqrt{B}$

d.

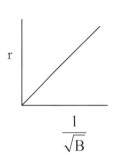

$\dfrac{1}{\sqrt{B}}$

34. The slope of the straight line graph can be used to determine the charge-to-mass ratio of the particle. Identify the expression that gives the value for the charge-to-mass ratio.
   a. velocity divided by slope
   b. slope divided by velocity
   c. slope times velocity
   d. slope squared times velocity

Use the information below to answer questions 35 – 41.

A compass needle is a small magnet. If it is constructed so it is free to turn, it will always align itself with the Earth's magnetic field (i.e., its north end always points to the Earth's Arctic magnetic pole).

- The Arctic magnetic pole is a south magnetic pole.
- The Earth's geographical North Pole is at a different location than its Arctic magnetic pole.
- The location of the Earth's magnetic poles is constantly changing.
- Dip angle or angle of inclination is the angle of the magnetic field relative to the ground (i.e., vertical magnetic field direction).

35. Identify the magnetic pole (N or S) that is in Canada's Arctic region. [Appendix A]

Declination (a.k.a. magnetic variation) is the difference in degrees between the Arctic magnetic pole and geographic North Pole. This is different for different locations on the Earth. The first recorded use of using a compass for navigation was by Zhu Yu in 1117 AD. On a topographical map used for navigation the declination (i.e., magnetic variation) is given as shown in the diagram. True north (T.N.) or geographic north is indicated using a star.

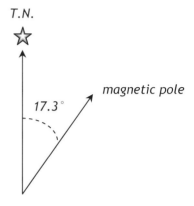

36.   Assume you are in the wilderness and need to hike towards the geographic north. In which direction should you walk relative to the direction your compass is pointing? [Appendix A]

37.   As you approach the Earth's Arctic magnetic pole the magnetic field weakens considerably. This can result in the magnetic force acting on the compass needle to be smaller than the force due to friction on the pivot supporting the compass needle. Explain how this might affect a compass' reliability in Canada's arctic. [Appendix A]

38.   The Apollo Moon flights during the late 1960s and early 1970s left the Earth's protective magnetic field to travel to the Moon. Explain why NASA did not schedule Lunar missions during times of high solar activity. [Appendix A]

39.   The Earth's magnetic field strength has decreased by 10 % over the last 150 years since it has been regularly measured and recorded. It has been predicted that it may decrease to zero in another 2000 years. Describe the possible consequences to life on Earth if the magnetic field strength continues to weaken. [Appendix A]

40. It is hypothesized that the Earth's magnetic poles are constantly moving because of a churning layer of molten iron about 4000 km below the Earth's surface which may be responsible for the magnetic field. This results in the magnetic declination (a.k.a magnetic variation) continually changing.

    a. Use the data in the chart to plot a graph of declination as a function of year.

    b. Use the graph to predict the declination in Stony Plain in the year 2040. [~8.5°]

Magnetic declination in Stony Plain

Year	Declination (degrees)
1960	23.6
1970	23.1
1980	21.7
1990	20.2
2000	18.4
2005	17.4
2010	16.2

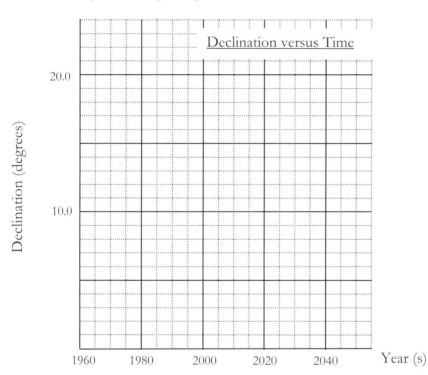

41. Charged particles from the Sun enter the Earth's magnetic field and then travel to the Earth's poles. When the particles contact gasses in the atmosphere, northern or southern lights are produced. Explain why the lights are produced only near the Earth's poles. [Appendix A]

Northern Lights

4.4 Summary Notes – Conductors in Magnetic Fields

Notes:

_____

_____

_____

_____

_____

_____

A force is exerted on a current carrying wire inside a magnetic field.

A moving charge creates a magnetic field. If the charged particle passes through an external magnetic field the two fields may interact to produce a force on the particle.

The magnitude of the magnetic force on a current carrying conductor is given by

$$F_m = I\ell_\perp B$$

Where:

F_m is the magnetic force acting on the wire (N)

B is the magnetic field strength in tesla (T)

I is current through the conductor (A)

$\ell_\perp$ is the length of the conductor perpendicular to the magnetic field (m)

N.B., The magnetic field, magnetic force, and current are all perpendicular to each other.

Examples

1. A wire is placed between two magnetic poles. The wire is attached to a battery and electrons flow into the page as shown in the diagram. Use a vector arrow to indicate the direction of the magnetic
   a. field between the poles.
   b. force acting on the wire.

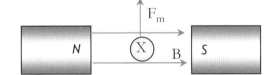

2. A 30 cm long copper wire has a mass of 40 g and is carrying a current of 5.0 A at right angles to a uniform magnetic field. This apparatus is placed in a strong magnetic field and the wire is found to levitate. Calculate the magnetic field strength.

$f_m = f_g$

$BI\ell = mg$

$B = \dfrac{mg}{I\ell}$

$B = \dfrac{40 \cdot 10^{-3} kg \cdot 9.81 N/kg}{5.0A \cdot 0.30m}$

$B = 0.2616 T$

The magnetic field strength must be 0.26 T.

Problems

1. A wire is placed between two magnetic poles. The wire is attached to a battery and electrons flow through the wire from right to left as shown in the diagram. Use vector arrows to indicate the direction of the magnetic
    a. field between the poles. [Appendix A]
    b. force acting on the wire. [Appendix A]

2. A wire is placed between two magnetic poles. The wire is attached to a battery and electrons flow through the wire into the page as shown in the diagram. Use vector arrows to indicate the direction of the magnetic
    a. field between the poles. [Appendix A]
    b. force acting on the wire. [Appendix A]
        (note e.g., #1 p. 162)

3. A wire is placed between two magnetic poles. The wire is attached to a battery and electrons flow through the wire from right to left as shown in the diagram. The wire experiences a magnetic force into the page. Label the polarity of the magnets. [Appendix A]

    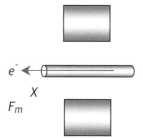

4. A wire in an electric motor is 0.500 m long and is perpendicular to a 0.30 T magnetic field. Determine the magnitude of the magnetic force on the wire when it carries a current of 1.0 A. [0.15 N]

---

5. A wire in an electric motor is 13.0 cm long and is perpendicular to the magnetic field of 0.250 T. Determine the magnitude of the current through the wire when it experiences a force of 0.350 N. [10.8 A]

6. A 60.0 cm long wire in an electric motor is perpendicular to a magnetic field and experiences a force of 0.12 N. Determine the magnitude of the magnetic field if the wire carries a current of 1.2 A. [0.17 T]

7. A 0.120 m long copper wire has a mass of 9.02 g and is carrying a current of 5.10 A perpendicular to a uniform magnetic field. This apparatus is placed in a strong magnetic field and the wire is found to levitate. Calculate the magnetic field strength. [0.145 T]

8. A 30 cm long copper wire has a mass of 40 g and is at right angles to a 0.262 T uniform magnetic field. This apparatus is placed in a strong magnetic field and the wire is found to levitate. Calculate the current through the wire. [5.0 A]

9. A 22.0 cm long aluminium wire carries a 2.10 A conventional current from east to west Assuming the component of the Earth's magnetic field strength directly into the ground is 3.01 x 10^{-5} T, determine the
   a. magnitude of the magnetic force produced on the wire. [1.39 x 10^{-5} N]
   b. direction of the magnetic force produced on the wire. [south]

Use the information below to answer question 10.

The two ends of a short wire are attached to the two ends of a 1.5 V battery. The wire is then brought close to a strong neodyminum magnet attached to the wall as shown in the picture.

A few simple measurements allow for a rough determination of the magnet's strength near its surface:

Mass of wire (m):	0.91 g
Diameter of magnet (L):	1.2 cm
Current through wire (I):	2.56 A

10. The gravitational force on the wire is equal in magnitude to the magnetic force causing the wire to levitate. Determine the magnet field strength of the magnet in units of tesla. [0.29 T]

11. A 20 cm wire is bent in the middle to form a right-angle and placed in a 0.61 T uniform magnetic field directed into the page as shown in the diagram. Determine the net magnetic force acting on the wire if it carries a current of 3.0 A. [0.26 N, 45° S of W]

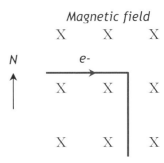

Magnetic field

Use the information below to answer questions 12 – 16.

The interaction between a current carrying wire and an external magnetic field is sometimes called the motor effect. This phenomenon was used by Michael Faraday to invent the electric motor. A basic DC (direct current) electric motor uses a loop of wire inside a magnetic field so that the force will cause the wire to turn.

- The armature is the coiled current carrying wire rotating on an axis.
- A split-ring commutator is needed to change the current direction every half of a rotation to keep the forces acting in the same direction.
- Brushes provide a strong electrical contact between the power source and the commutator.

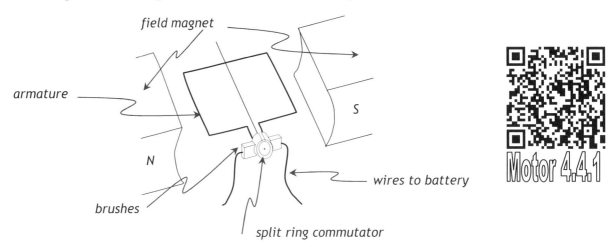

12. A motor is designed to have its armature rotate at a frequency of 60 Hz. Determine the time required for one complete rotation. [0.017 s]

13. The cross section of a simple DC electric motor is shown in the diagram. A single loop of wire is inside the magnetic field and the current direction (conventional current) within the loop is shown using a dot and an X. Use arrows to represent the forces on the two sections of wire, A and B. [Appendix A]

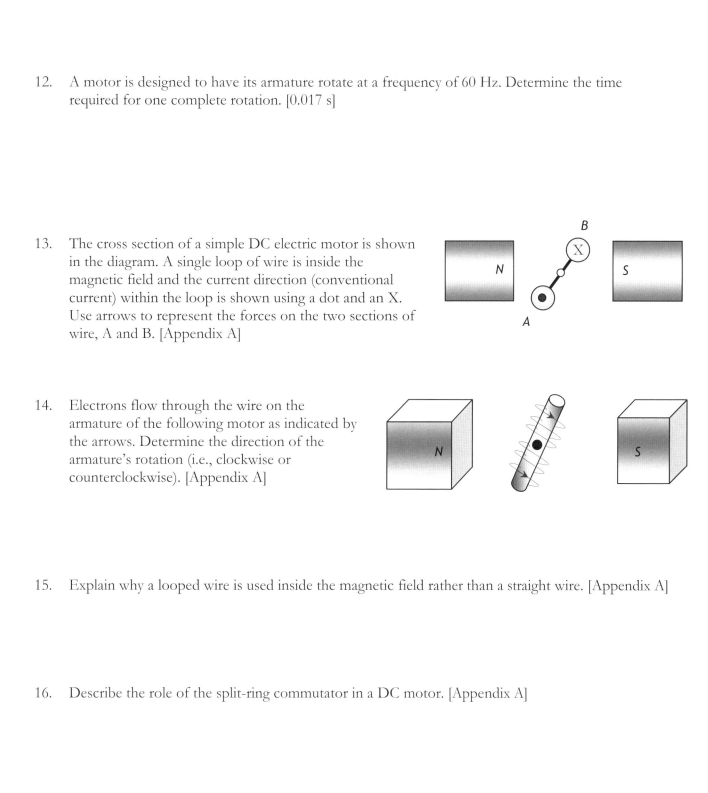

14. Electrons flow through the wire on the armature of the following motor as indicated by the arrows. Determine the direction of the armature's rotation (i.e., clockwise or counterclockwise). [Appendix A]

15. Explain why a looped wire is used inside the magnetic field rather than a straight wire. [Appendix A]

16. Describe the role of the split-ring commutator in a DC motor. [Appendix A]

A speaker converts electrical energy into sound energy. The force produced on a current carrying wire by an external magnetic field causes the wires of the voice coil, which are attached to the paper cone, to move which in turn causes the entire sound cone to oscillate. The oscillations are controlled to produce the desired sound waves.

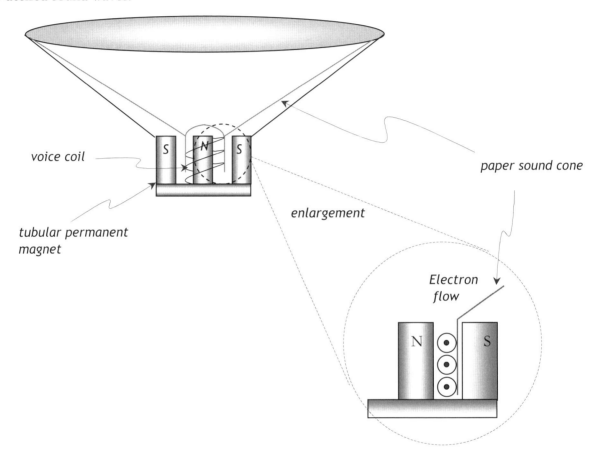

17. Describe the motion of the sound cone (i.e. up or down relative to the enlargement) when the current (i.e., electron flow) travels through the voice coil wires as shown. [Appendix A]

18. A small (1.2 cm in diameter) neodymium magnet is placed on an electronic balance. A wire is placed directly next to the magnet as shown in the picture.

The balance was zeroed when the current was off. The current was then turned on and manipulated. The corresponding balance readings were recorded. The experimental variables are provided in the table below.

Current (A)	Balance reading (g)
1.5	0.55
3.0	1.09
3.5	1.27
4.4	1.59
5.1	1.91

a. Graph the data.
b. Determine the slope of the graph. [~4.0 x 10^{-4} kg/A]
c. Use the slope to determine the strength of the magnetic field acting on the wire. [~0.32 T]

Balance reading as a function of Current for a Current Balance

Balance reading (x 10^{-3} kg)

2.0

1.0

1.0   2.0   3.0   4.0   5.0

Current (A)

4.5 Summary Notes – Lenz's Law

☐ Notes:

_____

_____

_____

_____

_____

_____

_____

_____

_____

_____

_____

Current may be induced through a conductor if the conductor is in a changing magnetic field.

Lenz's law helps explain induced current: An induced current flows in such a direction that the induced field it creates opposes the action of the inducing field.

Using Lenz's Law for coils:

> i.   Draw an imaginary bar magnet inside the coil that opposes the motion of the inducing magnetic field.
>
> ii. Use a hand rule to determine current direction (e.g., the thumb points to the north pole of the induced field and the fingers curl around to show direction of the current).

The magnitude of the induced voltage is a matter of the law of conservation of energy.

Examples

1. A copper rod shown is moving at 5.0 m/s to the right along conducting rails perpendicularly to a magnetic field that is directed out of the page as shown in the diagram. Determine the direction of the electron flow through the circuit.

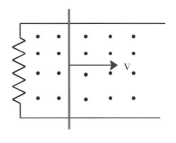

The electron flow is counter clockwise.

2. A bar magnet is moved into a coil, north end first. Determine the direction of the conventional current flow through the galvanometer.

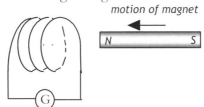

From left to right.

Problems

1. A wire that forms part of a circuit is moved through a magnetic field (represented by the dots and the Xs) as shown below. The arrows (labelled v) indicate the direction the wire is moved. Determine the direction of the induced current. [Appendix A]

    a.   b.   c.   d.

    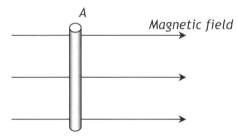

2. The cross section of two wires (P and Q) are forced to move through a magnetic field as shown in the diagram. Describe the induced current direction for each wire. [Appendix A]

    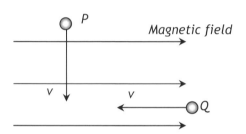

3. Determine the direction the wire must be forced to move in order to induce electrons to flow along the wire towards point A. [into the page]

    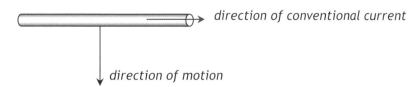

4. A section of wire that is part of a circuit is forced to move in a direction as shown in the diagram below. It enters a magnetic field that causes current to move from left to right through the wire. Determine the direction of the magnetic field. [into the page]

5.   A horseshoe magnet is on the ground as shown from a side view. A wire is pulled through the magnet towards geographic north, causing electrons to flow through the wire in a direction that is into the page. Label the poles of the horseshoe magnet. [Appendix A]

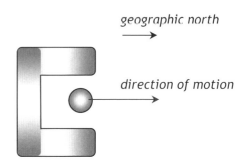

6.   The diagram to the right shows the cross section of two conducting wires (P and Q) moving towards a bar magnet as indicated by the arrows. Determine the direction of the induced current (electron flow) through wire
     a.   P. [into the page]
     b.   Q. [out of the page]

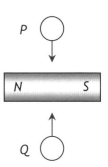

7.   At the equator, the Earth's magnetic field is nearly parallel to the surface with a magnitude of 4.45×10^{-5} T. A truck is driven due east starting from a point on the equator. Determine the electron flow direction through the truck's vertical antenna. [down, towards the ground]

8.   A copper ring is placed in a rapidly changing magnetic field. The copper ring becomes hot. Explain why the temperature of the copper increases. [Appendix A]

9. A bar magnet is moved relative to a coil, as depicted in the diagrams below. Determine the direction of the electron flow across through the galvanometer for each situation. [Appendix A]

a.   b.

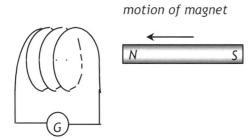

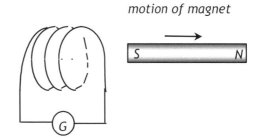

10. A magnet is moved out of a coil of wire (formed around a cardboard tube) causing the electrons to flow through the coil as indicated by the arrow on the wire by the galvanometer. Identify (north or south) the polarity of the magnet at the end labelled P. [north]

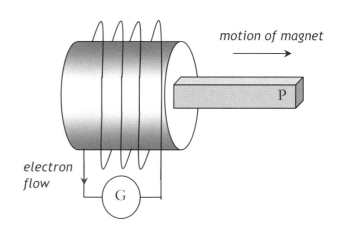

11. A magnet is moved through a coil causing electrons to flow as indicate by the arrow on the wire by the galvanometer. Determine the direction the magnet must be moved (left or right) to produce the indicated current. [to the right]

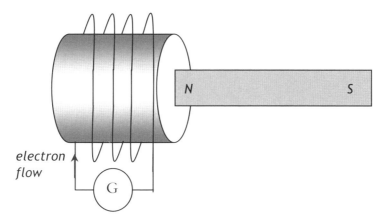

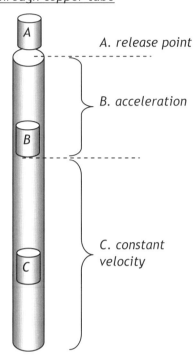

*Magnet falling
through copper tube*

A. release point

B. acceleration

*C. constant
velocity*

12. A non-magnetic object and a magnet are each dropped through a copper tube. The non-magnet free-falls through the tube while the magnet requires more time to fall. [Appendix A]

    a. Draw free-body diagrams for the magnet as it falls at the three locations (A, B, and C) on the given diagram.

    b. Describe the non-magnet's fall in terms of its
        i. kinetic energy.
        ii. gravitational potential energy.

    c. Describe the magnet's fall in terms of its
        i. kinetic energy.
        ii. gravitational potential energy.

    d. Explain why the magnet falls at constant velocity while the non-magnet simply free-falls through the tube.

4.6 Extensions

1. Two metal rods, A and B, are connected to separate batteries and placed near to each other as shown in the diagram. Determine if the rods will attract or repel each other. [Appendix A]

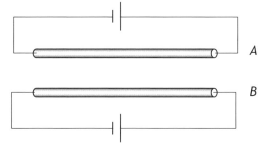

2. The cross-sectional diagram shows a current (assume electron flow) carrying wire inside a magnetic field. Each side of the electromagnet requires its own battery to create the electromagnetic poles.
Label the polarity of the electromagnets, indicate the direction of electron flow, and draw in the batteries so that the polarity will cause the wire to move downward.
[Appendix A]

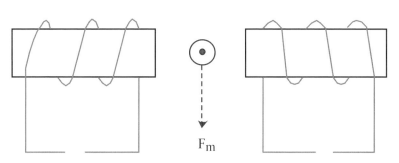

Use the information and diagram to answer questions 3 – 5.

A beam of electrons is passed between the electromagnets as shown below coming out of the page. A current is induced according to Lenz' law in the lower coil.

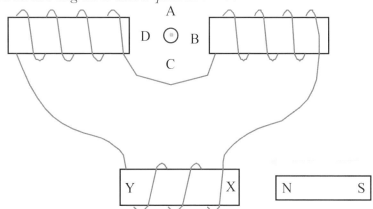

3. Identify the polarity of Y on the lower coil, N or S. [Appendix A]

4. Label the polarity on the upper electromagnets, N or S. [Appendix A]

5. Determine the direction the electron beam deflects, A, B, C, or D or no deflection. [Appendix A]

Use the information and diagram below to answer question 6.

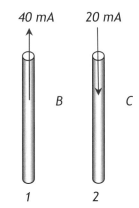

Two identical parallel copper wires, 1 and 2, carry currents of 40 mA and 20 mA in opposite directions as shown in the diagram.

6.   Identify the area, A, B, or C, where the magnetic field is most likely strongest. [Appendix A]

7.   A 40 cm long wire is oriented at 35° relative to magnetic field lines which have a value of 0.300 T. Calculate the magnitude of the magnetic force acting on the wire if the wire carries a current of 1.4 A. [0.096 N]

Use the information below to answer question 8.

A current carrying wire has a magnetic field surrounding it. The magnitude of this field can be found using the following formula:

$$B = \frac{\mu_o}{2\pi}\left(\frac{I}{r}\right)$$

Where:
    B is the magnetic field strength (T)
    I current through the wire (A)
    r is the distance to the wire (m)
    μ_o is a constant (1.26×10^{-6} N/A^2)

The Earth's magnetic field strength in the horizontal component is 4.3×10^{-5} T.

8.   A compass is placed near a vertically orientated wire as shown in the top view diagram below. The compass was pointing directly to the Earth's arctic magnetic pole before the current is turned on (the dark end of the compass needle is its north end). The wire then carries a current producing a magnetic field that makes the compass point 36° E of N. Determine the magnitude of the current through the wire at the compass' location. [5.0 A]

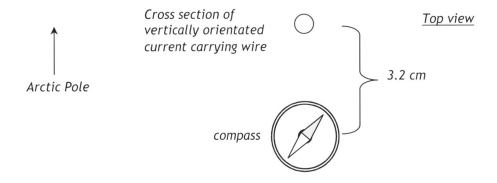

4.7 Review

1. In Alberta the north end of a compass needle points to (approximately) the geographic
    a. north
    b. south
    c. east
    d. west

2. A negatively charged droplet is travelling at a speed of 2.0×10^3 m/s. The field(s) that acts on this droplet is/are
    a. electrical only
    b. electrical and magnetic only
    c. magnetic and gravitational only
    d. electrical, magnetic, and gravitational

3. A charged particle experiences a magnetic force only when it
    a. moves in the same direction as the magnetic field
    b. crosses magnetic field lines
    c. goes against gravity
    d. moves against an electric field

4. A proton beam travels at a constant velocity to the right as shown below. Use a drawing to help describe the magnetic field created by the beam. [Appendix A]

    p+

5. The electromagnet on the right has its poles as labelled.
    a. Draw in the battery (between terminals A and B) so that the magnet's polarity will be as shown in the diagram. [Appendix A]
    b. Draw the magnetic field lines produced around the electromagnet. [Appendix A]

    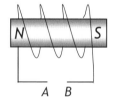

6. Three particles (A is a neutron, B is an electron and C is a proton), enter a magnetic field (B) at the same speed as shown in the diagram. Identify the direction the particle will be forced. Explain your choice. [Appendix A]

    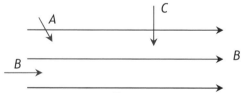

7. Determine the magnetic field strength acting on a positron travelling at 7.31×10^7 m/s that experiences a magnetic force of 5.38×10^{-13} N. [0.0460 T]

8. A beam of alpha particles is accelerated across a potential difference of 7.50 kV. They are then passed perpendicularly through a magnetic field and turn a circle with a radius of 15.1 cm. Determine the magnetic field strength. [0.117 T]

---

9. A 6.0 cm long copper wire has a mass of 5.04 g and is carrying a current of 14.10 A perpendicular to a uniform magnetic field. This apparatus is placed in a strong magnetic field and the wire is suspended motionless in the air.
   a. Draw a free-body diagram for the wire. [Appendix A]
   b. Calculate the magnetic field strength. [0.058 T]

10. A bar magnet is moved relative to a coil, as depicted in the diagrams below. Determine the direction of the electron flow through the galvanometer for each situation. [Appendix A]

   a.   b.

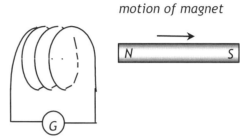

11. A mass spectrometer is used to determine the mass of triply charged negative ions. The ions were first accelerated through a potential difference of 90.0 V, and then injected into a 70.0 mT magnetic field where they have a radius of curvature of 11.6 cm. Determine the mass of the unknown ions. [1.76 x 10^{-25} kg]

Use the information below to answer question 12.

One end of an iron bar is coiled with insulated wires and attached to a 10 V AC power supply. The other end of the iron bar is coiled with twice the length of wire and is attached to a voltmeter as shown in the diagram

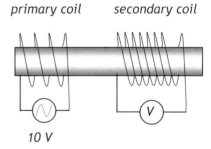

12. Using the diagram, explain how electrical power is induced in the secondary coil even though no current can transfer from the primary. [Appendix A]

4.8 Review Assignment

1. Determine the fundamental unit equivalent of the tesla.

2. Two electromagnets are place by a compass as shown. Draw the needle on the compass pointing in the appropriate direction.

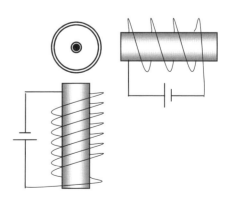

3. Determine the polarity of the battery that must be inserted to create the magnetic field lines shown on the electromagnet.

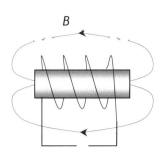

4. The Earth's magnetic field not only changes in direction it also changes in strength. If the present weakening trend continues the magnetic field may reduce to zero strength in 1500 years. It would then gradually gain strength and the north and south poles will be reversed. Considering that the Earth's magnetic field protects us and our technology from harmful solar radiation, how might technology and life on Earth be affected when this happens?

Use the information below to answer question 5.

The equation below describes the magnitude of the magnetic field around a current carrying wire.

$$B = \frac{K_m I}{r}$$

Where:

K_m is the magnetic constant
I is current in the wire
r is distance from the wire

5. Determine the units of the constant K_m.

6. A proton passes by a current carrying wire as shown in the diagram. Determine the direction of the magnetic
   a. field around the wire on the same side as the proton.
   b. force on the moving proton as it passes the wire.

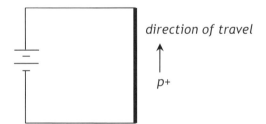

7. A current carrying wire has a magnetic field surrounding it. The magnitude of this field can be found using the following formula:

$$B = \frac{\mu_o}{2\pi}\left(\frac{I}{r}\right)$$

Where:
B is the magnetic field strength (T)
I current through the wire (A)
r is the distance to the wire (m)
μ_o is a permeability constant

An experiment is done to establish the value of the constant, μ_o. The current was constant through the wire at 5.0 A and the following data was collected:

Trial	Distance from wire (m)	Magnetic field strength (x 10^{-5} T)
1	0.10	6.28
2	0.20	3.14
3	0.30	2.09
4	0.40	1.57
5	0.50	1.26

a. Plot the variables that would give you a straight line.
b. Use the graph to determine the value, with units, of the constant μ_o.

Use the information below to answer question 8.

CERN is the *European Organization for Nuclear Research*, the world's largest centre for particle physics founded in 1954. The World Wide Web (www) was first developed at CERN as a method of communicating on the Internet for the 3000 people who work there. CERN uses the world's largest particle accelerated, 27 km in circumference, buried 100 m below the ground and is in both France and Switzerland. The high speed particles are used to determine how the atom works; what matter is made of and how the four fundamental forces work.

Protons travelling through the CERN accelerator can travel close to the speed of light. According to Einstein's theory of special relativity as they speed of light they become much more massive. Protons travelling through CERN's main accelerator obtain a relativistic mass of 8.01 x 10^{-25} kg.

8. Determine the strength of the magnetic field necessary to keep the 8.01 x 10^{-25} kg protons moving in a uniform radius.

9. When the velocity of a charged particle is parallel to the magnetic field it travels through the magnetic force on the charge is _____.

10. Determine the radius of curvature for an electron travelling at 8.30 x 10^7 m/s perpendicularly through a 0.11 T magnetic field.

Ernest Lawrence, working at the University of California, built the first cyclotron in 1931. It had a diameter of 28 cm and produced protons with energy of one million eV. The cyclotron is composed of two semi-circular plates called Ds (dees). These two plates are placed in a vacuum between two powerful magnets causing the charged particles to travel in a circular path inside the Ds. A changing electric field is produced across the gap. This allows the charged particles to be accelerated without using extremely high voltages.

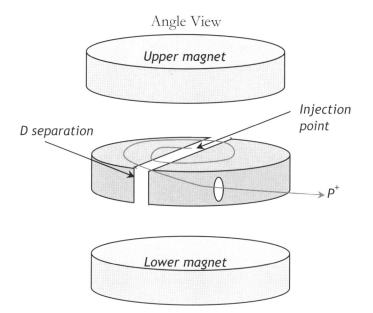

Angle View

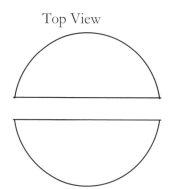

Top View

A changing electric field is placed across the Ds. When a positively charged particle crosses the gap from one D to another, the first D is positive and the second is negative.

The negative charge attracts the particle and it speeds up. By the time it circles through the second D to re-cross the gap, the electric field has reversed. Now the second D is positive and the first is negative, so the particle speeds up a little more. As it moves faster, the radius of its path increases. It spirals from the injection point at the centre to the edge of the cyclotron.

11. Determine the polarity of the upper and lower magnets in the diagram above.

12. A proton starts from rest and gains a kinetic energy of 5.00 keV after completing 600 orbits in a cyclotron. If the radius of its final orbit was 25.0 cm, determine the
    a. magnitude of the magnetic field in the "Ds" of the cyclotron.
    b. potential difference maintained across the "Ds" of the cyclotron.

13. If the separation of the cyclotron "Ds" is small compared to their radius, the time for each orbit is the same even though the radius of the orbit increases. An electron orbits a cyclotron at 5.00×10^7 Hz. If the radius of its final orbit is 5.00 cm, determine the final energy of the electron in eV.

Use the following information to answer questions 14 & 15.

The magnetic field produced at the centre of a solenoid (i.e., coil) may be calculated using:

Where:

$$B = \mu_o \left(\frac{n}{L} \right) I$$

B is the magnetic field strength in the coil (T)

I is the current through the wire (A)

n is the number of turns in the solenoid

L is the length of the solenoid (m)

μ_o is the magnetic permeability constant which is dependent on the material composing the core of the solenoid. (1.26×10^{-6} N/A^2 for vacuum or air)

14. Calculate the magnetic field strength in units of tesla (T) produced at the centre of a 30.0 cm long solenoid with 100 turns carrying a current of 1.20 A.

15. An experiment is done using a compass inside a coil to establish the value of the constant, μ_o. The dark end of the compass needle is its north end.

Problem: Determine the magnetic permeability constant μ_o.

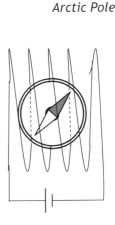

Arctic Pole

Equipment:
Coil
Ammeter
DC power supply
Compass

Procedure:
1. Orientate the equipment so that the compass needle points to the Arctic pole when the coil is off.
2. Adjust the current and note the angle of deflection of the compass.
3. Gradually increase the current and note the compass orientation.

Observations:

Number of coils: 16
Length of solenoid: 7.9 cm
Horizontal component of the Earth's Magnetic field: 4.3×10^{-5} T

The following data was collected:

Current (A)	Angle of deviation (degrees)	tanθ
0	0	
0.07	22	
0.18	40	
0.33	54	
0.63	64	
1.00	72	

Analysis:

a. Complete the labelling of the vector diagram that includes the Earth's magnetic field (horizontal component) and the two experimental variables.

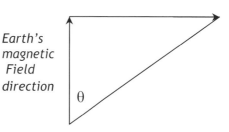

Earth's magnetic Field direction

θ

b. Plot the variables that would give you a straight line.
c. Use the graph to determine the value, with units, of the constant μ_o.
d. Compare your value with the accepted value of 1.26×10^{-6} N/A^2.

This 44-page booklet is designed to prepare you for the Physics 30 Diploma Exam. It provides:

- a summary of each unit.
- tips and tricks to help with problems and avoid common difficulties.
- sample questions designed in the same way as actual diploma exam questions.

Available from the Learning Resources Centre (LRC)

Product number 755869

Phone: 780-427-2767
toll-free access within Alberta,
first dial 310-0000

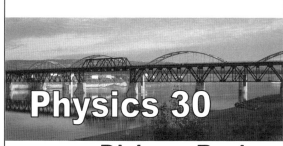

Diploma Review

This booklet summarizes your Physics 30 course and gives you helpful tips to prepare you to write your physics 30 diploma exam.

The Physics 30 Diploma exam will be written:

Date: _____

Time: _____

Location: _____

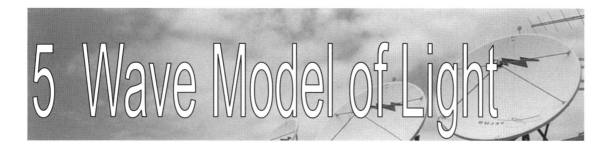

5 Wave Model of Light

Introduction

In physics light is referred to as electromagnetic radiation which is a natural phenomenon that can also be produced and detected through technological means. It has proven invaluable for many uses in medicine, communications and much more.

5.1 Summary Notes – The Nature of EMR

- Electromagnetic radiation (EMR) is caused by accelerating charges.
- The greater the acceleration, the higher the energy and frequency of the EMR and the shorter the wavelength.
- EMR are transverse waves.
- EMR has a changing electric field component and a changing magnetic field component.
- The changing electric field generates a changing magnetic field perpendicular to the direction the wave is travelling (i.e., the direction it propagates).

🗋 Notes:

_____

_____

_____

_____

_____

_____

_____

_____

_____

_____

_____

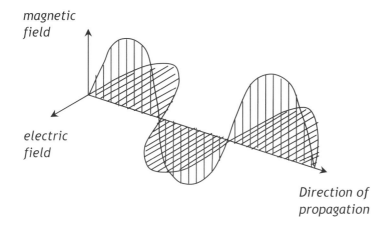

magnetic field

electric field

Direction of propagation

While electromagnetic radiation is a three-dimensional wave, it is often drawn two-dimensionally:

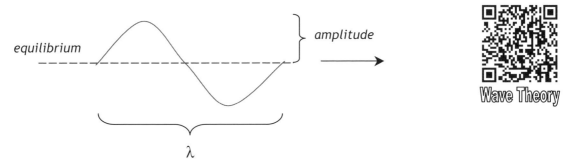

☐ Notes:

_____

_____

_____

_____

_____

_____

_____

_____

_____

_____

_____

The **wavelength** (λ) is the measured distance between successive crests (peaks) or troughs.

A **source** is anything that vibrates to create a disturbance and a wave. Vibrating charges or changing electric fields are sources for EMR.

A **medium** is the substance a wave travels through.

Wave **propagation** is the movement of a wave through a medium.

The **frequency** of a wave (Hz) is equal to the number of waves that pass a certain point in a given time.

The **speed** of a wave depends on the nature of the medium it is travelling through. All EMR travels at 3.00 x 10^8 m/s in a vacuum.

A range of wavelengths can be organized in the electromagnetic spectrum:

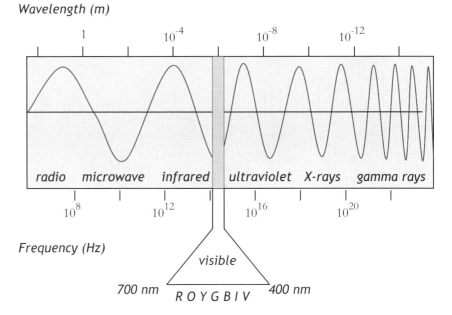

Wave-particle nature

Light is pure energy. As light (EMR) becomes more energetic the frequency increases and the wavelength decreases allowing it to behave more like a particle than a wave. Generally:

- EMR having a frequency less than visible light is treated as a wave.
- EMR having a frequency greater than visible light is treated as a particle.
- Visible light is treated both as a wave and a particle depending on the experiment or phenomenon being investigated.

The universal wave equation and the period-frequency relationship apply to light waves:

$$v = \lambda f \ \text{ or } \ c = \lambda f$$

$$T = \frac{1}{f}$$

Where:
    v is the speed of the wave
    c is the speed of light in a vacuum
    f is the frequency of the wave (cps, s^{-1} or Hz)
    λ is the wavelength (λ is the Greek letter "lambda")
    T is the period of the wave (s)

- The colour of visible light is usually associated with its frequency, wavelength or energy.
- **Monochromatic** light is light consisting of a single frequency (or wavelength).

Examples

1. An electromagnetic wave is travelling directly upwards, normal to the Earth's surface. The electric field component of this wave is oscillating in an east-west plane. Use a diagram to determine the direction of oscillation of its magnetic field component.

3-dimensional   2-dimensional

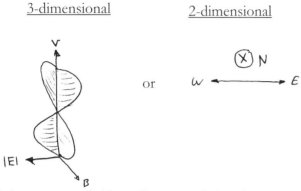

or

The magnetic field oscillates North-South.

2. Ultraviolet light travels through a vacuum at a speed of 3.00×10^8 m/s with a wavelength of 3.47×10^{-7} m. Determine its
    a. frequency.
    b. period.

$$V = 3.00 \times 10^8 \, m/s \qquad V = \lambda f \qquad\qquad f = \frac{1}{T}$$

$$\lambda = 3.47 \times 10^{-7} m \qquad f = \frac{V}{\lambda} \qquad\qquad T = \frac{1}{f}$$

$$T = ? \qquad\qquad f = \frac{3.00 \times 10^8 \, m/s}{3.47 \times 10^{-7} m} \qquad T = \frac{1}{8.6455 \times 10^{14} Hz}$$

$$f = ? \qquad\qquad f = 8.6455 \times 10^{14} Hz \qquad T = 1.15\overline{6} \times 10^{-15} s$$

a. The frequency is 8.65×10^{14} Hz.
b. The period is 1.16×10^{-15} s.

Problems

1. List the seven colours of the visible light spectrum from high energy to low energy. [Appendix A]

2. The Inuit of the Canadian Arctic protected their eyes from bright sunlight reflected off snow by constructing snow goggles made from ivory or wood with carved narrow slits. By blocking much of the light, snow blindness could be avoided. Identify the region of the EMR spectrum that might be most responsible for damaging the eyes causing snow blindness. Explain. [Appendix A]

3. An electromagnetic wave is travelling directly east parallel to the Earth's surface producing an electric field oscillating in a north-south plane. Use a diagram to determine the direction of oscillation of its magnetic field component (see example problem 1 for help). [Appendix A]

4. Fill in the blanks. EMR is produced by _____ charged particles. The wave is made from a changing electric field that produces a changing _____ field that travels at the speed of _____ m/s. [Appendix A]

5. Moving charges may create fields. Complete the chart below for an electron exhibiting the described motion. [Appendix A]

Description of motion	Description of field(s) created
Stationary	
Uniform motion	
Accelerating	

Cell phones typically operate on a frequency between 800 Hz to 900 Hz. Cell phones only transmit their signal to nearby cell phone towers that then incorporate the phone call into the regular phone system. Location-tracking technologies make it possible to determine where a cell phone is. One method involves a global positioning satellite sending a unique signal that only your cell phone can pick up (a.k.a "pinging"). The cell phone will then send a signal to nearby cell towers that determines your position through triangulation.

6. Cell phone tower A is at grid location I-13 and tower B is at M-3 on the map shown below. Tower A detects a signal coming from a bearing of 350° (80° N of W). Tower B detects the same signal coming from a bearing of 264° (84° W of S). Determine the most likely grid location of the cell phone. [Appendix A]

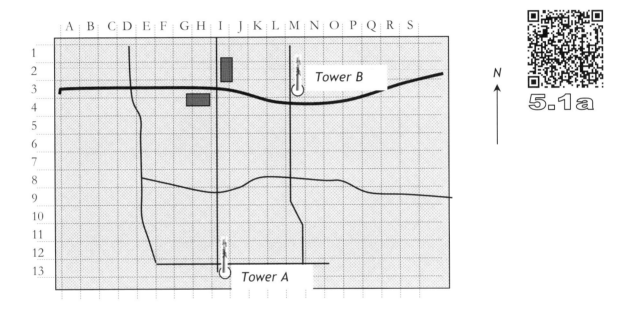

7. Calculate the period of the wave for a blue laser diode having a frequency of 4.23 x 10^{14} Hz. [2.36 x 10^{-15} s]

8. The frequency of a certain monochromatic beam of visible light in a vacuum ($v = 3.00 \times 10^8$ m/s) is found to be 5.50×10^{14} Hz. Determine the wavelength. [545 nm]

9. An X-ray travels at a speed of 3.00×10^8 m/s in a vacuum with a wavelength of 6.53×10^{-10} m. Determine its
    a. frequency. [4.59×10^{17} Hz]
    b. period. [2.18×10^{-18} s]

10. Street lamps are typically sodium vapour lamps or mercury vapour lamps. Sodium vapour lamps emit a visible wavelength of 590 nm. Calculate the frequency of this sodium light. [5.08×10^{14} Hz]

11. A common pen laser has a wavelength of 680 nm.
    a. Calculate the frequency of the laser light. [4.41×10^{14} Hz]
    b. Identify the colour of the laser beam. [Appendix A]

12. Some people have the ability to see greater wavelength range than most: from 380 nm to 780 nm. Calculate the frequency of the longer wavelength. [3.85×10^{14} Hz]

13. Many cordless telephones and baby monitors use a radio frequency of 2.4 GHz. Calculate the magnitude of the phone's wavelength. [13 cm]

14. AM radio stations broadcast between 535 kHz and 1700 kHz while FM radio stations broadcast from 88 MHz through 108 MHz. A local radio station broadcasts at a frequency of 90.9 MHz. Calculate the
    a. wavelength of the 90.9 MHz radio waves. [3.30 m]
    b. number of complete 90.9 MHz radio waves over a 1.50 km distance. [454]

15. Sketch the graphs shapes illustrating the following relationships for EMR travelling through a vacuum. [Appendix A]

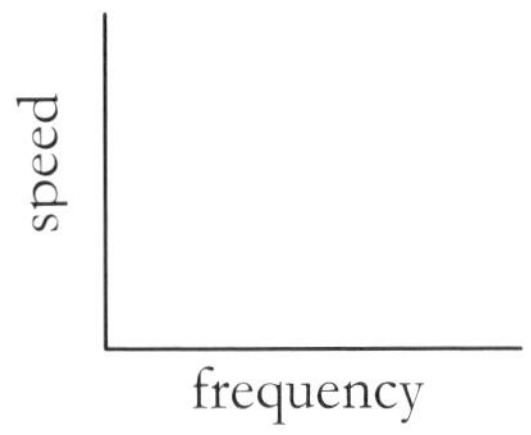

speed

frequency

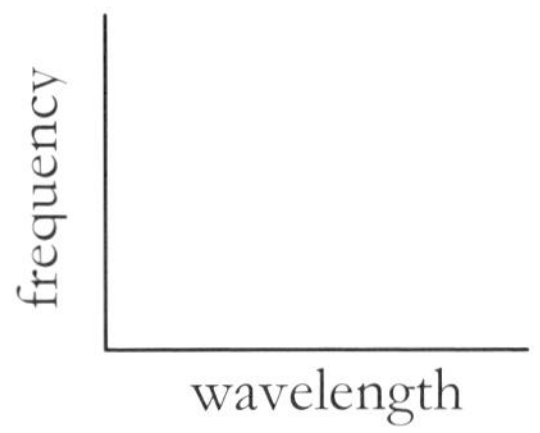

frequency

wavelength

16. Frequency is plotted as a function of the inverse of wavelength.
    a. Sketch the graph of the relationship. [Appendix A]
    b. Identify what the slope would represent. [Appendix A]

Inverse of Wavelength

17. Electromagnetic waves may be detected by the current they produce in a conducting wire called an antenna. The most efficient antenna is one that is one-half the size of the wavelength it is to detect. Calculate the most efficient antenna length for a radio signal of 630 kHz. [238 m]

18. The first radios were called spark gap transmitters because they produced a spark (accelerating electrons) to create radio waves. Spark gap transmitters are now illegal because they create radio waves across a large part of the spectrum and interfere with radio communications. In a modern electronic device radio waves are produced by accelerating electrons along a conductor which is called the antenna. Calculate the wavelength of a radio station broadcasting at 100.3 MHz. [2.99 m]

19. Alex and Fiona measure the speed of microwaves in air using a microwave oven. They first place cheese cubes on a paper plate and place it in the microwave on high for 20 s. They identify hot spots in the cheese spread to be 6.08 cm apart. Knowing that the hot spots are areas of constructive interference that occurs every half a wavelength, together with the frequency of the microwave listed on the back of the device as 2450 MHz, determine the speed of the microwaves. [2.98×10^8 m/s]

5.2 Summary Notes – Speed of EMR

🗋 Notes:

_____

_____

_____

_____

_____

_____

Early attempts to measure the speed of light proved difficult due to its speed being so great. As equipment improved it was possible to measure the speed of light with increasing precision.

The speed of visible light was determined before other parts of the Electromagnetic spectrum.

Examples

1. A disk with 600 cogs must be spun at 111.0 Hz for light to travel a distance of 1164 m, reflect off a mirror and travel the return trip of 1164 m to be blocked or eclipsed by the adjacent cog. The beam of light requires 7.5075×10^{-6} s for the round trip. Calculate the speed of light as determined by this experiment.

    $n = 600$

    $f = 111 \, Hz$

    $d = 1164 m$

    $t = 7.5075 \times 10^{-6} s$

    $v = ?$

    $v = \dfrac{d}{t}$

    $v = \dfrac{2(1164m)}{7.5075 \times 10^{-6} s}$

    $v = 3.100899 \times 10^{8} \, m/s$

    The speed of light was measured to be 3.101×10^{8} m/s.

2. An eight-sided mirror is used to measure the speed of light. The first image (minimum frequency) occurred when the mirror was rotating 610 Hz. Calculate the speed of light if the fixed mirror is 30.0 km from the rotating mirror.

    $n = 8$

    $d = 30 km$

    $f = 610 Hz$

    $v = ?$

    $T = \dfrac{1}{f}$

    $T = \dfrac{1}{610 Hz}$

    $T = 0.001639 s$

    fraction of turn $\dfrac{1}{8}$

    time for fraction of turn

    $0.001639 s \times \dfrac{1}{8}$

    $= 0.00020 49 s$

    $v = \dfrac{d}{t}$

    $v = \dfrac{2(30 \times 10^{3} m)}{2.0492 \times 10^{-4} s}$

    $v = 2.928 \times 10^{8} \, m/s$

    The speed of light was found to be 2.93×10^{8} m/s.

Problems

1. Determine the speed of light if light requires 1.187 s to travel a distance of 3.56×10^8 m from the Moon to the Earth. [3.00×10^8 m/s]

2. Calculate the time for light to travel from the Sun to the Earth if they are separated by a distance of 1.49×10^{11} m. Assume a speed of light of 3.00×10^8 m/s. [497 s]

Use the information below to answer question 3.

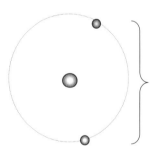

Jupiter

Io

Olaf Römer made the first known determination for the speed of light using the eclipse of Jupiter's moon, Io, by Jupiter in 1676. Astronomical data allowed him to predict when the eclipses would occur, but due to the time required for light to travel to the Earth, the eclipses appeared later than they actually occurred. A simplified diagram of this situation is shown on the right.

Extra distance light must travel when the Earth is on the side of the Sun away from Jupiter.

3. Assume Römer made his initial observations of Io when Earth was in its closest approach to Jupiter and his second observation six months later. Römer thought that light required 22 minutes to cross Earth's orbit. Determine Römer's value for the speed of light if the diameter of the Earth's orbit around the Sun is 2.82×10^{11} m. [2.14×10^8 m/s]

Use the information below to answer question 4.

Römer's value of light's time lag of 22 minutes to cross the Earth's orbit was too large. When the Earth and Jupiter are on the same side of the Sun they are separated by 6.28 x 10^{11} m and when they are on opposite sides they are separated by 9.28 x 10^{11} m. Jupiter's eclipse of Io is 16 minutes later when the Earth is farther away than when it's at the closest approach.

4.   Determine the speed of light using the more precise data. [3.1 x 10^8 m/s]

Use the information below to answer questions 5 – 7.

In 1849 Armand Fizeau performed the first terrestrial experiment to determine the speed of light. He used an extremely bright lamp and pulsed the light using a rotating wheel constructed with 720 cogs. He separated the rotating wheel and a reflecting mirror a distance of 8.63 km between Montmartre and Suresnes in Paris, France. He observed the light source through the gaps between the cogs and then gradually increased the rotational speed of the wheel until he could not see the light source. The light had been eclipsed (i.e., blocked) by a cog in the wheel.

5.   Fizeau gradually increased the wheel's frequency of rotation to 12.6 Hz, which showed that the light travelled the 8.63 km, and back in a time of 5.51 x 10^{-5} s. Calculate the speed of light as determined by Fizeau. [3.13 x 10^8 m/s]

6.   In an experiment similar to Fizeau's a spinning wheel with 360 cogs and a distance of 450 m between the wheel and the mirror, was used to measured the speed of light to be 3.00 x 10^8 m/s. Determine the time required for light to travel from the spinning wheel to the mirror and back. [3.00 x 10^{-6} s]

7. A spinning wheel with 360 cogs can be used to determine distance. The light used requires a total of 2.15×10^{-6} s to travel from the wheel to the mirror and back to the mirror. Assuming a speed of light of 3.00×10^{8} m/s determine the distance between the wheel and the mirror. [323 m]

Use the information below to answer questions 8 & 9.

Foucault's method for finding the speed of light in 1862 was similar to Fizeau's but Foucault used a rotating plane mirror as shown in the diagram. This greatly improved the results.

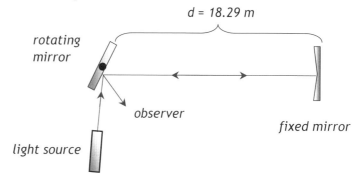

8. Foucault separated the rotating mirror and fixed mirror by 18.29 m. If the total time for the light beam to travel the distance between the rotating mirror and fixed mirror (there and back) was 1.221×10^{-7} s, determine Foucault's measurement for the speed of light. [2.996×10^{8} m/s]

9. In 1850 Foucault used the same apparatus to measure the speed of light through water and showed that it moved slower, which added support to the idea that light was a wave. The total time to travel the separation distance of 18.29 m in water was 1.62×10^{-7} s. Calculate the speed of light in the water. [2.26×10^{8} m/s]

10. Albert Michelson was born in Poland and moved to the United States to avoid persecution due to his Jewish heritage. His first attempt to measure the speed of light was in 1878 at the U.S. Naval Academy in Annapolis and was based on Foucault's rotating mirror apparatus. Michelson obtained better results, however, by improving the precision of his measurements.

Michelson used a \$10 mirror rotating at 128.00 Hz placed 152.40 m away from a plane mirror. The light beam required a total time of 1.0153×10^{-6} s to travel from the rotating mirror to the fixed mirror and back. Determine Michelson's first value for the speed of light. [3.0021×10^{8} m/s]

11. In 1879 Michelson improved his experiment by using a longer distance, more precisely measured at 605.4029 m, and better equipment. The light beam required a total time of 4.0380×10^{-6} s to travel from the mirror rotating at 257.39 Hz to the fixed mirror and back. Determine Michelson's improved value for the speed of light. [2.9985×10^{8} m/s]

Use the information below to answer question 12.

Michelson won a Nobel Prize for his work in 1907. His value for the speed of light was widely used for 40 years until he repeated his experiment many times between 1926 and 1931 using the 35.51 km distance between Mount Wilson and Mount San Antonio in California. This time he used a rotating 8-sided mirror which again improved his results.

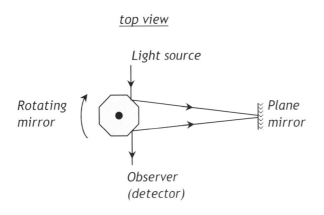

top view

Light source

Rotating mirror

Plane mirror

Observer (detector)

An eight-sided mirror must rotate through at least 1/8 of a rotation for the light beam to be reflected off the rotating mirror, to the plane mirror and return to the rotating mirror.

12. Determine Michelson's value for the speed of light using an 8-sided mirror rotating at 527.6 Hz placed 35.51 km from the plane mirror. (Note example #2, page 194) [2.998×10^8 m/s]

13. Michelson experimented with several types of rotating mirrors to produce observed images when measuring the speed of light. Determine the frequency of rotation necessary to produce an image at a fixed distance of 25.0 km from a rotating 12-sided mirror. [500 Hz]

14. Michelson's final experiment before he died was to measure the speed of light in a vacuum. He took years constructing precision instrumentation and obtaining exact measurements. He set up a 1594.2658 m long vacuum tube in Orange County, California. A system of mirrors caused the light beam to reflect back and forth along the tube a total of 10 times while a 32-sided mirror revolved at 587.60395 Hz. Determine Michelson's value for the speed of light in a vacuum. [$2.997\ 750\ 0 \times 10^8$ m/s]

Use the information below to answer question 15.

The metre was originally defined in 1793 as one ten-millionth of the distance between the Earth's equator and pole as it passes through Paris, France. Later it was redefined as the distance between two marks on a platinum-iridium bar kept in Paris, France. This became the standard that all length measurements were referenced to. In 1983 the metre was re-defined as the distance light travels in 1/299 792 458 of a second in a vacuum.

15.   List two benefits to referencing the length of a metre to the speed of light rather than the length of a metal bar. [Appendix A]

Use the following information to answer question 16.

In 1969 the Apollo 11 crew left a reflector on the Moon as part of the "Laser Ranging Retro-reflector Experiment". Laser pulses from the Earth are aimed at this reflector to determine the distance between the Earth and the Moon. It has been found that the Moon has been gradually moving away from the Earth at a rate of 3.8 cm per year.

16.   A laser pulse aimed at a reflector on the Moon requires a total travel time of 2.72 s between the initial pulse and the detection of the reflected signal when the Moon is at its apogee. Calculate the separation distance between the Earth and the Moon at its apogee (i.e., where it is furthest from the Earth). [4.08×10^8 m]

17.   Microwaves are used in telecommunications to transmit signals. Radar (an acronym for radio detection and ranging) uses microwave radiation. Radar was invented during the Second World War and can be used to determine the distance and speed of an object. A radar signal with a wavelength of 4.0 cm is reflected off a distant object and returns for a total travel time of 4.0 ms. Determine the distance separating the radar source and the object. [6.0×10^5 m]

Lasers and extremely precise timing devices used to be nonexistent, then prohibitively expensive. Now, laser ranging has become affordable enough that many department stores sell lasers for determining distance. They emit a short laser pulse, which is timed by an extremely accurate clock. When the beam contacts a target it is reflected and scattered in many directions, some of the reflected beam returns to the ranger, which detects it and measures the total time between emission and detection. The detector must be very sensitive and a highly reflective target will enable a longer range and better measurement.

18. Determine the total time for a pulse of laser light to be emitted and detected from a range finder measuring a distance of 13.2 m. [8.80×10^{-8} s]

19. Determine the distance measured by a laser rangefinder if the total time between the light emission and detection is 2.83×10^{-7} s. [42.5 m]

Use the information below to answer question 20.

Hertz could only produce and detect waves in his laboratory. Guglielmo Marconi helped the communications revolution by producing and detecting radio waves over much longer distances. He is often credited with receiving the first transatlantic signal that was sent from Cornwall England to Signal Hill St. Johns Nfld. on December 12, 1901, a distance of 3425 km.

20. Calculate the time required for Marconi's radio signal to be transmitted across the Atlantic. [11.4 ms]

21. A television transmitting tower is 5.0 km from a receiving TV set as shown below. The person watching has to use "rabbit ear" antennas since he does not have cable or satellite TV. The television signal can take more than one path to get to the receiving set. It can take the direct path and it can also reflect off a nearby high rise building and then return to the set. As a result, the TV receives multiple signals producing multiple pictures called "ghosting." Calculate the time difference between the direct signal and reflected signal. [2.7×10^{-5} s]

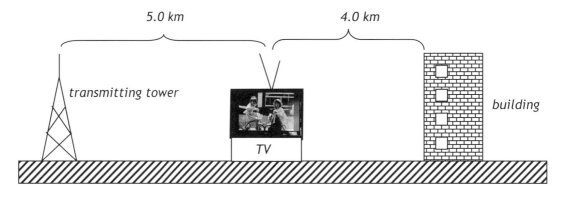

Use the information below to answer question 22.

Electromagnetic radiation can be used for communication by changing (modulating) some aspect of the wave. Three common methods have been used:

  i.   pulse modulation (PM) changes the time the wave is on. This method is used to produce dots and dashes in Morse Code.
  ii. amplitude modulation (AM) where changes in amplitude carry the message.
  iii. frequency modulation (FM) where changes in frequency carry the message.

22. A radio wave having a wavelength of 2.5 cm is pulsed for a time of 0.60 s. Determine the number of complete wavelengths in the pulse. [7.2×10^{9} wavelengths]

5.3 Summary Notes – Reflection & Refraction

Light obeys the **law of reflection:** $\theta_i = \theta_r$.

incident ray   reflected ray

θ_i | θ_r

barrier

Refraction is the changing of direction or bending of a ray as it passes from one medium to another. It is caused by a sudden change in speed as the waves pass from one medium to another.

Snell's Law

$$\frac{\sin \theta_1}{\sin \theta_2} = \frac{n_2}{n_1} = \frac{v_1}{v_2} = \frac{\lambda_1}{\lambda_2}$$

Where:

n_1 is the refractive index of the medium where the incidence ray comes from (no units)

n_2 is the refractive index of the medium where the refractive ray exists (no units)

θ_1 is the angle of incidence (degrees)

θ_2 is the refracted angle (degrees)

☐ Notes:

_____

_____

_____

_____

_____

_____

_____

_____

_____

_____

_____

_____

N.B., frequency will not change.

Speed decreases	Speed increases
• Bends towards the normal $\theta_2 < \theta_1$ • Wave is faster in medium 1 • Refractive index of 1 is less than 2	• Bends away from the normal $\theta_2 > \theta_1$ • Wave is slower in medium 1 • Refractive index of 1 is greater than 2
θ_1 medium 1 medium 2 θ_2	θ_1 medium 1 medium 2 θ_2

Critical angle is the angle of the incident ray that causes the refracted ray to be 90° relative to the normal line. When the incident ray is at an angle greater than the critical angle, total internal reflection occurs. This can only occur when light goes from a <u>high</u> index of refraction to a <u>low</u> index of refraction.

Examples

1. A wave contacts two surfaces as shown below. Draw the reflected wave off of each surface.

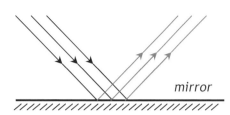 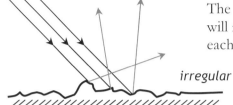

The reflected waves will not be parallel to each other.

mirror

irregular

2. A ray of light from air strikes the surface of a block of glass, having a refractive index of 1.50, at an angle of 67°. Determine the angle of refraction. (The refractive index of air is on your data sheet.)

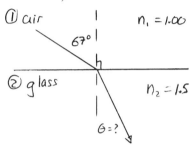

$$\frac{\sin\theta_1}{\sin\theta_2} = \frac{n_2}{n_1}$$

$$\sin\theta_2 = \frac{n_1 \sin\theta_1}{n_2}$$

$$= \frac{(1)\sin 67°}{1.5}$$

$$\theta_2 = 37.855$$

The angle of refraction is 38°.

3. Lucite is a strong clear plastic used for many windows. Determine the critical angle for a water-lucite system if the refractive index of water is 1.33 and 1.51 for Lucite.

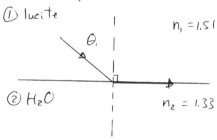

$$\frac{\sin\theta_1}{\sin\theta_2} = \frac{n_2}{n_1}$$

$$\sin\theta_1 = \frac{n_2 \sin\theta_2}{n_1}$$

$$= \frac{(1.33)\sin 90°}{1.51}$$

$$\theta_1 = 61.738°$$

The critical angle is 61.7°.

Problems

1. If the angle of reflection from a mirror is 35.0°, determine the angle of incidence. [Appendix A]

---

2. A light ray is reflected of a system of two mirrors as shown in the diagram. If the angle between the surface of mirror A and mirror B is 120°, complete the chart for the angle θ_2 and θ_3. [Appendix A]

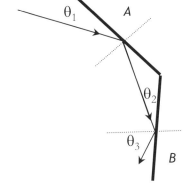

θ_1 (degrees)	θ_2 (degrees)	θ_3 (degrees)
30		
40		
50		

3. Define refraction. [Appendix A]

4. A student sets up a system where laser light is travelling from air and strikes a block of clear gelatin as shown in the diagram below. Determine the speed of light in the gelatin. [2.3 x 10^8 m/s]

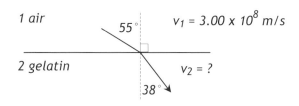

5. A layer of ice is next to a piece of flint glass. A ray of light in the flint enters the ice at an angle of 15.0°. Determine the angle of refraction in ice. (Use your data sheet in Appendix C, page 377 for index of refractions.) [18.4°]

6. A green laser has a wavelength of 532 nm in air and is 50 times brighter than the more common red lasers. Determine the speed of the 532 nm laser light in a transparent plastic if its refracted wavelength is 480 nm in the plastic. [2.71 x 10^8 m/s]

7. Light travelling from air enters a layer of water. The speed of light through water is 2.25 x 10^8 m/s. Calculate the water's index of refraction relative to air. [1.33]

8. Inuit, along with many other Native Americans, have long used spear fishing for gathering food. Spear fishing not only requires skill in throwing a spear but also knowledge of the phenomenon of refraction. Consider the diagram below. The spear-fisher sees an image of the fish represented in the diagram below. Should the spear fisher throw the spear where he sees the fish to be? Explain using the diagram below. [Appendix A]

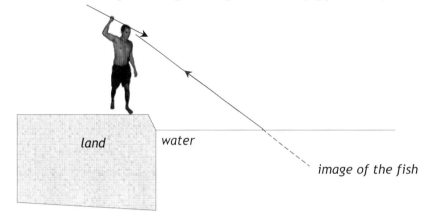

9. A Bose-Einstein condensate is a gaseous superfluid near absolute zero. It was used in 1999 to slow light to a speed of 17 m/s. Calculate the refractive index of this substance. [1.8 x 10^7]

10   A swimmer (while underwater) views rays of
       light entering the ocean water from the air at a
       refracted angle of 25.0°. Calculate the incident
       angle of the light as it enters the water. [34.2°]

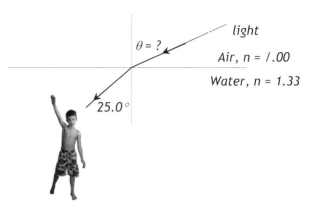

11.   Light from air strikes the surface of water (n = 1.33) at an angle of 34° relative to the surface
       as it comes from the air. Calculate the angle of refraction. [39°]

12.   A beam of light travels from air to a liquid in which the speed of light is 2.65×10^8 m/s.
       Determine the index of refraction of the liquid. [1.13]

13. Green laser light travels from air into an unknown material. If the angle between the beam and the normal is 48.0° in air and 29.0° in the unknown material, determine the
    a. index of refraction of the unknown material. [1.53]
    b. speed of light in the unknown material. [1.96 x 10^8 m/s]

Use the information below to answer questions 14 – 16.

The index of refraction of a substance may be defined as the ratio of the speed of light in a vacuum to the speed of light through the substance.

$$n = \frac{c}{v}$$

14. Determine the refractive index of a substance where light travels at 2.45 x 10^8 m/s. [1.22]

15. The Northwest Territories has three large diamond mines near Yellowknife. Diamonds may be cleaned in ethanol. The refractive index of ethanol is 1.36 and 2.42 for diamond. Calculate the difference in the speed for light travelling through ethanol into a diamond. [9.66 x 10^7 m/s]

16. State the relationship between the index of refraction of a material and the speed of light. [Appendix A]

17. Monochromatic light travels from air to water. Describe what happens to the light wave's
    a. speed. [Appendix A]
    b. wavelength. [Appendix A]
    c. frequency. [Appendix A]

18. The diagram on the right represents light travelling through a glass windowpane. The index of refraction of the glass is 1.50 and it is 2.0 mm thick. Determine the
    a. angle of refraction in the glass. [26.5°]
    b. distance "d". [1.0 mm]

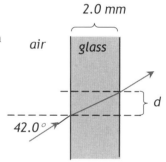

19. Aidan sets out to determine the speed of light in a viscous fluid by using the principles of refraction. Using a red pen laser he manipulates the angle of incidence and records the angle of refraction.

Incident angle (degrees)	Sine of incident angle	Refracted angle (degrees)	Sine of refracted angle
15.0		12.0	
25.0		20.0	
35.0		28.0	
45.0		36.0	

a. Determine the sine of the angles and place data in the chart.
b. Plot the sine of the angles.
c. Determine the slope of the line. [~0.864]
d. Use the slope to determine the speed of light in the viscous fluid. [~2.59 x 10^8 m/s]

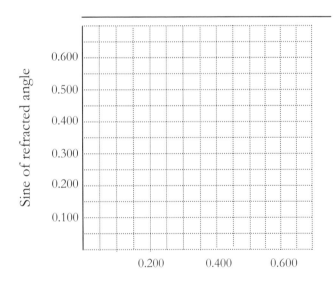

20. A critical angle may occur if a waves travels from a substance having a high refractive index to a substance with low refractive index. The critical angle for a given liquid-air system is 49.5°. Calculate the refractive index of the liquid. [1.32]

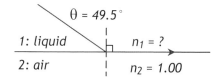

21. The speed of light in a clear liquid is three-quarters the speed of light in air. Determine the critical angle of the liquid. [48.6°]

22. Determine the critical angle for a diamond/air system. [24.4°]

23. Describe what will happen when the angle of the incident ray is greater than the critical angle. [Appendix A]

24. A monochromatic light ray is incident on the interface between two substances at the critical angle as shown in the diagram below. Determine the missing index of refraction. [2.0]

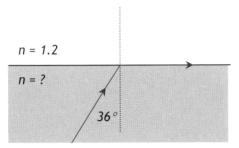

25. A researcher created an experiment to determine the critical angle of an unknown substance using a variable wavelength light emitter and detector. The angle of incident is held constant.

Incident wavelength (nm)	Refracted wavelength (nm)
400	665
450	747
500	830
550	913
600	996

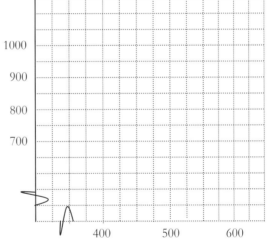

Incident wavelength (nm)

a. Plot the information.
b. Determine the slope of the line. [~1.62]
c. Use the slope to determine the critical angle. [~38.1°]

Use the information below to answer question 26.

Honey that contains too much water will easily spoil. The moisture content may be determined using the honey's refractive index. The refractive index is proportional to the moisture content as shown in the chart.

26. Determine the percent moisture in honey which shows a critical angle of 41.819° with air. Use a refractive index of 1.0003 for air. [Appendix A]

Refractive index at 20 °C	Moisture content (%)
1.5044	13.0
1.5028	13.6
1.5018	14.0
1.5002	14.6
1.4992	15.0
1.4976	15.6
1.4966	16.0
1.4951	16.6
1.4940	17.0

27. A beam of monochromatic light strikes a prism at a right angle as shown in the diagram below. A critical angle is obtained as the light travels from the prism to the air. Determine the refractive index of the prism. [1.15]

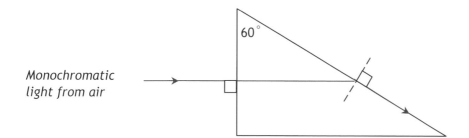

5.4 Summary Notes - Lenses

Notes:

_____

_____

_____

_____

_____

_____

_____

_____

_____

_____

Characteristics of an image: An object placed in front of a lens may produce an image that has different characteristics than the object. The characteristics are:

- **Size:**   Larger, smaller, or same size as the original object (magnification is an expression of relative size)
- **Orientation:**   inverted or upright (erect)
- **Image type:**   real or virtual.

A **real image** is an image that can be projected onto a screen (light rays converge at one point). Real images are always inverted.

A **virtual image** cannot be projected onto a screen. You must look through the lens, or in the mirror to see a virtual image. Virtual images are always upright.

optical centre (O): The centre of the lens.
principal axis: A line drawn through the vertex and the optical centre.
focal point (F): The point where all the light rays meet.
focal length (f): The distance from the lens to the focal point. It is dependent on the refractive index of the material and the shape of the lens.

Convex Lens (a.k.a., converging lens)

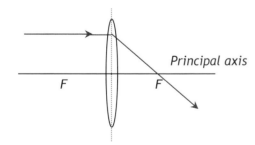

Concave Lens: (a.k.a., diverging lens)

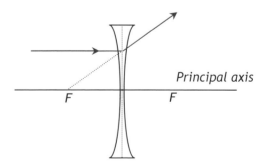

- All concave lenses produce images that are smaller, upright and virtual.
- Concave lenses have a negative focal length.

To draw ray diagrams:

i.   draw the lens showing the principal axis and the principal focal points.
ii.   place a vertical arrow on the principal axis to indicate the position, size and attitude of the object.
iii. draw two rays from the tip of the arrow to the lens. Where these two rays meet (real image) or appear to diverge from (virtual image) is the position of the image. Any two of the following three rays may be used:
- A ray coming in parallel to the principal axis emerges towards the focus.
- A ray coming through the focus emerges parallel to the principal axis.
- A ray passing through the optical centre is left unchanged.

The characteristics of an image in a lens may be determined algebraically:

$$\frac{1}{f} = \frac{1}{d_o} + \frac{1}{d_i}$$

Notes:

_____

_____

Where:

d_o is the distance from the object to the lens

d_i is the distance from the image to the lens

f is the focal length of the lens

_____

_____

_____

_____

_____

_____

Sign Convention:

_____

Distance (d)		Height (h)	
real focal points or images	+	upright images	+
virtual focal points or images	-	inverted images	-

Magnification

$$M = \frac{h_i}{h_o} = -\frac{d_i}{d_o}$$

N.B.,
- All real images are inverted and all virtual images are upright.
- Any units may be used as long as they are consistent.
- The negative sign is needed due to sign convention.
- A concave lens has a negative focal length.

Examples

1. An object 3.0 cm high is 15 cm from a convex lens of 6.0 cm focal length. Complete the chart.

1 div. = 1.0 cm

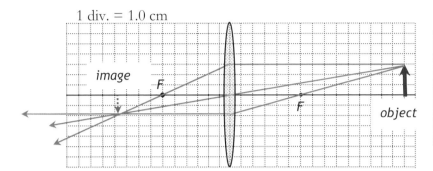

Image Dimensions

	Graphically	Algebraically
d_i	9.6 cm	10 cm
h_i	-1.8 cm	-2.0 cm
M	0.60 X	0.67 X

Characteristics
inverted
smaller
real

$$h_o = 3.0 \text{ cm}$$
$$d_o = 15 \text{ cm}$$
$$f = 6 \text{ cm}$$
$$d_i = ?$$
$$h_i = ?$$

$$\frac{1}{f} = \frac{1}{d_i} + \frac{1}{d_o}$$
$$\frac{1}{d_i} = \frac{1}{f} - \frac{1}{d_o}$$
$$\frac{1}{d_i} = \frac{1}{6 \text{ cm}} - \frac{1}{15 \text{ cm}}$$
$$d_i = 10 \text{ cm}$$

$$\frac{h_i}{h_o} = -\frac{d_i}{d_o}$$
$$h_i = -\frac{d_i h_o}{d_o}$$
$$h_i = \frac{-10 \text{ cm} * 3 \text{ cm}}{15 \text{ cm}}$$
$$h_i = -2 \text{ cm}$$

2. A 6.0 cm tall object is 11.0 cm from a concave lens of 4.0 cm focal length. Complete the chart.

1 div. = 1.0 cm

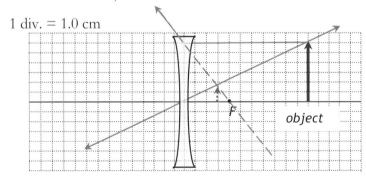

Image Dimensions

	Graphically	Algebraically
d_i	2.9 cm	2.9 cm
h_i	1.4 cm	1.6 cm

Characteristics
upright
smaller
virtual

$$h_o = 6 \text{ cm}$$
$$d_o = 11 \text{ cm}$$
$$f = 4 \text{ cm}$$
$$d_i = ?$$
$$h_i = ?$$

$$\frac{1}{f} = \frac{1}{d_i} + \frac{1}{d_o}$$
$$\frac{1}{d_i} = \frac{1}{f} - \frac{1}{d_o}$$
$$\frac{1}{d_i} = \frac{1}{-4 \text{ cm}} - \frac{1}{11 \text{ cm}}$$
$$d_i = -2.933 \text{ cm}$$

$$\frac{h_i}{h_o} = -\frac{d_i}{d_o}$$
$$h_i = -\frac{d_i h_o}{d_o}$$
$$h_i = \frac{2.93 \text{ cm} * 6 \text{ cm}}{11 \text{ cm}}$$
$$h_i = 1.6 \text{ cm}$$

Problems

1. Determine the dimensions and characteristics by drawing ray diagrams for the following objects placed in front of concave and convex lenses. Assume 1 division = 1.0 cm. Complete the charts. [Appendix A]

    a.

    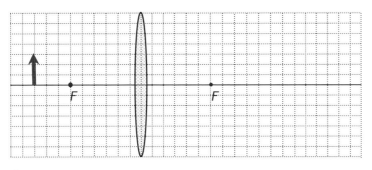

Characteristics	Dimensions
	$d_i =$
	$h_i =$

    b.

    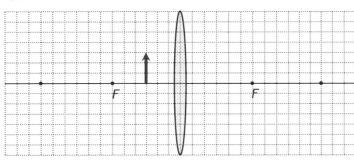

Characteristics	Dimensions
	$d_i =$
	$h_i =$

    c.

    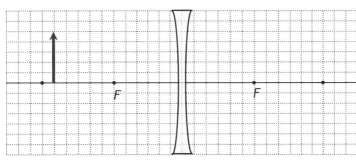

Characteristics	Dimensions
	$d_i =$
	$h_i =$

2. Use a ray diagram to find the size and position of an image projected by a 10.0 cm object, 30.0 cm from a thin positive lens with a 10.0 cm focal length. Complete the chart. [Appendix A]

    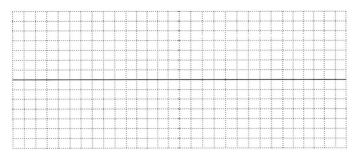

Characteristics	Dimensions
	$d_i =$
	$h_i =$

3. Fill in the blanks. A _____ image is an image that can be projected onto a screen. A _____ image can only be viewed when looking through a lens. [Appendix A]

4. A 15 cm tall object is 30 cm away from a concave lens that has a focal length of 5.0 cm. (Hint: a concave lens has a negative focal length.) Determine the
   a. image's distance from the lens. [-4.3 cm]
   b. image size. [2.1 cm]
   c. image magnification. [0.14 X]

5. An old camera allows light to reflect off of the object it focuses on and then refract through its lens onto sensitive film. Consider a 3.5 m tall object that is placed 6.5 m from the convex lens that allows a 1.1 cm tall real image to be exposed onto the film inside the camera. Determine the
   a. distance to the image. [2.0 cm]
   b. focal length of the lens. [2.0 cm]

6. The cornea of the eye acts as a convex lens. An eye with a radius of curvature of 8.00 mm observes an object from a distance of 45 cm.
   a. Determine the characteristics of the image that forms on the back of the eye. [Appendix A]
   b. What must the brain do to correctly interpret the image? [Appendix A]

7. A 2.0 m tall object is 12.0 m from a convex lens that has a 1.0 m focal length. Determine the
   a. image's characteristics. [Appendix A]
   b. image distance from the lens. [6.0 m]
   c. image size. [-1.0 m]

8. A 25 cm tall object is 50 cm from a convex lens with a focal point that is twice the distance of the object's height. Will there be an image visible? Explain. [Appendix A]

9. A 6.5 cm high object is 22.0 cm in front of a lens with a -10.5 cm focal length. Determine the image's
   a. characteristics. [Appendix A]
   b. distance from the lens. [-7.1 cm]
   c. size. [2.1 cm]

10. In an experiment a student inserts a concave lens into an old camera. Describe what the student would observe if an object 8.5 m away from the lens is brought into focus considering the lens has a focal length of 4.0 cm. [Appendix A]

11. Reading glasses are often sold using a unit called "dioptre". The larger the dioptre number the stronger or more powerful the reading glasses. The dioptre is the inverse of the focal length. Determine the dioptre of reading glasses having a focal length of 0.67 m. [1.5]

Use the information below to answer question 12.

While Galileo never invented the telescope he was one of the first to use it to observe the night sky. One of his telescopes used two lenses (a convex and concave) to produce a magnification of 20 X. When using it to observe the Moon he noted that it was "marked here and there with chains of mountains and depths of valleys."

12. Identify the type of lens used as the objective lens. [Appendix A]

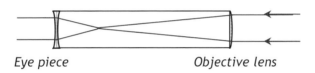

Eye piece   Objective lens

13. The refractive index for water is 1.33 while the refractive index for the cornea in the eye is 1.37. Explain why this makes focusing underwater without the aid of goggles difficult. [Appendix A]

14   Zoë conducted an experiment to determine the focal length of a convex lens. She used an optics bench to illuminate an object and project a real image of it onto a screen and recorded the data in the chart below:

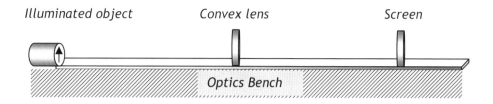

Object distance (cm)	Inverse of distance to object (cm^{-1})	Image distance (cm)	Inverse of distance to image (cm^{-1})
25.0		100.0	
27.0		77.1	
31.0		56.4	
35.0		46.7	
42.0		38.2	

a. Complete the chart above.
b. Graph the data to produce a straight line.
c. Use the graph to determine the focal length of the convex lens. [~19 cm]

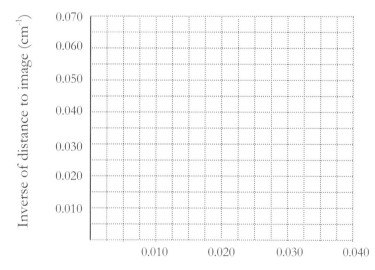

The Italian, Giambattista della Porta wrote the first systematic work on lenses, *Magia Naturalis* (Natural Magic), in 1589. In it he designs an optical system composed of two lenses. Multi-lens systems, such as Giambattista's, make up telescopes and microscopes. Janssen of Holland, in 1590, is credited with actually building the first compound microscope.

15. A certain compound microscope has two convex lenses that are 6.0 cm apart. The objective lens has a focal length of 1.0 cm, and the eyepiece has a focal length of 7.0 cm. The object under study is placed 1.5 cm from the objective lens as shown in the diagram below where 2 division = 1.0 cm. Determine the microscope's magnifying power. [~3.5 X]

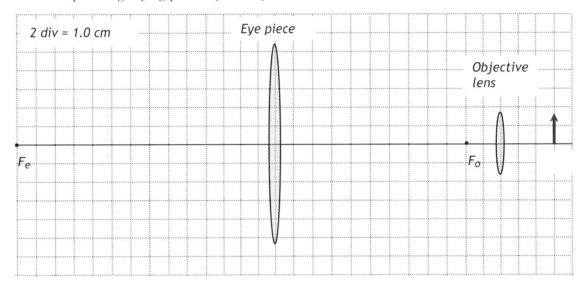

5.5 Summary Notes - Mirrors

Plane mirrors form images that are
- virtual and appear to be equal distances behind the mirror as the objects are in the front of the mirror.
- the same height as the object.
- horizontally inverted.

Curved mirrors may be described using the following terminology:

The vertex (V) is the centre of the mirror.

The centre of curvature (C) The centre of the sphere that was used to cut the mirror.

The principal axis is a line drawn through the vertex and the centre of curvature.

The focal point (F) is halfway between the mirror and the centre of curvature. It is the place where all the light rays meet.

The focal length (f) is the distance from the mirror to the focal point.

Notes:

_____

_____

_____

_____

_____

_____

_____

_____

_____

_____

_____

_____

_____

_____

_____

Concave Mirror: (a.k.a., converging mirror)

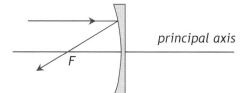

Convex Mirror (a.k.a., diverging mirror)

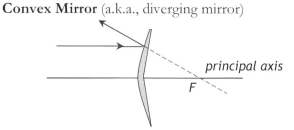

- All convex mirrors produce images that are smaller, upright and virtual.
- Convex mirrors have a negative focal length

How to draw a ray diagram

i.	Draw the mirror showing the principal axis, the centre of curvature, and the principal focus.
ii.	Place a vertical arrow on the principal axis to indicate the position, size and orientation of the object.
iii.	Draw two rays from the tip of the arrow to the mirror. Where these two rays meet (real image) or appear to diverge from (virtual image) is the position of the image. Any two of the following three rays may be used:

- The ray directly parallel to the principal axis will reflect through or appear to have come from **F**.
- The ray directed through **F** will reflect parallel to the principal axis.
- A ray passing through the centre of curvature is reflected back along the same path.

Notes:

_____
_____
_____
_____
_____
_____
_____
_____

The characteristics of an image in a mirror may be determined algebraically with the following equation.

$$\frac{1}{f} = \frac{1}{d_o} + \frac{1}{d_i}$$

Where:

d_o is the distance from the object to the mirror

d_i is the distance from the image to the mirror

f is the focal length of the mirror

Sign Convention:

Distance (d)		Height (h)	
real focal points or images	+	upright images	+
virtual focal points or images	-	inverted images	-

Magnification

$$M = \frac{h_i}{h_o} = -\frac{d_i}{d_o}$$

N.B.,

- All real images are inverted and all virtual images are upright.
- Any units may be used as long as they are consistent.
- The negative sign is needed due to sign convention.

Examples

1. A 5.0 cm tall object is placed 22.0 cm in front of a concave mirror that has a focal length of 6.0 cm. Determine the characteristics and dimensions of the image (complete the charts) using
   a. a scale diagram.
   b. the curved mirror formula (algebraically).

1 div. = 1.0 cm

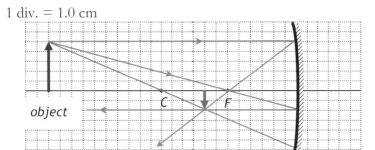

object

Image Dimensions

	Graphically	Algebraically
d_i	8.0 cm	8.3 cm
h_i	-2.0 cm	-1.9 cm
M	0.40 X	0.38 X

$h_o = 5cm$

$d_o = 22cm$

$f = 6cm$

$h_i = ?$

$d_i = ?$

$M = ?$

$\frac{1}{f} = \frac{1}{d_i} + \frac{1}{d_o}$

$\frac{1}{d_i} = \frac{1}{f} - \frac{1}{d_o}$

$= \frac{1}{6cm} - \frac{1}{22cm}$

$d_i = 8.25 cm$

$\frac{h_i}{h_o} = -\frac{d_i}{d_o}$

$h_i = \frac{-d_i h_o}{d_o}$

$h_i = \frac{-(8.25cm)(5cm)}{22cm}$

$h_i = -1.875 cm$

$M = \frac{h_i}{h_o}$

$= \frac{1.875 cm}{5cm}$

$M = 0.375 X$

Characteristics
inverted
smaller
real

2. A 5.0 cm tall object is placed 11.0 cm in front of a convex mirror that has a focal length of 5.0 cm. Determine the characteristics and dimensions of the image (complete the charts) using
   a. a scale diagram.
   b. the curved mirror formula (algebraically).

1 div. = 1.0 cm

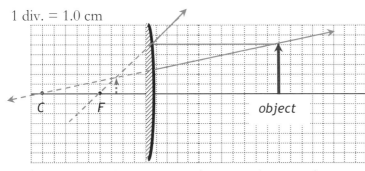

object

Image Dimensions

	Graphically	Algebraically
d_i	-3.6 cm	-3.4 cm
h_i	1.8 cm	1.6 cm
M	0.36 X	0.31 X

$f = -5cm$

$d_o = 11cm$

$h_o = 5cm$

$d_i = ?$

$h_i = ?$

$M = ?$

$\frac{1}{f} = \frac{1}{d_o} + \frac{1}{d_i}$

$\frac{1}{d_i} = \frac{1}{f} - \frac{1}{d_o}$

$= \frac{1}{-5cm} - \frac{1}{11cm}$

$d_i = -3.4375cm$

$\frac{h_i}{h_o} = -\frac{d_i}{d_o}$

$h_i = \frac{-d_i h_o}{d_o}$

$= \frac{3.4cm \times 5cm}{11cm}$

$h_i = 1.5625cm$

$M = \frac{h_i}{h_o}$

$= \frac{1.56cm}{5cm}$

$M = 0.3125 X$

Characteristics
upright
smaller
virtual

Problems

1. Locate the image and identify its characteristics by drawing ray diagrams for the following objects placed in front of a mirror. For each question assume 1 scale division = 1.0 m Complete the charts. [Appendix A]

a.

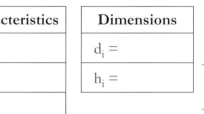

Characteristics	Dimensions
	$d_i =$
	$h_i =$

b.

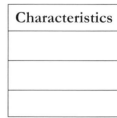

Characteristics	Dimensions
	$d_i =$
	$h_i =$

c.

Characteristics	Dimensions
	$d_i =$
	$h_i =$

2. A 2.0 cm tall candle, is placed 12 cm in front of a concave mirror with a focal length of 8.0 cm. Use a scale diagram to determine the image's characteristics. Complete the chart. [Appendix A]

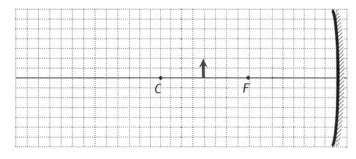

Characteristics	Dimensions
	$d_i =$
	$h_i =$

3. An object, 5.0 cm high, is located 15.0 cm from a converging (concave) mirror with a focal length of 10.0 cm. Determine the characteristics and dimensions of the image (complete the charts) using
    a. a scale diagram.
    b. the curved mirror formula (algebraically). [Appendix A]

Image Dimensions

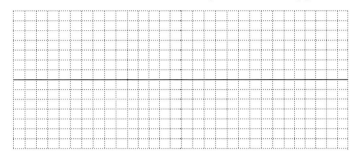

	Graphically	Algebraically
d_i		
h_i		
M		

Characteristics

4. An object, 2.0 cm high, is located 3.0 cm from a diverging (convex) mirror with a focal length of 4.6 cm. Determine the characteristics and dimensions of the image (complete the charts) using
    a. a scale diagram.
    b. the curved mirror formula (algebraically). [Appendix A]

Image Dimensions

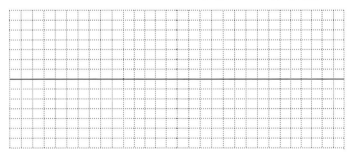

	Graphically	Algebraically
d_i		
h_i		
M		

Characteristics

5. A 6.5 cm high object is 15 cm from a concave mirror with a 20.0 cm radius. Determine the
   a. image distance from the mirror. [30 cm]
   b. image size. [-13 cm]

6. An object is placed 20 cm from a spherical concave mirror. It produces an image that is 15 cm away from the mirror. Determine the focal length of the mirror. [8.6 cm]

7. A 5.0 cm tall object is placed 4.0 cm in front of a mirror having a focal length of -6.0 cm.
   a. Identify the type of mirror used. [Appendix A]
   b. Identify the type of image produced. [Appendix A]
   c. Determine the distance to the image produced. [-2.4 cm]
   d. Determine the size of the image produced. [3.0 cm]

8. Fill in the blank. The main mirror on the Hubble's Space Telescope has a radius of curvature of 115.2 m. Its focal length is _____. [Appendix A]

9.	A 5.0 cm high object is 20.0 cm in front of a mirror with a -15 cm focal length. Determine the
	a.	image distance from the mirror. [-8.6 cm]
	b.	image size. [2.1 cm]

10.	A 5.00 cm tall object is 10.3 cm from a concave mirror with a 10 cm focal length. Determine the
	a.	distance to the image. [343 cm]
	b.	size of the image. [-167 cm]

11.	An object is placed at the focal point of a concave mirror. Will an image be observed? Explain. [Appendix A]

12.	A 3.0 cm tall object is placed 6.0 cm in front of mirror. A virtual image is produced that is 1.0 cm tall.
	a.	Determine the focal length. [-3.0 cm]
	b.	Identify the type of mirror. [Appendix A]

5.6 Summary Notes – Dispersion & Polarization

Newton explained that light is composed of many colours. He demonstrated this through the following experiment:

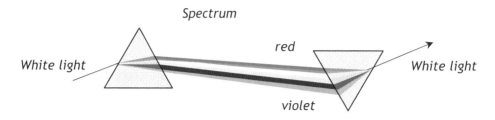

☐ Notes:

_____

_____

_____

_____

_____

_____

_____

Dispersion is the separation of EMR into individual wavelengths.

A prism disperses EMR because the refractive index of an object is different for each wavelength causing each frequency (colour for visible light) to refract a different amount, thus spread out and separate.

The wavelength range of visible light is from approximately 4.00×10^{-7} m to 7.00×10^{-7} m (400 nm to 700 nm).
nanometre: 1 nm = 10^{-9} m

R   O   Y   G   B   I   V
700 nm   **400 nm**
velocity   constant
wavelength   decreases
frequency   increases
bending (refraction)   increases
energy   increases
diffraction   decreases
scattering   increases

Polarization

Polarized waves vibrate in one plane only. A wave on a rope can be produced so that the wave vibrates in all directions. It is possible to filter out all directions but one with the following arrangement:

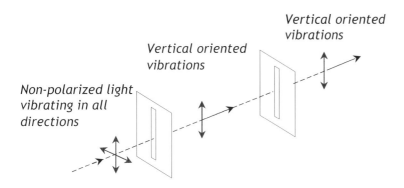

When the filters are orientated at right angles relative to each other, no light will get through.

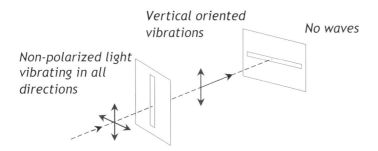

Polarized light may be produced naturally through:

Reflection: Light reflected from shiny surfaces is often polarized. This polarized light causes glare, which polarizing sunglasses can reduce.

Scattering: Blue light that is scattered by the atmosphere is polarized.

This works only for transverse waves. If, therefore, light is a transverse wave, it too should demonstrate these phenomena.

Example

1. Sunglasses used as driving glasses or boating glasses are polarized to reduce glare. Describe a simple procedure (that could be done at the store when buying them) for testing sunglasses to make sure they are polarized.

    Hold two sets of identical glasses up to the light, both in line with your one eye, rotate one of the sets and if the intensity of light changes they are polarized.

Problems

1. A visible spectrum may be produced using a prism. The different wavelengths refract different amounts since the index of refraction is different for each wavelength. Use the diagram below to identify the colour (red or violet) that has the largest index of refraction in the glass prism. [Appendix A]

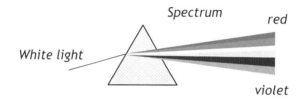

2. Define dispersion. [Appendix A]

3. A ray of monochromatic light enters and exits a water droplet as shown in the diagram below. Identify the location (i, ii, or iii) where
    a. total internal reflection occurs.
    b. light crosses a boundary to a higher refractive index.
    c. light crosses a boundary to a lower refractive index.

    [Appendix A]

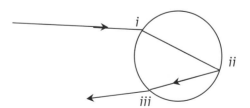

Use the information below to answer question 4.

The refractive index for a substance is different for different wavelengths, though often an average value is used. When white light from air enters a diamond it disperses to form a spectrum because each wavelength has its own refractive index and therefore bends to different angles.

4. Determine the difference in degrees ($\Delta\theta$) between a red light of 687 nm (n = 2.407) and a violet light of 431 nm (n = 2.452) if white light is incident on the diamond at 25° relative to the normal. [0.19°]

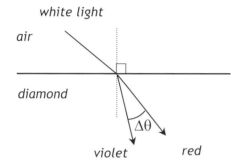

5. The first use of diamonds as gemstones was in India during the fourth century B.C. Diamond cutting became possible in fifteenth century Europe that helped ensure their popularity. Diamonds are not rare but they are expensive due to effective marketing and control by a few large companies. Diamonds are extremely hard and have very high refractive index. The diamond is cut to ensure that light that enters it exits back out the top giving it a sparkle.

Light ray through a diamond

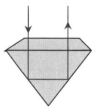

a. Explain why white light spreads out as it passes through the diamond to produce visible spectra. [Appendix A]
b. Explain why a high refractive index is important to make the light follow the path shown in the diagram. [Appendix A]

6.   Lap-top screens, calculator displays and flat panel monitors use liquid crystal displays (LCD) which use the phenomena of polarization to either let light through or to block it. The liquid crystal is a polarizer that is controlled using an electric field. Explain how you could test if the light coming from a flat panel monitor is polarized or non-polarized light. [Appendix A]

7.   A beam of light is incident upon a clear viscous fluid at an angle of 47.3°. Its refracted angle in the fluid is measured to be 21.8°. Determine the ratio of wavelengths ($\lambda_{fluid}/\lambda_{air}$) for this fluid. [0.505]

8.   Explain how the polarization of light can support the transverse wave nature of light. [Appendix A]

9.   Newton studied optics and realized one of the problems with Galileo's telescope was that the white light often separated out to produce a spectrum. This effect is called chromatic aberration. Explain why this effect occurs. [Appendix A]

5.7 Summary Notes – Diffraction & Interference

Diffraction is the spreading out of a wave as it passes a corner or through an opening. If light is a wave it should diffract.

For diffraction of a wave to be noticeable the wavelength should be larger than the opening it passes through. Since light has very small wavelengths, its diffraction can easily go undetected.

straight waves   *diffracted waves*

Wave **interference** occurs when two or more waves pass each other and superimpose to produce a new wave of different amplitude.

Thomas Young developed an experiment to show that light is a wave by having it diffract and interfere.

Young's apparatus
- Maxima are bright areas called bright fringes (i.e., antinodal or areas of constructive interference). They occur at n = 1, 2, etc.
- Minima are dark areas (i.e., nodal or areas of destructive interference) between the bright areas.
- Alternating bright and dark lines are projected onto the screen.

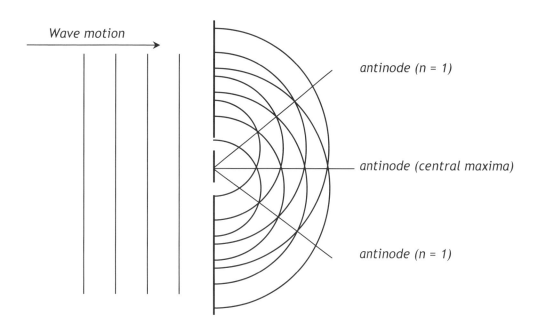

Wave motion

antinode (n = 1)

antinode (central maxima)

antinode (n = 1)

Two equations are used with Young's double slit experiment:

$$\lambda = \frac{dx}{nl}$$

$$\lambda = \frac{d\sin\theta}{n}$$

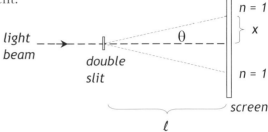

Where:

λ is the wavelength of the light (m)

d is the distance between the two slits (m)

θ is the angle from the centre of the two slits to the bright fringe in question (degrees)

n is the order number of the bright fringe

x is the distance from the central bright fringe to another bright fringe (m)

l is the distance from the double slit to the screen (m) if the angle is small.

N.B., The derivation of the first equation relies on an approximation. It is assumed that d is very small in comparison to l. This approximation is good unless large angles (> 10°) or large n values are used. With the angle being less than 10°, the screen to slit distance is assumed to be identical to the path length of the light from double slit to screen.

Notes:

_____

_____

_____

_____

_____

_____

_____

_____

_____

_____

_____

_____

_____

_____

Diffraction Gratings (a.k.a. interference gratings)

Rather than a double slit to perform Young's experiment, multiple slits, called diffraction gratings, are more commonly used.

• The bright maxima are much sharper and narrower for a grating than for a double slit, and, therefore, better for measuring wavelength.

• The angle of diffraction depends on wavelength.

• If light of multiple wavelengths is used, the grating sorts out the wavelengths and produces a spectrum.

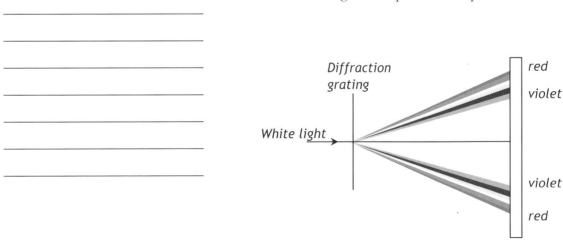

Examples

1. Light falls on a pair of slits 1.35 μm apart. The maxima are measured to be 41.0 cm apart and the screen is a distance of 1.00 m from the slits. Determine the wavelength of light using each diffraction equation:

a. $\lambda = \dfrac{d \sin \theta}{n}$

b. $\lambda = \dfrac{dx}{n\ell}$

c. Explain why the answers in part a and b are different.

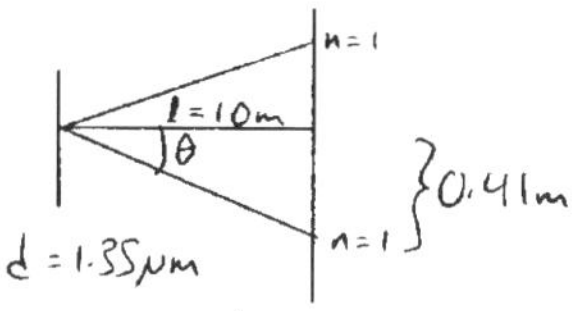

a) $\lambda = \dfrac{d\sin\theta}{n}$

$\lambda = \dfrac{1.35 \cdot 10^{-6}m \sin 22.2936°}{(1)}$

$\lambda = 5.1213 \cdot 10^{-7} m$

b) $\lambda = \dfrac{dx}{\ell n}$

$\lambda = \dfrac{1.35 \cdot 10^{-6}(0.41m)}{(1.0m)(1)}$

$\lambda = 5.535 \cdot 10^{-7} m$

$d = 1.35 \mu m$

$\tan\theta = \dfrac{opp}{adj}$

$\tan\theta = \dfrac{0.41m}{1.0m}$

$\theta = 22.29°$

a. The light's wavelength is 512 nm.
b. The light's wavelength is 554 nm.
c. Since the angle of deviation is greater than 10°, the small angle approximation gives large errors. Therefore the wavelength of 512 nm should be the better answer.

2. A glass grating is ruled with a line density of 5500 lines/cm. Monochromatic light striking the grating forms a second order image diffracted at 50.0°. Determine the wavelength of the light used.

$R = 5500 \text{ lines}/cm$

$n = 2$

$\theta = 50°$

$\lambda = ?$

$d = \dfrac{1}{R}$

$d = \dfrac{1}{5500 \text{ lines}/cm}$

$d = 1.81 \times 10^{-4} cm$

$\lambda = \dfrac{d\sin\theta}{n}$

$\lambda = \dfrac{1.81 \times 10^{-4} cm \sin 50°}{(2)}$

$\lambda = 6.964 \times 10^{-5} cm$

The light has a wavelength of 696 nm.

Problems

1. A monochromatic beam of light travels through a double slit and produces a diffraction pattern on a screen as shown in the diagram below. Determine the wavelength of the light if the two slits are 3.12 x 10⁻⁶ m apart. [471 nm]

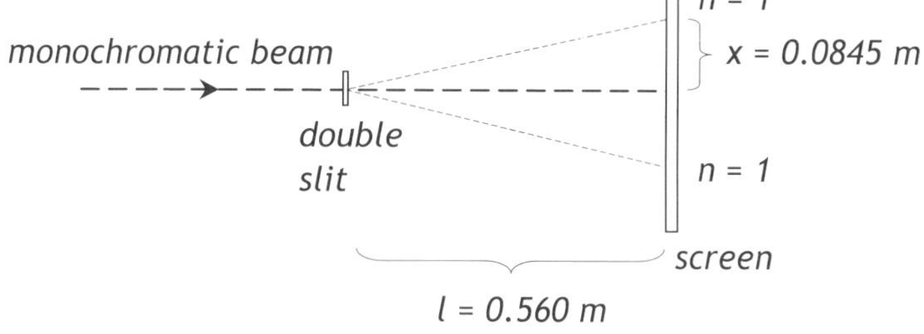

monochromatic beam

double slit

n = 1

x = 0.0845 m

n = 1

screen

l = 0.560 m

2.	The spacing between two slits is 5.90 x 10^3 m in a Young's double slit experiment. The distance from the slits to the screen is 1.00 m, and the distance from the central bright maximum to the third maxima is 2.50 x 10^{-4} m. Determine the wavelength of the incident light used in the experiment. [492 nm]

3.	A monochromatic beam of light is passed through two slits and forms an interference pattern on a screen. The distance between the slits is 0.0550 cm and the distance to the screen is 5.00 m. The distance from the central bright to the third bright fringe is 2.38 cm.
    a.	Determine the wavelength of the incident light. [873 nm]
    b.	Identify the colour of the incident light if it is visible. [Appendix A]

4.	Monochromatic light of 520 nm is passed through two narrow slits imprinted onto a slide. The distance between the two slits is 0.75 mm and the screen is located 110 cm away from the slide. Determine the separation distance between bright lines in the interference pattern formed on the screen. [7.6 x 10^{-4} m]

5. Determine the angle of deviation of the 1st order maxima produced when monochromatic light of 440 nm is directed through two slits that are 6.2 μm apart. [4.1°]

6. Determine the spacing of the rulings on an interference grating if the third order maximum is observed to deviate 26° from the central maxima using monochromatic light of 548 nm. [3.8 x 10^{-6} m]

7. A CDROM acts as a diffraction grating as it reflects light since it has many small imprints lined up as a way of storing data. An experiment is performed to determine the line spacing on a CDROM using a pocket laser pointer. The following data was recorded:

    | wavelength of laser pointer: | 680 nm |
    | distance from the screen to the CDROM: | 94.0 cm |
    | distance from the bright central max to the first maximum: | 42.5 cm |

    Determine the spacing of the lines on the CDROM. (Hint: is the angle greater than 10°?) [1.65 x 10^{-6} m]

8. A student is asked to determine the line spacing in a diffraction grating using a pen laser. The apparatus is set up as shown in the picture to the right. She sets the laser on a piece of paper so she can mark the locations of the laser, double slit, the screen and the bright lines on the screen.

She then uses the pen marks as shown in the diagram below to calculate the diffraction grating's line spacing. The label on the pen laser claimed a wavelength of 670 nm. [1.64×10^{-6} m]

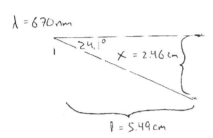

$\lambda = 670$ nm

$24.1°$

$x = 2.46$ cm

$l = 5.49$ cm

9. A diffraction experiment is performed where it is determined that the 2nd order maxima is at an angle of deviation of 56.0° using a diffraction grating having a line density of 1.00×10^{6} lines/m.
   a. Determine the wavelength of light used. [415 nm]
   b. Identify the colour of the light if it is visible. [Appendix A]

10. A grating ruled with 12 000 lines per cm produces a first order image at an angle of 32.0°. Determine the wavelength of light used. [442 nm]

11. An argon laser used in retinal surgery has a frequency of 6.148 x 10^{14} Hz. It is incident on a diffraction grating ruled with 6000 lines/m. The diffraction grating and screen are 1.50 m apart. Determine the
    a. wavelength of the argon laser. [488 nm]
    b. angle between bright lines. [0.2°]
    c. distance between the bright lines in the diffraction pattern. [4.39 mm]

12. Use the terms refraction and diffraction to fill in the blanks for the following statements. [Appendix A]
    a. Blue light is affected more by _____.
    b. Red light is affected more by _____.

13. Monochromatic laser light of 650 nm is directed through a diffraction grating that a line density of 4500 lines/cm. Determine the angle of the second order fringe relative to the central bright fringe. [35.8°]

14. A glass grating is etched with 5400 lines/cm. Monochromatic light is incident on the grating and forms a second order image with a diffracted angle of 30.0°. Determine the wavelength of the monochromatic light used. [463 nm]

15. A second order image is formed by a diffraction grating at an angle of 64°. The grating is ruled with 10 000 lines/cm.
    a. Calculate the wavelength of the light. [4.5×10^{-7} m]
    b. Will an image also appear at a smaller angle? If so, what is the angle? [Yes, 27°]
    c. Can a third order image be seen? Show your work to prove it either way. [Appendix A]

Use this information to answer question 16.

Sir Isaac Newton thought that light was composed of tiny particles which he referred to as "corpuscles". Christiaan Huygens proposed a wave theory for light. However the particle theory of light dominated science due to Newton's reputation.

16. Considering Thomas Young's observations of light interference, explain how these observations eventually changed common scientific knowledge or theory of his day. [Appendix A]

17. An experiment is done to determine the spacing between lines on a DVD video using a laser beam. The line spacing on a DVD is closer together than on a CD allowing DVDs to contain more data. The experimental set-up is shown below and the data collected is given in the chart.

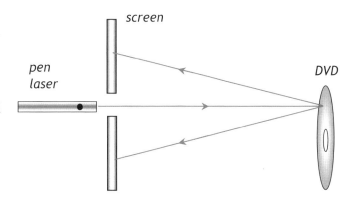

Screen-disk separation distance (cm)	Distance from central bright fringe to n = 1 (cm)
20.0	46.6
25.0	58.2
30.0	69.9
35.0	81.5
40.0	93.1

a. Plot the data.

Distance to Central Fringe as a Function of Separation Distance

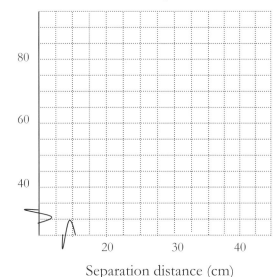

b. Determine the slope of the line. [~2.38]

c. Since the slope of the line is equal to the tangent of the angle, use the slope to calculate the angle. [~67.2°]

d. The angle calculated in part c may be considered an average angle for all the trials. Using a red laser with a wavelength of 680 nm and the angle found from the slope, determine the spacing between data lines on the DVD. [~7.38 x 10^{-7} m]

5.8 Extensions

1. This is a research question. Why do radio waves travel further at night than during the day? (Hint: ionosphere.) Your explanation must include a diagram. [Appendix A]

2. Two hockey fans are watching a playoff game being played in Edmonton. The first fan is at the game in Edmonton and the second is at home in Dallas watching on satellite TV. The signal to Dallas is being sent via a communication satellite in a geosynchronous orbit 36 000 km above the earth's equator. How much sooner does the Edmonton fan hear the play-by-play than the Dallas fan? You'll have to make some approximations to answer this question. [0.24 s]

3. An oscilloscope can be attached to an antenna and represent EMR as a picture on a computer screen. The following electromagnetic wave is shown on an oscilloscope's cm grid.
   a. Determine the frequency of the wave being analyzed by the oscilloscope. [4.0×10^{14} Hz]
   b. Identify the region of the electromagnetic spectrum the wave is found in. [Appendix A]

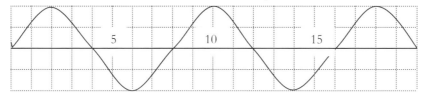

wavelength (x 10^{-7} m)

4. A ray of light is reflected in series from two mirrors as shown below. Determine the angle of reflection off the second mirror. (The diagram is not drawn to scale.) [28°]

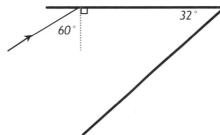

5. Some companies provide a service to track cell phones. For a small fee a cell phone can be "pinged" and located. Discuss the risks and benefits of this feature. [Appendix A]

6. Small microchip implants in called radio frequency identification (RFID) are useful for keeping track of people, animals and consumer goods and have been widely used in the 21 century. It has been shown, however, that they can carry and transmit computer viruses. Discuss the risks and benefits of the widespread use of RFIDs. [Appendix A]

7. Determine the angle of refraction or reflection as light strikes the opposite side of the equilateral piece of cut glass (n = 1.55). [41°, reflection]

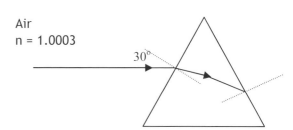

8   A student uses various mirrors and lenses to produce images of an object that are one half the object's original size.
   a.   If the student uses a concave mirror with a focal point of 10 cm, determine the distance from the mirror the object should be placed. [30 cm]
   b.   If the student uses a convex lens with a focal length of 5.0 cm, determine the distance from the lens the object should be placed. [15 cm]

9.   Explain why the sky is blue. [Appendix A]

10.   Locating your blind spot.

Where the optic nerve joins the eye, there are no rods or cones. This is called the *blind spot* because any light incident here cannot be converted into electrical signals. The following exercise can help you locate your blind spot.

•   Hold this page at arm's length and close your left eye while you look directly at the picture of the triangle on the left side of the page out of your right eye. You should be able to see the picture of the circle using your peripheral vision (don't turn your right eye towards it).

•   Gradually bring the page closer to your right eye. There will be a location where the circle suddenly disappears. If you move the paper further or closer away from that distance, the circle will reappear.

The circle disappears when the page is at this distance from your eye because light reflecting from the circle is falling on your blind spot.

5.9 Review

1. Maxwell proposed that a changing electric field generates a
    a. uniform current
    b. direct current
    c. changing magnetic field
    d. permanent magnetic field

2. Radio waves in the FM band are from 50 MHz to 500 MHz. Identify the wavelength below that could be a FM radio wave.
    a. 3 km
    b. 3 cm
    c. 3 m
    d. 3 mm

3. Red light having a wavelength of 680 nm has a frequency of
    a. 4.41×10^{-14} Hz
    b. 2.27×10^{-15} Hz
    c. 2.27×10^{15} Hz
    d. 4.41×10^{14} Hz

4. The visible spectrum of light is commonly generated by
    a. movements of microwaves in the sun
    b. scattering of light in the atmosphere
    c. dispersion of light through droplets of water
    d. transitions of electrons within the atom

5. A polarizing filter
    a. filters out all light except wavelengths that are oriented with the filter
    b. causes light to behave like a particle reflecting between two mirrors
    c. generates electromagnetic fields
    d. releases energy in the form of EMR in all directions

6. The frequency of a certain monochromatic beam of visible light in a vacuum is found to be 5.50×10^{14} Hz. Determine the light's wavelength. [545 nm]

7. The wavelength of a certain monochromatic beam of visible light in a vacuum is found to be 510 nm. Calculate the wave's frequency. [5.88×10^{14} Hz]

8. List the seven colours of visible light from high frequency to low frequency. [Appendix A]

9. Determine the speed of light if Michelson's used an 8-sided mirror rotating at 545.0 Hz placed 36.20 km from the plane mirror. [3.157×10^{8} m/s]

10. Determine the minimum frequency of rotation necessary to produce an observed image if the distance separating a rotating 32-sided mirror from the fixed mirror is 12.0 km. [391 Hz]

11. A blue laser has a wavelength of 485 nm. Determine the speed of the laser light in a transparent plastic if its refracted wavelength is 442 nm in the plastic. [2.73 x 10^8 m/s]

12. Determine the critical angle for a diamond/water system. [33.3°]

13. A 6.50 cm tall object produces a 10.5 cm tall image behind the mirror. If the radius of curvature of this mirror is 10.0 cm determine the
    a. magnification of the object. [1.62 X]
    b. characteristics of the image. [Appendix A]
    c. kind of mirror used. [Appendix A]

14. A 5.0 cm high object is 10.5 cm from a convex lens with a 20.0 cm focal length. Determine the
    a. image's characteristics. [Appendix A]
    b. image distance. [-22.1 cm]

15. A monochromatic beam of light is passed through two slits and forms an interference pattern on a screen with a special detector. The distance between the slits is 0.0620 cm and the distance to the screen is 4.50 m. The distance from the central bright to the second bright fringe is 2.65 cm.
    a. Determine the wavelength of the incident light. [1.83 x 10^{-6} m]
    b. Identify the region of the EMR spectrum the light is coming from. [Appendix A]

16. A glass grating is ruled with 5700 lines/cm. Monochromatic light striking the grating forms a second order image diffracted at 28.0° to the normal. Determine the wavelength of light used. [412 nm]

5.10 Review Assignment

1. Low frequency radiation possibly produced by cosmic radiation and lightning is called Shuman resonance. Determine the wavelength of a Shuman resonance wave at 7.8 Hz. [3.8 x 10^7 m]

2. Calculate the period of the wave for a blue laser diode having a frequency of 4.23 x 10^{14} Hz.

3. Radio frequency identification (RFID) tags are small microchips (less than 0.4 mm thick) that are attached to many consumer goods and animals. They have also been implanted in people to track their movements. The device is activated by a sensor and then emits a radio signal which is detected by a scanner (i.e., antenna). Determine the wavelength of an RFID emitting a radio signal at 134.2 kHz.

4. Sketch a graph showing the relationship between the frequency of an electromagnetic wave and wavelength.

5. Satellite phones (a.k.a satphones) do not require cell phone towers and can receive and transmit signals directly to geosynchronous satellites 36 000 km above the equator. Determine the time for a signal to travel from the satphone to the satellite.

6. Determine Michelson's value for the speed of light using an 8-sided mirror rotating at 527.8 Hz placed 35.512 km from the plane mirror.

7. Heinrich Hertz used an induction coil to obtain a high voltage to cause electrons to jump a gap and produce EMR in the form of radio waves as shown in the diagram below. This allowed him to determine the speed of the radio waves. Assuming a distance of 12.0 m between the spark gap and the antenna and a travel time of 4.01×10^{-8} s, calculate the speed of the radio waves.

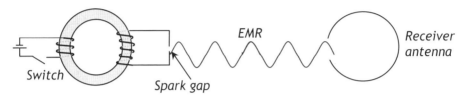

8. Shivani wrapped a cell phone in a thin layer of aluminium foil. She then called the cell phone. Predict what Shivani should observe.

9. Fill in each blank with one of the seven colours of the visible spectrum.
   a. The colour _____ is most affected by refraction.
   b. The colour _____ is most affected by diffraction.

10. Determine the angle of refraction of the light ray as it leaves the opposite side of the equilateral piece of cut glass (n = 1.52).

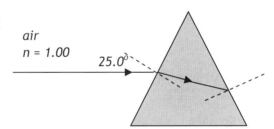

11. Design an experiment to determine the focal length of a metal spoon.

12. Light is travelling from air to a substance with a different refractive index. Describe what happens to speed, wavelength and angle in the substance when its index of refraction increases (i.e., increase, decrease, or stay the same). Complete the chart.

speed	wavelength	angle	frequency

13. Derive the equations for the diffraction of waves through a double slit.

14. Derive the thin lens formula.

6 Particle Model of Light

Introduction

Matter and energy have a dual nature: wave and particle. Understanding the particle nature of light is necessary for learning about modern physics and technology.

6.1 Summary Notes – The Quantum

A **quantum** (plural quanta) is a discrete (individual or separate) amount.

A **photon** is a quantum (particle) of light.

A photon is a quantum of light energy. The energy of a photon is described as:

$$E = hf \quad E = \frac{hc}{\lambda}$$

Where:

E is the energy (J or eV)

h is Planck's constant (6.63 x 10^{-34} J•s or 4.14 x 10^{-15} eV•s)

f is frequency (Hz)

λ is wavelength (m)

c is the speed of light (m/s)

☐ Notes:

_____

_____

_____

_____

_____

_____

_____

_____

_____

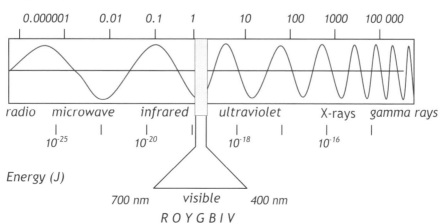

Examples

1. Some wavelengths of infrared light are produced by molecules vibrating at 3.75×10^{14} Hz. Determine the amount of quantized energy for each photon.

    $$f = 3.75 \times 10^{14} \text{ Hz} \qquad\qquad E = hf$$
    $$E = ? \qquad\qquad\qquad = 6.63 \times 10^{-34} \text{ J} \cdot \text{s} \times 3.75 \times 10^{14} \text{ Hz}$$
    $$E = 2.486 \times 10^{-19} \text{ J}$$

    Each photon's energy is 2.49×10^{-19} J.

2. A beam of monochromatic light having a wavelength of 560 nm is incident on a detector. The beam delivers 1.28×10^{-16} J of energy to the detector each second. Determine the number of photons incident on the detector each second.

    $$E = 1.28 \times 10^{-16} \text{ J} \qquad E = \frac{hc}{\lambda}$$
    $$\lambda = 560 \times 10^{-9} \text{ m}$$
    $$\text{\# photons} = ? \qquad = \frac{6.63 \times 10^{-34} \text{ J} \cdot \text{s} \times 3 \times 10^{8} \text{ m/s}}{560 \times 10^{-9} \text{ m}}$$
    $$E = 3.5518 \times 10^{-19} \text{ J}$$

    $$\text{\# photons} = \frac{\text{total energy}}{\text{energy of 1 photon}}$$
    $$\text{\# photons} = \frac{1.28 \times 10^{-16} \text{ J}}{3.5518 \times 10^{-19} \text{ J/photon}}$$
    $$\text{\# photons} = 360.38$$

    360 photons are incident on the detector each second.

Problems

1. Determine the energy of a photon with a frequency of 5.05×10^{14} Hz. [3.35×10^{-19} J or 2.09 eV]

2. Welders must shield their eyes from the intense ultraviolet radiation emitted from the molten hot metals they work with. Determine the energy of a photon with a frequency of 1.75×10^{15} Hz. [1.16×10^{-18} J or 7.25 eV]

3.   Determine the frequency of a photon that has an energy of 1.15×10^{-18} J. [1.73×10^{15} Hz]

4.   Determine the energy of a photon that has a wavelength of 650 nm. [3.06×10^{-19} J or 1.91 eV]

5.   Determine the wavelength of a photon having an energy of 4.00×10^{-19} J. [497 nm]

6.   Complete the following energy conversions. (Hint: Note question 8 on page 109.) [Appendix A]

	Energy (J)	Energy (eV)
a.	1.80×10^{-18}	
b.	4.52×10^{-19}	
c.		2.00
d.		5.60

7. Determine the wavelength a photon having an energy of 2.80 eV. [444 nm]

8. Assuming visible light is between 400 nm and 700 nm, determine the maximum frequency of the visible light. [7.50 x 10^{14} Hz]

9. The three primary colours for light are arranged in a spectrum as shown in the diagram. Complete the chart that follows for three particular wavelengths. [Appendix A]

visible spectrum

red   green   violet

	red	green	violet
Wavelength (nm)	690		
Frequency (Hz)		5.56 x 10^{14}	
Energy (J)			5.23 x 10^{-19}
Energy (eV)			

10. A laser produces 4.05×10^5 photons each second to give a total energy of 1002 keV/s. Calculate the energy of each photon in units of eV. [2.47 eV]

11. A photon has an energy of 4.05×10^{-16} J. A beam of these photons is produced from a laser to give a total energy of 3.27×10^{-13} J/s. Calculate the number of photons emitted by the laser in 2.0 s. [1615 photons]

12. The human eye is capable of detecting as few as 6 photons as long as they are all received by the retinal cells within 100 ms. A beam of monochromatic light of 560 nm provides energy to a detector at a rate of 1.28×10^{-17} J/ms. Determine the number of photons incident on the detector each ms. [36 photons/ms]

13. A green pen laser has a wavelength of 532 nm and a power output of 0.48 mW. Determine the number of photons emitted each second from the laser. [1.3×10^{15} photons per second]

14. Identify the items from the list below that best represent an analogue (i.e., continuous) system and the items that best represent a quantized system. Use A for analogue and Q for quantized and place the appropriate letter in the blank before the item. [Appendix A]

a. _____ stairs

b. _____ ramp

c. _____ vending machine that accepts coins only

d. _____ clock

e. _____ clock

Use the information below to answer question 15.

A **blackbody** is an object that absorbs all energy that contacts it when it is cool and emits (radiates) all wavelengths of light when hot.

Based on the theory that light is a wave, Planck predicted the EMR intensity as a function of wavelength for a radiating blackbody. The results from experiment did not match his prediction. Planck showed that to make the prediction match what actually happened, the energy had to be **quantized** – that is, the energy only occurred in whole number multiples of a basic amount.

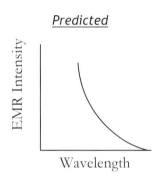

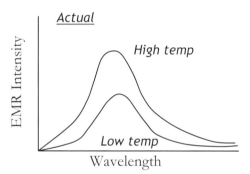

15. Explain what should be done when a theory is not supported by the evidence from experiment. [Appendix A]

6.2 Summary Notes – The Photoelectric Effect

The **photoelectric effect** occurs when light energy contacts a metal and releases electrons from the metal. This can be done using two parallel plates enclosed in an evacuated glass tube. This may be called a phototube.

Description:

- When light illuminates a metal surface electrons are emitted immediately.

- Each metal has its own **threshold frequency** where electrons are emitted only at a certain frequency or above.

- When the EMR is at or above the threshold frequency the energy of the emitted electrons will increase as the frequency of the incident EMR increases.

- When the **intensity** of light is increased the current of electrons will increase (if above the threshold frequency). This is detected as an increase of current.

Explanation:

Einstein explained the photoelectric effect based on the idea that light is quantized (i.e., a particle):
- One electron is liberated from the metal surface for every photon absorbed.
- In order for electrons to leave the metal a photon must have enough energy to knock it out of its position around the metal nuclei (this explains the threshold frequency required by the metal).
- If the energy of a photon is too low an electron will not be emitted.
- The brighter the light, the more photons hit the metal and therefore more electrons are liberated as long as the photons have enough energy.

☐ Notes:

_____

_____

_____

_____

_____

_____

_____

_____

_____

_____

_____

_____

_____

_____

_____

_____

_____

_____

_____

_____

_____

_____

_____

_____

_____

_____

_____

_____

_____

_____

_____

_____

_____

_____

The photoelectric effect may be explained using the particle model of light in conjunction with the Law of Conservation of Energy:

Photon energy = kinetic energy of electron + work function

At the threshold frequency the energy of the photon is equal to the work function so the kinetic energy of the emitted electron is zero.

$$W = hf_o$$

$$E_{k_{max}} = qV_{stop}$$

Where:

W is the work function (J or eV)

h is Planck's constant (J•s or eV•s)

f_o is the threshold frequency (Hz)

q is the charge of an electron (C)

V_{stop} is the voltage required to stop (turn back) the electron (V)

$E_{k_{max}}$ is the energy of emitted electrons (J)

Example

1. Cesium metal has a work function of 2.10 eV. Determine the maximum wavelength of light required to produce emission of photoelectrons.

$W = 2.10 eV$

$\lambda_{max} = ?$

$W = h f_o$

$f_o = \dfrac{W}{h}$

$f_o = \dfrac{2.10 eV}{4.14 \times 10^{-15} eV \cdot s}$

$f_o = 5.0725 \times 10^{14} Hz$

$c = \lambda f$

$\lambda = \dfrac{c}{f}$

$= \dfrac{3 \times 10^8 m/s}{5.0725 \times 10^{14} Hz}$

$\lambda = 5.914 \times 10^{-9} m$

The maximum wavelength that would produce photoelectrons is 591 nm.

Problems

1. A photon having an energy of 6.0 eV contacts the photoelectric surface of a metal having a work function of 2.0 eV. Determine the kinetic energy of the ejected photoelectron. [4.0 eV]

2. Photons having energy of 3.20 eV are incident on cesium metal having a work function of 2.02 eV resulting in the emission of electrons. Use the Law of Conservation of Energy to determine the
    a. kinetic energy of the emitted electrons in electron volts. [1.18 eV]
    b. speed of the emitted electrons. [6.44 x 10^5 m/s]

3. The carbon in an HB pencil has a work function of 4.81 eV. A 6.21 eV photon is incident on the carbon. Determine the
    a. energy in electron volts of the emitted photoelectrons. [1.40 eV]
    b. speed of the emitted photoelectrons. [7.01 x 10^5 m/s]

4. Einstein's explanation of the photoelectric effect based on the idea that light was a particle was not quickly accepted by many scientists. Millikan spent 10 years performing sophisticated photoelectric experiments in an effort to disprove Einstein's photon interpretation. In the end he provided verification of the photon interpretation. Light falls on a photoelectric surface with a work function of 1.60 eV resulting in the emission of electrons with a kinetic energy of 3.78 eV.
    a. Determine the energy of each photon of the incident light. [5.38 eV]
    b. Identify the region of the electromagnetic spectrum where the photon belongs. [Appendix A]

5. Electrons are emitted with a kinetic energy of 1.90 eV from a photoelectric surface having a work function of 2.12 eV. Determine the incident
    a. photon's energy. [4.02 eV]
    b. light's frequency. [9.71 x 10^{14} Hz]
    c. light's wavelength. [309 nm]
    d. light's location in the electromagnetic spectrum. [Appendix A]

6.   A photon having a frequency of 8.2×10^{14} Hz contacts the photoelectric surface of a metal having a work function of 1.1×10^{-19} J. Determine the kinetic energy of the ejected photoelectron. [1.0×10^{-19} J]

7.   A graph of kinetic energy as a function of frequency for a photoelectric experiment is shown to the right. Label the sections of the graphs indicated. [Appendix A]

a. _____

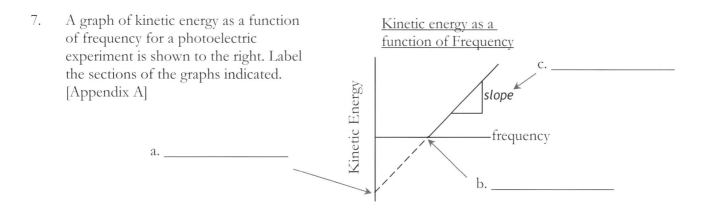

Kinetic energy as a function of Frequency

c. _____

slope

frequency

b. _____

Use the graph to answer questions 8 – 11.

Hertz discovered the photoelectric effect while investigating EMR. Millikan spent 10 years precisely examining the effect. A graph of kinetic energy of emitted electrons versus frequency of incident light is plotted for a photoelectric tube.

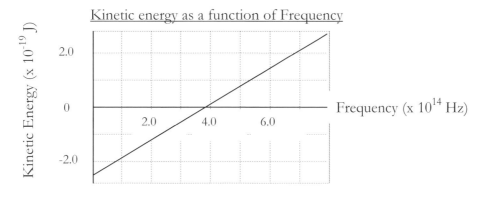

Kinetic energy as a function of Frequency

8.   Determine the work function of the metal used in the phototube. [~2.6×10^{-19} J]

9.   Determine the metal's threshold frequency. [~3.8×10^{14} Hz]

10.   Calculate the threshold wavelength of the metal. [~7.9 x 10^{-7} m]

11.   Use the graph to determine Planck's constant. [~8.2 x 10^{-34} J•s]

12.   The work function of three different metals was determined in a lab to be 1.30 eV, 2.60 eV, and 4.10 eV. The values for the work functions were obtained from a graph of energy versus frequency. Compare the slopes of the three lines. [Appendix A]

13.   Convert Planck's constant in units of J•s to units of eV•s. [4.14 x 10^{-15} eV•s]

14.   Fill in the blank. Incoming photons strike a photoelectric surface. If the energy of the photons is greater than the work function of the metal, _____are ejected. [Appendix A]

15. A photoelectric experiment uses a metal having a work function 1.24 eV. It was determined that the threshold frequency of the metal is 3.00×10^{14} Hz. Draw a graph of kinetic energy of the photoelectrons as a function of frequency for sodium. [Appendix A]

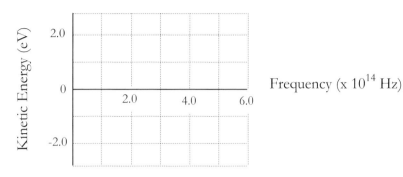

Kinetic energy as a function of Frequency

16. Determine the work function of platinum having a threshold frequency of 1.28×10^{15} Hz. [8.49×10^{-19} J or 5.30 eV]

17. The threshold frequency or wavelength of light may be used to help identify an unknown substance in a photoelectric experiment. Complete the chart below. [Appendix A]

Element	Work Function (x 10^{-19} J)	Threshold Wavelength (nm)	Threshold Frequency (x 10^{15} Hz)
Beryllium	8.00		
Iron		276	
Uranium			0.870

18. Assume the three substances listed in the previous question are used in an experiment. Each substance has the identical light of 220 nm incident on their surface. Identify the substance that would result in photoelectrons with the greatest kinetic energy. [Appendix A]

19. Heinrich Hertz first observed the photoelectric effect in the latter part of the 19th century while working with his spark gap generator. He found that his spark-gap generator worked better in the presence of visible light and even better with UV light. Determine the threshold frequency of light shining on a metal with a work function of 4.32 eV. [1.04×10^{15} Hz]

20. Fill in the blanks. As the intensity of light increase the number of photoelectrons _____, as long as the frequency of incident light is _____ than the threshold frequency. [Appendix A]

21. Light, having a frequency greater than the threshold frequency is incident on a metal's surface and photoelectrons are emitted. Sketch the graph shapes below as the intensity of the incident light is manipulated and frequency is held constant. [Appendix A]

22. Electrons are emitted from a photoelectric surface at speed of 5.20×10^5 m/s. If the work function of the metal surface is 3.39×10^{-19} J, determine the frequency of the incident photons. $[6.97 \times 10^{14}$ Hz]

23. Light with a wavelength of 610 nm falls on a photoelectric surface with a work function of 2.56 $\times 10^{-19}$ J. Determine the maximum kinetic energy of the emitted photoelectrons in units of
    a. joules. $[7.01 \times 10^{-20}$ J]
    b. electron volts. [0.438 eV]

24. Old film projectors used the photoelectric effect to synchronize the sound image as the projector was played. Consider a certain metal being used in an old film projector that has a threshold frequency of 2.10×10^{15} Hz. Calculate the maximum kinetic energy of electrons emitted by light with a frequency 3.40×10^{15} Hz. $[8.62 \times 10^{-19}$ J or 5.38 eV]

25. Determine the stopping voltage of an electron having a kinetic energy of 3.1 eV. [Appendix A]

26. The stopping voltage of electrons released through a photoelectric process may be determined using the following apparatus. Identify the type of meter used in position
    a. P. [Appendix A]
    b. Q. [Appendix A]

27. Light with a wavelength of 470 nm is directed on a photoelectric surface having a work function of 1.40 eV. Determine the stopping voltage needed to reduce the current through the cell to zero. [1.24 V]

28. Define, [Appendix A]
    a. photocurrent:

    b. photoelectron:

29. Explain how the photoelectric effect supports the particle nature of light. [Appendix A]

30. In the equation for the photoelectric effect, the expression "maximum kinetic energy" is used. Explain the use of the word "maximum". [Appendix A]

31. In a photoelectric experiment a variable frequency light source was incident upon a photoelectric metal and the following stopping voltages were recorded.

a. Graph the data.
b. Use the graph to determine
   i. the threshold frequency of the metal. [~2.4 x 10^{14} Hz]
   ii. the work function of the metal. [~1.0 eV]
   iii. Planck's constant. [~ 4.3 x 10^{-15} eV•s or ~8.0 x 10^{-34} J•s]

Frequency (x 10^{14} Hz)	Stopping Voltage (V)
2.6	0.15
2.9	0.31
3.3	0.45
3.5	0.59
4.0	0.80

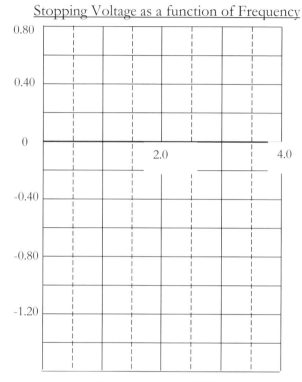

Stopping Voltage as a function of Frequency

Frequency (x 10^{14} Hz)

32. Sketch graphs for the following photoelectric relationships. [Appendix A]

a. Photocurrent as a function of frequency

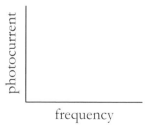

b. Photocurrent as a function of intensity

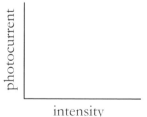

c. Photocurrent as a function of stopping voltage

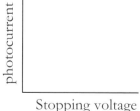

6.3 Summary Notes – The Compton Effect

☐ Notes:

_____

_____

_____

_____

_____

_____

_____

_____

_____

_____

_____

_____

_____

_____

_____

_____

_____

_____

Compton's experiment confirmed the particle nature of EMR.

A beam of high energy X-rays is incident on a thin metal foil causing electrons to be ejected. Lower energy X-rays are also emitted.

The interaction between an X-ray photon and an electron may be treated as an elastic collision:

According to the classical definition of momentum photons should have no momentum since they have a zero mass.

However, photons have a mass equivalence using $E = mc^2$; therefore they have momentum:

$$p = \frac{h}{\lambda}$$

$$E = pc$$

Where:
  p is momentum (kg•m/s)
  h is Planck's constant (6.63×10^{-34} J•s)
  λ is wavelength (m)
  c is the speed of light (m/s)
  E is energy (J)

Using the law of conservation of energy and the law of conservation of momentum, the Compton scattering equation is derived:

$$\Delta\lambda = \frac{h}{mc}\left(1 - \cos\theta\right)$$

$\Delta\lambda = \lambda_f - \lambda_i$ is the change in wavelength (m)

θ is the angle between the initial and final wavelength paths
m is the mass of an electron (kg)

Examples

1. Determine the momentum of a photon whose wavelength is 1.25 nm.

$$\lambda = 1.25 \times 10^{-9}\,m \qquad p = \frac{h}{\lambda}$$

$$p = ?$$

$$p = \frac{6.63 \times 10^{-34}\,J \cdot s}{1.25 \times 10^{-9}\,m}$$

$$p = 5.304 \times 10^{-25}\,kgm/s$$

The momentum of the photon is 5.30×10^{-25} kg•m/s.

2. A 1.24×10^{-11} m X-ray hits a section of foil metal and scatters at an angle of 40.0°. Calculate the wavelength of the scattered X-ray photon.

$$\lambda_i = 1.24 \times 10^{-11}\,m \qquad \Delta\lambda = \frac{h}{mc}(1-\cos\theta) \qquad \Delta\lambda = \lambda_f - \lambda_i$$

$$\theta = 40° \qquad \qquad \lambda_f = \Delta\lambda + \lambda_i$$

$$\lambda_f = ? \qquad \Delta\lambda = \frac{6.63 \times 10^{-34}\,J \cdot s\,(1-\cos 40°)}{9.11 \times 10^{-31}\,kg \times 3 \times 10^{8}\,m/s}$$

$$= 5.6755 \times 10^{-13}\,m + 1.24 \times 10^{-11}\,m$$

$$= 5.6755 \times 10^{-13}\,m \qquad \qquad \lambda_f = 1.2968 \times 10^{-11}\,m$$

The wavelength of the scattered X-ray photon is 1.30×10^{-11} m.

Problems

Use the information below to answer questions 1 & 2.

Röntgen discovered X-rays when experimenting with high voltage cathode ray tubes. X-rays are produced when high energy electrons are decelerated quickly. (Assume that 100% of the electrical energy is transformed into high energy X-rays).

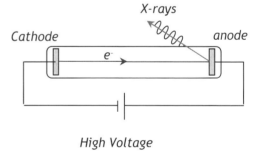

1. An X-ray tube produces EMR having a maximum frequency of 2.50×10^{18} Hz. Determine the
   a. energy of the X-rays. [1.66×10^{-15} J or 10.4 keV]
   b. potential difference required for this tube. [10.4 kV]

2. In Germany X-rays are sometimes called Röntgen-rays. Determine the operating potential (voltage) of a Röntgen-ray machine used to provide photons with a minimum wavelength of 8.60×10^{-11} m. [14.5 kV]

Use the following information to answer question 3.

Ionizing radiation such as X-rays and gamma rays has enough energy to damage human tissue. It is often measured in units of millirems (mrem), which measures the effect on living tissue. The average person in Canada receives about 360 mrem each year from normal background radiation. Here are some other sources of ionizing radiation:

Source	Amount of radiation
cross country air travel	5 mrem
living in a brick house	10 mrem per year
smoke detectors	1 mrem per year
dental X-ray	2 - 3 mrem

3. The number of mrems from dental X-rays is a factor of the frequency of the radiation and its intensity. A typical dental X-ray may have a wavelength of 2.07×10^{-11} m. Determine the minimum voltage required to create this X-ray in a cathode ray tube. [60.1 kV]

4. Determine the momentum of a photon of light having an energy of 7.57×10^{-16} J. [2.52×10^{-24} kg•m/s]

5. Determine the momentum of a 7.2 MeV photon. [3.8×10^{-21} kg•m/s]

6. Determine the momentum of a photon having a wavelength of 3.00×10^{-8} m. [2.21×10^{-26} kg•m/s]

7. Determine the momentum of a photon having a frequency of 3.40×10^{23} Hz. [7.51×10^{-19} kg•m/s]

8. A photon has a momentum of 3.52×10^{-24} kg•m/s. Determine the photon's
   a. energy. [1.06×10^{-15} J]
   b. wavelength. [1.88×10^{-10} m]

9. A Crookes tube (CRT) is used with a potential difference of 60.0 kV between the cathode and anode. Determine the maximum momentum of each X-ray photon produced. [3.20×10^{-23} J•s/m]

10. An alpha particle is travelling at 6.3×10^5 m/s. Calculate the wavelength of a photon with the same momentum as the alpha particle. [1.6×10^{-13} m]

Use the following information for question 11.

The Compton Gamma Ray Observatory was a satellite was a NASA satellite used to obtain gamma-ray measurements from every section of the sky with greater precision than had previously been done. This would enable scientists to better understand quasars, pulsars and black holes. On January 31, 1993 a gamma ray burst (called the super bowl burst) was detected that radiated more energy in less than one second than the Sun can radiate in 1000 years.

11. Gamma rays with energies up to 1.0 GeV were detected at the observatory. Determine the gamma ray's
    a. frequency. [2.4×10^{23} Hz]
    b. momentum. [5.3×10^{-19} J•s/m]

Use the information below to answer questions 12 – 14.

When X-rays or gamma rays strike an electron within a metal the work function of the electron is small relative to the energy of the EMR and therefore is often left out of the conservation of energy expression. The kinetic energy of the electron within the atom before the collision is also small and typically left out.

12. X-ray photons having an energy of 18.0 keV strike a metal plate causing electrons to be ejected along with X-ray photons of 16.0 keV. Calculate the
    a. kinetic energy of the ejected electrons. [2.0 keV]
    b. speed of the ejected electrons. [2.65×10^7 m/s]

13. X-rays having a wavelength of 5.20×10^{-11} m strike a metal plate. By striking the plate electrons are ejected along with X-rays having a wavelength of 8.20×10^{-11} m. Calculate the
    a. kinetic energy of the ejected electrons. [1.40×10^{-15} J]
    b. speed of the ejected electrons. [5.54×10^7 m/s]

14. X-rays having a wavelength of 6.30×10^{-11} m strike a metal plate. Electrons are ejected at a speed of 6.24×10^7 m/s along with scattered X-rays. Calculate the wavelength of the scattered X-rays. [1.44×10^{-10} m]

15. X-rays strike a metal plate causing the ejection of electrons as shown in the diagram. Determine the wavelength of the scattered X-rays. [4.34 x 10^{-11} m]

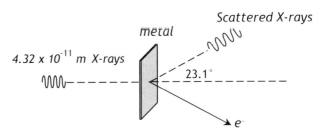

16. A 0.0650 nm X-ray scatters at an angle of 40.2°. Calculate the wavelength of the scattered X-ray photon. [6.56 x 10^{-11} m]

17. A 0.0113 nm X-ray collides with a stationary neon atom that is at rest. The X-ray photon bounces directly backwards. Determine the wavelength of the scattered X-ray. [1.62 x 10^{-11} m]

18. X-rays moving to the east are incident perpendicularly upon a metal foil. Scattered X-rays having a wavelength of 0.0300 nm are detected at 50.0° N of E of the foil. Determine the wavelength of the incident X-ray. [2.91 x 10^{-11} m]

19. In a Compton Effect experiment the following data was collected:

 - Wavelength of incident photon: 5.00×10^{-11} m
 - Wavelength of scattered photon: 5.12×10^{-11} m

Determine the X-ray's scattering angle. [59.6°]

20. X-rays of 0.0124 nm are incident on a metal foil. The scattered X-rays have a wavelength of 0.0129 nm. Determine the X-ray's scattering angle. [37.4°]

21. Compare the Compton Effect to the Photoelectric Effect. [Appendix A]

Use the information below to answer questions 22 & 23.

X-rays strike a metal plate causing electrons to be ejected along with scattered X-rays as shown in the diagram. Momentum must be conserved.

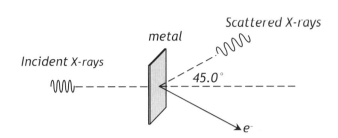

22. Complete the chart. [Appendix A]

Momentum	Incident X-ray	Scattered X-ray	Target Electron	Scattered Electron
x-component (x 10^{-23} kg•m/s)	3.52		0	
y-component (x 10^{-23} kg•m/s)	0	2.40	0	

23. Determine the velocity of the ejected electron. [2.91×10^7 m/s, at 65.0°]

24. A bubble chamber is a device that shows the path of electrons and other charged particles but not the path of photons. The spiral track shown below is called a Compton electron because it is produced through the Compton Effect. Determine the direction of the magnetic field that is causing the electron to spiral in the bubble chamber. [Appendix A]

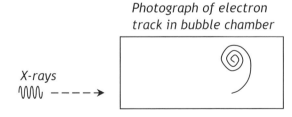

Photograph of electron track in bubble chamber

6.4 Extensions

1. Light, having a frequency greater than the threshold frequency is incident on a metal's surface and photoelectrons are emitted. Sketch the graph shapes below as the intensity of the incident light is manipulated and frequency is held constant. [Appendix A]

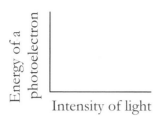

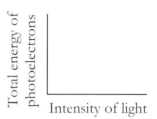

2. X-ray photons with a wavelength of 2.035×10^{-10} m collide elastically with electrons initially at rest. After the collision the electrons recoil at a speed of 4.21375×10^{6} m/s as shown in the diagram below.

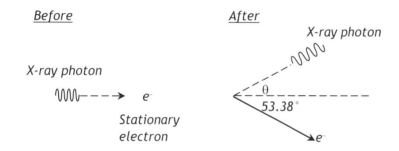

a. Calculate the momentum of the scattered X-ray photon after the collision.* (Assume the original photon was heading due east.) [3.229×10^{-24} kg•m/s]

b. Determine the scattered photon's
    i.   energy. [9.680×10^{-16} J]
    ii. wavelength. [2.052×10^{-10} m]

*Use the following data:

Planck's constant:	6.626×10^{-34} J•s
Mass of electron:	9.1095×10^{-31} kg
Speed of light:	2.998×10^{8} m/s

6.5 Review

1. A quantum of EMR is called a
   a. pronoun
   b. transverse wave
   c. wave
   d. photon

2. Planck's constant expressed in base units are
   a. $kg \cdot m^2/s^2$
   b. $kg \cdot m/s^2$
   c. $kg \cdot m^2/s$
   d. $kg \cdot m/s$

3. When the incident EMR is at or above the threshold frequency of a photoelectric cell, the energy of the emitted electrons
   a. decrease as the wavelength of the incident EMR decreases
   b. increase as the frequency of the incident EMR increases
   c. is constant as long as photons are increasing in energy
   d. increase as the stopping voltage increases

4. At the threshold frequency the energy of the photon is
   a. greater than the work function of the metal
   b. equal to the stopping voltage
   c. smaller than the maximum kinetic energy of the electron
   d. equal to the work function

5. Photons have mass equivalence due to
   a. $Ft = m\Delta v$
   b. $E = 1/2mv^2$
   c. $E = mc^2$
   d. $E = mgh$

6. Determine the energy in electron volts of a photon with a frequency of 7.15×10^{14} Hz. [2.96 eV]

7. A photon is produced having an energy of 7.50 eV.
   a. Determine its wavelength. [166 nm]
   b. Identify its location in the electromagnetic spectrum. [Appendix A]

8. Photons having an energy of 5.10 eV are incident on magnesium metal having a work function of 3.70 eV resulting in the emission of electrons. Determine the
   a. kinetic energy of the emitted electrons in electron volts. [1.40 eV]
   b. kinetic energy of the emitted electrons in joules. [2.24×10^{-19} J]
   c. speed of the emitted electrons. [7.01×10^5 m/s]

9. Electrons are emitted with a kinetic energy of 2.63 eV from a photoelectric surface having a work function of 2.79 eV. Determine the incident light's
    a. frequency. [1.31×10^{15} Hz]
    b. wavelength. [229 nm]
    c. location in the electromagnetic spectrum. [Appendix A]

10. The kinetic energy of photoelectrons is graphed as a function of frequency of incident light. Complete the chart below to communicate how to correctly interpret the graph. [Appendix A]

Graph of kinetic energy versus frequency	Photoelectric interpretation
slope	
y-intercept	
x-intercept	

11. Fill in the blanks.

    a. As the frequency of incident photons increases the kinetic energy of photoelectrons _____. [Appendix A]
    b. As the energy of incident photons decreases the kinetic energy of photoelectrons _____. [Appendix A]

12. Determine the momentum of a photon having a wavelength of 660 nm. [1.00×10^{-27} J•s/m]

13. A 0.0755 nm X-ray is incident on a metal surface causing Compton electrons to be produced. Calculate the wavelength of the scattered X-ray photon if they are scattered at an angle of 50°. [7.64×10^{-11} m]

6.6 Review Assignment

1. Determine the energy of a photon from a pen laser that has a wavelength of 680 nm.

2. A beam of monochromatic light having a wavelength of 580 nm is incident on a detector. The beam delivers 900 eV of energy to the detector each second. Determine the number of photons incident on the detector each second.

3. Complete the sentences regarding the photoelectric effect by filling in the blanks.

    When the kinetic energy of the photoelectron is plotted as a function of frequency of light incident on the metal's surface the x-intercept is the _____; the y-intercept is the _____; and the slope is _____ constant.

4. The Carbon in an HB pencil has a work function of 4.81 eV. Determine the maximum wavelength of light required to produce emission of photoelectrons from the surface of carbon.

5. Light falls on a photoelectric surface with a work function of 1.80 eV resulting in the emission of electrons with a kinetic energy of 3.88 eV.
   a. Determine the energy of the light in electron volts.
   b. Identify the type of EMR incident on the metal visible light.

6. Photons having a wavelength of 410 nm are incident on a metal's surface (W = 2.10 eV) at a rate of 120 000 per ms. Determine the maximum possible current in units of amperes provided by this photocell.

7. Use the Law of Conservation of Energy to write an energy statement about the two diagrams of a photon hitting an electron orbiting inside an atom.

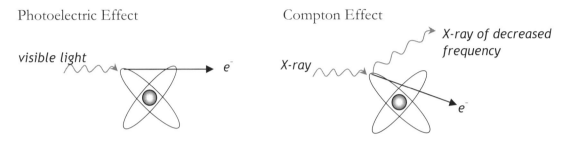

Photoelectric Effect

Compton Effect

8. Compare the momentum of a 7.2 MeV photon with a 7.2 MeV electron.

9. Calculate the frequency of a photon whose energy is 7.65 x 10^{-19} J.

10. Electrons can be emitted from a metal surface when it is irradiated with a maximum wavelength of 8.10 x 10^{-6} m. Determine the work function of the metal.

11. Electrons travelling at 1.37 x 10^{7} m/s strike the tungsten anode of an X-ray tube. Determine the operating potential difference of this tube.

12. Determine how many photons are emitted per second by a 1.5 W krypton-argon laser having a wavelength of 488 nm.

13. X-rays of 0.0134 nm are incident on a metal foil. The scattered X-rays have a wavelength of 0.0141 nm. Determine the X-ray's scattering angle.

14. Compare the particle model of light with the wave model of light in regards to energy distribution, amplitude and frequency.

15. Explain how the Compton Effect supports the particle model of light.

This 44-page booklet is designed to prepare you for the Physics 30 Diploma Exam. It provides:

- a summary of each unit.
- tips and tricks to help with problems and avoid common difficulties.
- sample questions designed in the same way as actual diploma exam questions.

Available from the Learning Resources Centre (LRC)

Product number 755869

Phone: 780-427-2767
toll-free access within Alberta, first dial 310-0000

Physics 30

Diploma Review

This booklet summarizes your Physics 30 course and gives you helpful tips to prepare you to write your physics 30 diploma exam.

Tips,

Tricks

& Helpful Hints

The Physics 30 Diploma exam will be written:

Date: _____
Time: _____
Location: _____

7 Atomic Structure

Introduction

An understanding of the composition of matter and the organization of the atom is necessary, not only to explain natural phenomena, but to control natural phenomena and to develop new technologies. The physical sciences did showed little progress using Aristotle's theories of matter.

7.1 Summary Notes – Early Atomic Models

Since atoms cannot be directly observed scientists develop atomic models to help visualize and understand the atom. A model relates something we are familiar with to something that is otherwise unfamiliar and not tangible. As new experimental evidence is obtained the models become more sophisticated.

☐ Notes:

Billiard Ball Model of the Atom
This model suggests that atoms are very small, indivisible particles.

_____

Raisin Bun (Plum Pudding) Model of the Atom
Developed by J. J. Thomson

_____

Experimental Evidence:

_____

Cathode rays are beams of electrons produced at the cathode. They are produced using a high voltage and a cathode and anode inside a glass tube.

_____

_____

Cathode Ray Tubes (CRT)

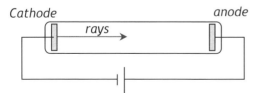

CRT 7.1.1

Properties of cathode rays:
- travel in straight lines.
- deflected by electric and magnetic fields.
- produce chemical reactions similar to that of light.

Interpretation of Evidence:

Since the cathode rays are deflected by electric fields and magnetic fields, they must be discrete (i.e., individual) charged particles.

Thomson determined the charge-to-mass ratio (q/m) for these cathode rays. The ratio was the same no matter what material was used for the cathode. Thomson interpreted this as meaning that all substances contained the same small discretely charged particles. These are now called electrons.

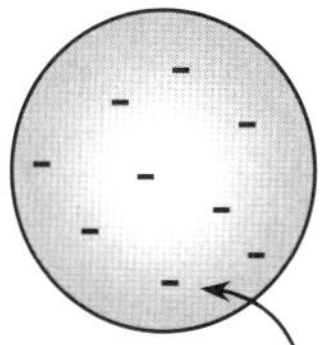

*electrons embedded in a
positive fluid*

Planetary (Nuclear) Model of the Atom
Developed by Rutherford

Experimental Evidence:

A thin gold foil scattered a beam of alpha particles. Most alpha particles went directly through, a few scattered at small angles, very few scattered at large angles.

Alpha-particle Scattering

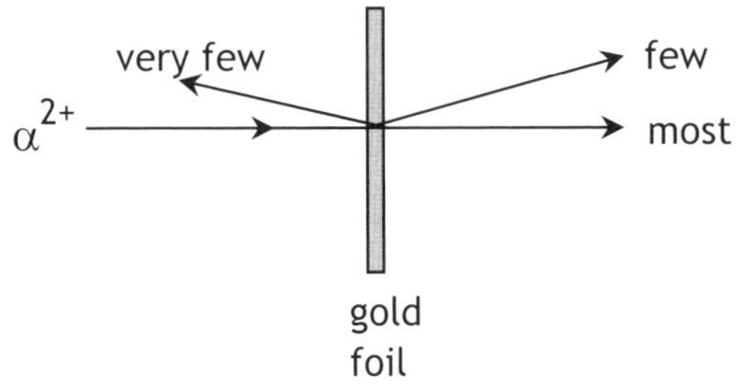

very few   few

α^{2+} most

gold
foil

Interpretation of Evidence:

Rutherford interpreted this as meaning the atom is mostly empty space with an extremely small positive nucleus with electrons orbiting it.

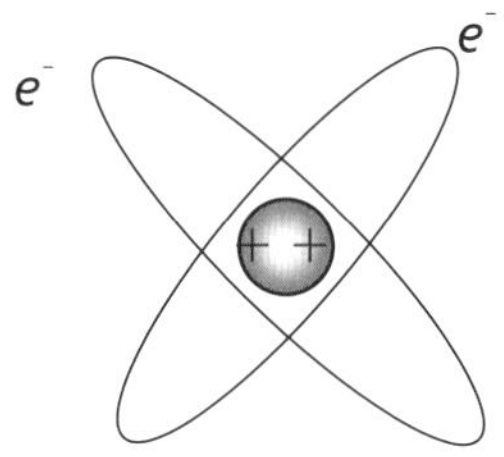

Electrons are interpreted as circling the nucleus which means they are undergoing a centripetal acceleration. Therefore the model must be invalid, as accelerating charges should be emitting EMR. As the electrons emit EMR they are losing energy and should spiral into the nucleus.

e^- e^-

e^-

Examples

1. A stream of charged particles having an initial speed of 5.7×10^6 m/s enters a magnetic field of 0.264 T. As they enter the magnetic field they deflect into a circular path with radius of 7.5 cm. Determine the charge-to-mass ratio of the charged particles.

$$V = 5.7 \times 10^6 \, m/s \quad F_{net} = ma_c = f_m \qquad \frac{q}{m} = \frac{5.7 \times 10^6 \, m/s}{0.264T \cdot 0.075m}$$

$$B = 0.264T \qquad \frac{mv^2}{r} = qvB$$

$$r = 7.5 \, cm \qquad \frac{q}{m} = \frac{v}{Br} \qquad \frac{q}{m} = 2.878 \times 10^8 \frac{C}{kg}$$

$$q/m = ?$$

The charge to mass ratio is 2.9×10^8 C/kg.

2. A fast moving stream of electrons enters a velocity selector with a 10000 N/C electric field and a 15.5 mT magnetic field and passes through without deflecting as shown in the diagram.
   a. Use arrows to draw the electric field between the charged plates.
   b. Determine the speed of the electrons.

$$f_m = f_e \qquad V = \frac{1000 \, N/C}{15.5 \, mT}$$

$$qvB = |E|q$$

$$V = \frac{|E|}{B} \qquad V = 64516 \, m/s$$

b. The electrons' speed is 6.45×10^4 m/s.

3. Explain why Rutherford suggested that the electron orbit the nucleus.

   Just as a satellite must orbit the Earth to maintain its altitude, Rutherford thought an electron should do the same.

Problems

A basic cathode ray tube consists of a thin filament carrying an electrical current. When the filament gets hot, electrons "boil" off the surface of the metal in a process called thermionic emission. They are then accelerated across a potential difference – from the cathode to the anode.

1. Use the rest mass of an electron and the elementary charge to determine the charge-to-mass ratio of an electron. [1.76×10^{11} C/kg]

2. A beam of charged particles travelling at 7.5×10^6 m/s enter a 0.651 T magnetic field perpendicular to the direction they are moving. As they enter the magnetic field they deflect into a circular beam with radius of 5.5 cm. Determine the charge-to-mass ratio of the charged particles. [2.1×10^8 C/kg]

3. J. J. Thomson performed an experiment to measure the charge-to-mass ratio of a hydrogen ion (p^+) and compared it with the charge-to-mass (q/m) ratio for an electron in order to determine how much more massive a proton was in comparison to an electron. Determine the
    a. charge-to-mass ratio (q/m) for a hydrogen ion (i.e., proton). [9.58×10^7 C/kg]
    b. mass of a proton relative to an electron (the charge-to-mass ratio for an electron is 1.756×10^{11} C/kg). [1833]

4. An electron enters a magnetic field of 75.0 mT and deflects in to a circular arc with a radius of 0.0075 m. Determine the kinetic energy of the electrons in electron volts. [28 keV]

Use the information below to answer question 5.

An electric field can be used to balance the magnetic field so that beams of charged particles go un-deflected in CRT experiments. To do this the electric field must be perpendicular relative to the magnetic field.

5. A stream of electrons enters a 7200 N/C electric field and a 6.5 mT magnetic field in a CRT and is not deflected as it passes through the two fields. (Note example 2, page 285)
   a. Draw a free-body diagram for the electron. [Appendix A]
   b. Determine the speed of the undeflected electrons. [1.1×10^6 m/s]

6. Unidentified ions enter a magnetic field of 0.800 T at 3.40×10^5 m/s and deflected with a radius of 8.50 cm. Determine the charge-to-mass ratio of the ions. [5.00×10^6 C/kg]

7. Electrons are accelerated from rest across a potential difference of 1200 V in a CRT. This beam of electrons then enter a magnetic field of 0.0450 T. Determine the radius of the beam's curvature (assume the beam and the magnetic field are perpendicular to each other). [2.60 mm]

CRT 7.1.1

8. The gold foil, in Rutherford's experiment gradually accumulated a positive charge. Explain why this happened and how it helped Rutherford determine atomic structure. [Appendix A]

9. Describe the major problem with Rutherford's Planetary Model. [Appendix A]

10. Determine the centripetal acceleration of an electron circling a proton if they are separated by a distance of 5.29×10^{-11} m. [9.03×10^{22} m/s^2]

7.2 Summary Notes – Atomic Spectra & the Quantized Model

The Bohr Atom
Developed by Bohr

Experimental Evidence:

The light produced (spectra) by various substances was used to develop this model. The light is analyzed using a prism or diffraction grating. There are three types of spectra:

Continuous Spectra

When a solid is heated it will produce a continuous spectra (blackbody radiation).

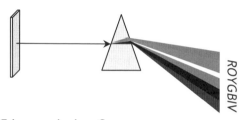

Line-emission Spectra

When a hot gas emits energy a bright line spectra is observed. Each element has its own characteristic line-emission spectrum which may be used to identify the elements.

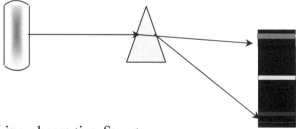

Line-absorption Spectra

White light (a continuous spectra) is passed through a gas at low temperature. A spectrum with lines of missing wavelengths (dark lines) is produced.

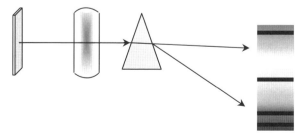

☐ Notes:

_____

_____

_____

_____

_____

_____

_____

_____

_____

_____

_____

_____

_____

_____

_____

_____

_____

_____

_____

□ Notes:

_____
_____
_____
_____
_____
_____
_____
_____
_____
_____

Interpretation of Evidence:

According to Bohr, only certain electron energies are allowed as an electron orbits a nucleus – the energy is quantized. At these energy levels Maxwell's law stating that accelerating charges must emit EMR does not apply.

When an electron absorbs energy (through the collision with a passing electron or a photon) it moves to higher energy levels. When an electron moves to lower energy levels it releases energy as a photon.

- A **line-emission** spectrum is produced when the electron in an atom releases energy as a photon.

- A **line-absorption** spectrum is produced when the electron in an atom absorbs photon energy.

Therefore, only light with certain frequencies and wavelengths can be emitted or absorbed by an atom.

Examples

1.   Two atomic spectra are provided below. Explain why they appear to be produced from the same substance.

Visible line-emission spectrum

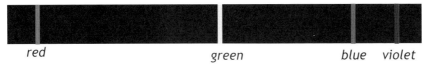

red   green   blue   violet

Visible line-absorption spectrum

red   green   blue   violet
(missing)   (missing)   (missing) (missing)

They are most likely from the same substance because the bright line spectrum has lines where the absorption spectrum does not.

Copyright © Kennedy/Oswald, 2008   Chapter 7 - 290

The energies of an electron within an atom are most often given relative to ionization as shown to the right.

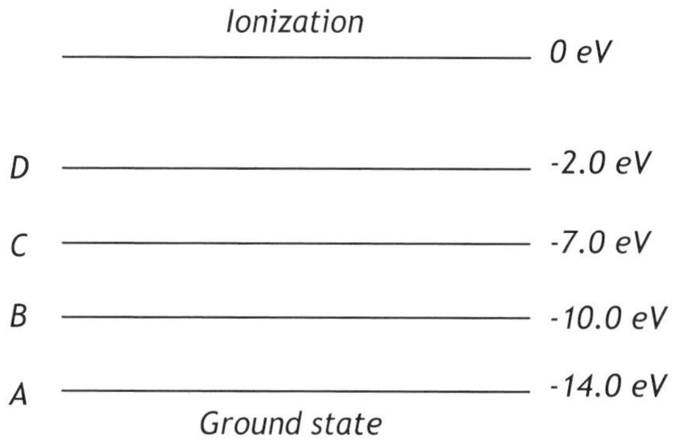

2. Determine the energy of a photon released as an electron makes a transition from D to B.

$$E_{photon} = E_D - E_B$$
$$= -2eV - {}^-10eV$$
$$E_{photon} = 8.0eV$$

The photon released has an energy of 8.0 eV.

3. Determine the number of photons of different wavelengths that could possibly be produced due to an electron at level C moving back to ground state.

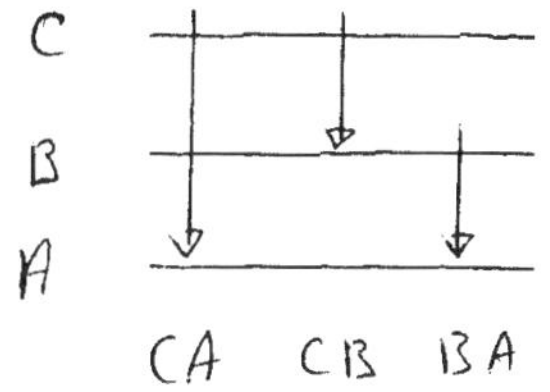

CA   CB   BA

Three transitions are possible; therefore, three different photons may possibly be released.

4. An electron at ground state in the atom is struck by a passing electron having an energy of 9.0 eV and the atom's electron absorbs as much of the energy as possible. Determine the
   a. kinetic energy of the passing electron after it collides with the electron in the atom.
   b. minimum possible wavelength of light that could be released from the atom.

$E_e = 9eV$ ∴

$A \to C$ abs 7eV,
2eV remaining

7eV released in a photon : $C \to A$

$E = \dfrac{hc}{\lambda}$

$\lambda = \dfrac{hc}{E}$

$\lambda = \dfrac{4.14 \times 10^{-15} eV \cdot s \times 3 \times 10^{8} m/s}{7eV}$

$\lambda = 1.774 \times 10^{-7} m$

   a. The kinetic energy of the passing electron after the collision is 2.0 eV.
   b. The minimum possible wavelength released is 1.8×10^{-7} m.

Problems

Use the information below to answer questions 1 & 2.

The energy levels for an atom are drawn below. The energy at each level is given relative to ground state and levels are labelled alphabetically.

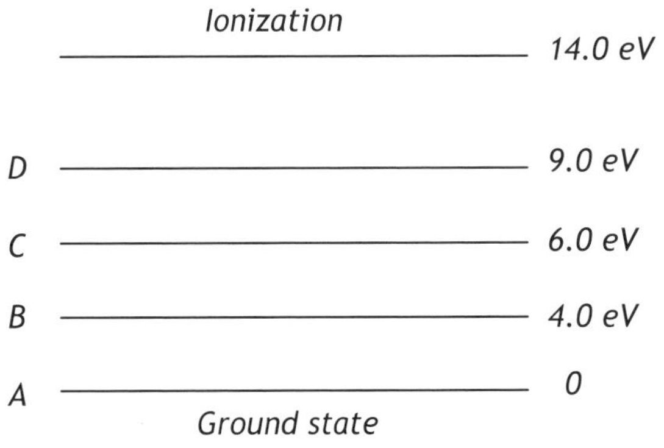

```
                    Ionization
         _____  14.0 eV


D        ———————————————————  9.0 eV

C        ———————————————————  6.0 eV

B        ———————————————————  4.0 eV

A        ———————————————————  0
              Ground state
```

1. A passing electron having a kinetic energy of 7.0 eV collides with an electron in the ground state of the atom. Determine the
    a. highest energy level the electron in the atom could obtain. [C]
    b. kinetic energy of the passing electron after the collision. [1.0 eV]

2. Determine the energy of the photon released as an electron makes a transition from
    a. D to A. [9.0 eV]
    b. C to B. [2.0 eV]

The energies of an electron within an atom are most often given relative to ionization as shown below.

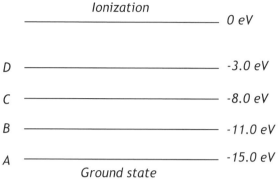

3. Determine the energy of the photon released as an electron makes a transition from
   a. D to A. [12.0 eV]
   b. C to B. [3.0 eV]

4. Determine the energy required to ionize the atom if its electron is originally in the ground state. [15.0 eV]

5. Determine the number of photons of different wavelengths that could possibly be produced due to an electron at level D moving back towards ground state. [Appendix A]

6. An electron at ground state in the atom is struck by a passing electron having an energy of 8.0 eV and the atom's electron absorbs as much of the energy as possible. Determine the
   a. kinetic energy of the passing electron after it collides with the electron in the atom. [1.0 eV]
   b. minimum possible wavelength of light that could be released from the atom. [1.8 x 10^{-7} m]

Mercury gas is used in fluorescent lights and many street lamps. Some of the possible transitions for an electron in a mercury atom are given in the energy level diagram.

	ionization	*0 eV*
F	————————	*-2.48 eV*
E	————————	*-2.68 eV*
D	————————	*-3.71 eV*
C	————————	*-5.52 eV*
B	————————	*-5.74 eV*
A	————————	*-10.38 eV*

7. The electron in a mercury atom drops (de-excites) from energy level E to energy level B. Determine the
   a. energy of the photon emitted. [3.06 eV]
   b. frequency of the photon emitted. [7.39 x 10^{14} Hz]
   c. wavelength of the photon emitted. [406 nm]
   d. region of the EMR spectrum where the photon is classified. [Appendix A]

8. Determine the quantity of energy required to ionize a mercury atom if its electrons are already excited to energy level E. [2.68 eV]

9. An electron with 5.00 eV of energy collides with an electron in the ground state of the mercury atom. Complete the chart below as the electron moves towards ground. [Appendix A]

	Transition	ΔE (eV)	Wavelength (m)	Spectral region
a.				
b.				
c.				

10. A gas is used to produce a bright line spectra and then is also used to produce a dark line spectra. Explain why the bright line and dark line spectra have lines at the same wavelengths. Use energy level diagrams as part of your explanations. [Appendix A]

11. A photon will be absorbed if a transition exists that is exactly the same amount of energy as the photon - the photon must be completely absorbed. Consider an excited mercury atom that absorbs a photon with 0.22 eV of energy. Identify the initial energy level of the mercury atom before being struck by the photon. [Appendix A]

12. A coin machine that requires exact change and a store that requires at least the cost of the item and can give change back may be analogous to an atom that can accept energy from a photon or an electron to excite the atom. Using this analogy, explain how the photon is analogous to money in a vending machine and how the electron is analogous to the coins used for the machine. [Appendix A]

13. A dark line absorption spectrum is shown below. Are any photons of light emitted at the locations of the dark lines in the spectrum? Explain. [Appendix A]

7.3 Summary Notes – Matter Waves

Notes:

_____

_____

_____

_____

_____

_____

_____

_____

_____

DeBroglie suggested that since waves can act as particles, perhaps particles could act like waves. This wave-particle duality allowed wavelength to be related to momentum:

$$p = \frac{h}{\lambda} \quad \text{and} \quad p = mv \quad \text{to give} \quad \lambda = \frac{h}{mv}$$

Small masses travelling at high speeds have noticeable wavelengths. Electrons were demonstrated to behave like waves in diffraction experiments using crystals as a diffraction grating.

Example

1. Use deBroglie's formula to determine the wavelength of a positron that has 6.56×10^{-19} J of kinetic energy.

$$E_k = \tfrac{1}{2}mv^2$$

$$v = \sqrt{\frac{2E_k}{m}}$$

$$= \sqrt{\frac{2 \times 6.56 \times 10^{-19} J}{9.11 \times 10^{-31} kg}}$$

$$v = 1.20 \times 10^6 \; m/s$$

$$p = \frac{h}{\lambda} \quad p = m$$

$$mv = \frac{h}{\lambda}$$

$$\lambda = \frac{h}{mv}$$

$$= \frac{6.63 \times 10^{-34} \; J \cdot s}{9.11 \times 10^{-31} kg \times 1.20 \times 10^6 m/s}$$

$$\lambda = 6.0644 \times 10^{-10} \; m$$

The positron's wavelength is 6.06×10^{-10} m.

Problems

1. Determine the deBroglie wavelength of an electron moving at 4.51×10^7 m/s. [1.61×10^{-11} m]

2. Determine the speed of an electron which has a deBroglie wavelength of 2.10×10^{-11} m.
   [3.47×10^7 m/s]

3. Compare the de Broglie wavelength of an electron moving at 4.0×10^6 m/s and a 50 kg physics student moving at 5.0 m/s. Would it be possible to diffract the physics student in an experiment like Young's double slit experiment? Explain. [Appendix A]

Use the following information to answer question 4.

The electron microscope uses electrons which have a wavelength much shorter than visible light in order to distinguish (i.e., resolve) and observe detailed features.

4. Determine the deBroglie wavelength of an electron accelerated from rest across a potential difference of 600 V. [5.01×10^{-11} m]

5. Determine the kinetic energy of an electron whose matter wavelength is 3.50 x 10^{-11} m. [1.97 x 10^{-16} J]

6. Calculate the potential difference that an electron would be accelerated across so that its deBroglie wavelength is 2.00 x 10^{-11} m. [3.77 kV]

7. Determine the deBroglie frequency of an electron after it is accelerated across a potential difference of 20.0 kV. [9.65 x 10^{18} Hz]

7.4 Summary Notes – Wave Mechanical Model

Quantum or Wave Mechanical Model

Classical physics does not adequately explain the wave behavior of atomic or sub-atomic particles due to their significant wave nature.

Experimental Evidence:

Moving electrons were observed to have wave properties.

Interpretation of Evidence:

DeBrogle explained that electrons were circular standing waves around a nucleus. An electron can exist where there is constructive interference and cannot exist where there is destructive interference. This explained Bohr's quantized orbits.

A probability interpretation was given – the electron is found in regions of constructive interference producing a probability cloud.

☐ Notes:

_____

_____

_____

_____

_____

_____

_____

_____

_____

_____

_____

_____

_____

Example

1. In order to constructively interference, the wavelength of the electron must fit evenly into the circumference of the orbit where the circumference is equal to the wavelength ($C = \lambda$). An electron in an atom may be interpreted as being a wave that surrounds the nucleus. Draw the electron standing wave for the 2nd energy level around an atom's nucleus.

    $n = 1$ $n = 2$

    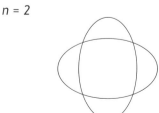

Problems

1. An electron orbits a proton at a distance of 1.06×10^{-10} m. Use the planetary model of the atom to determine the
   a. speed of the electron in circular motion. $[1.54 \times 10^{6}$ m/s]
   b. deBroglie wavelength of the electron as it moves around the nucleus. $[4.71 \times 10^{-10}$ m]

2. An analogy can be made between standing waves on a rope and electron standing waves around a nucleus. The diagrams below show a rope between two fixed points. Select the diagram of the rope producing waves of the highest energy if it analogous to an electron standing wave. [Appendix A]

   a   b   c

    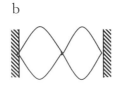 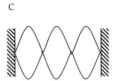

3. The diagram to the right represents an electron as a standing wave circling the nucleus of an atom. Determine the number of complete wavelengths the electron is producing around the nucleus. [Appendix A]

   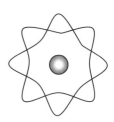

---

4. Fill in the blank. The amplitude of an electron wave surrounding the nucleus of an atom may be interpreted as the _____ of finding the electron at that location. [Appendix A]

5. The two diagrams below represent identical atoms with their electrons at different energy states. Identify the atom having the electron at the higher energy state. Explain. [Appendix A]

a   b

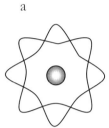 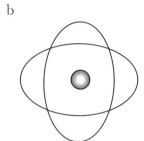

6. Explain the diagrams from the previous question in terms of constructive and destructive interference to explain how an energy level is "quantized". [Appendix A]

Use the information below to answer questions 7 & 8.

When an electron is treated as a matter wave it may be interpreted as acting as a standing wave around the nucleus of an atom. The relationship of its radius of orbit, quantum number and deBroglie wavelength is given by:

$$2\pi r = n\lambda$$

Where:

    $2\pi r$ is the circumference of the orbit (m)
    n is the quantum number or energy level (always a whole number)
    λ is the de Broglie wavelength (m)

7. Determine the wavelength of an electron orbiting a hydrogen atom at a distance of 5.29×10^{-11} m from the nucleus when the electron is in its first energy state (n = 1). [3.32×10^{-10} m]

8. If an electron moves around a nucleus with a velocity of 3.8×10^{6} m/s determine
   a. its deBroglie wavelength. [1.92×10^{-10} m]
   b. the orbital radius if it is at its 3rd energy level. [9.14×10^{-11} m]

9. Describe how the diffraction and interference of electrons in a double slit experiment may be interpreted as meaning that electrons may be thought of as waves. [Appendix A]

10. The Bohr model of the atom was unable to explain why only certain electrons orbits around a nucleus are allowed. Explain how the wave interpretation of an electron helps explain quantized energy levels for the electrons in orbit about a nucleus. [Appendix A]

Use the information below to answer question 1.

James Franck and Gustav Hertz provided more evidence for the quantized structure of the atom. They supplied energy to the atom through collision with a fast moving electron.

The following diagrams show the collision between a fast moving electron and a mercury atom. The collisions are shown on an atomic level and again on a subatomic level. The electron's kinetic energy is measured before and after the collision. As the initial kinetic energy of the electron increased the following happened:

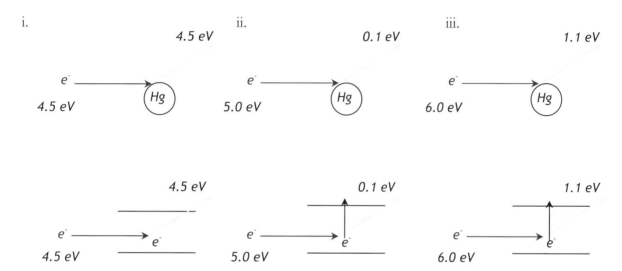

i.

ii.

iii.

    The Hg atom could only absorb 4.9 eV; no more, no less.

As the electron's velocity was increased, it was found that other energies could also be absorbed.

1.   A certain atom can absorb energies of 4.90 eV, 6.81 eV, and 10.38 eV. If an incoming electron with kinetic energy of 5.97 eV is used to bombard this atom, determine the
    a.   energy of the incoming electron after the collision. [1.07 eV]
    b.   wavelength of light emitted. [254 nm]

7.6 Review

1. To determine the speed of charged particles in a cathode ray tube, J. J. Thomson balanced the force produced by a(n)
    a. electromagnetic field and a gravitational field
    b. magnetic field and a gravitational field
    c. electric and a gravitational field
    d. electric field and a magnetic field

2. The charge and the approximate diameter of a nucleus can be estimated from
    a. alpha particle scattering experiments
    b. X-ray diffraction experiments
    c. photoelectron experiments
    d. cathode ray experiments

3. An absorption spectrum is produced when white light is passed through a cool gas and then the light is viewed through a diffraction grating. The EMR for an absorption spectrum of an element is produced by
    a. centripetal acceleration of the electrons within the element
    b. electrons within the element dropping down from the excited state as they absorb energy
    c. electrons within the element moving up to an excited state as they absorb energy
    d. the nucleus of an atom moving from a low energy to a high energy state as it absorbs energy

4. An electron moving with a kinetic energy of 5.2 eV strikes an atom and rebounds with a kinetic energy of 3.1 eV. The atom then releases a photon of light. The most likely frequency of the emitted light is
    a. 1.25×10^{15} Hz
    b. 2.00×10^{15} Hz
    c. 5.07×10^{14} Hz
    d. 7.07×10^{14} Hz

5. Constructive and destructive interference of electrons help support the
    a. nuclear model
    b. Bohr model
    c. wave mechanical model
    d. billiard ball model

6. Use the mass and charge of an alpha particle to determine its charge-to-mass ratio.
    [4.82×10^7 C/kg]

7. Calculate the charge-to-mass ratio of a particle travelling at 3.60×10^5 m/s that is deflected with a radius of 7.40 cm as it travels through a perpendicular magnetic field of 0.420 T.
    [1.16×10^7 C/kg]

Consider the following energy level diagram for an element under investigation.

ionization _____ 0 eV

F _____ -2.44 eV
E _____ -2.59 eV

D _____ -3.73 eV

C _____ -5.67 eV
B _____ -5.81 eV

A _____ -10.45 eV

8. When the element de-excites from energy level D to energy level A. Determine the
    a. energy of the photon emitted. [6.72 eV]
    b. frequency of the photon emitted. [1.62×10^{15} Hz]
    c. wavelength of the photon emitted. [185 nm]
    d. region of the EMR spectrum where the photon is classified. [Appendix A]

9. Determine the quantity of energy that would be required to ionize the element if its electrons are already excited to energy level C. [5.67 eV]

10. An electron with 5.50 eV of kinetic energy collides with an electron in the ground state of the investigated element. Complete the chart below that includes the possible transitions. [Appendix A]

	Transitions	ΔE (eV)	Wavelength (m)	Spectral region
a.				
b.				
c.				

11. Calculate the wavelength of a photon that has the same momentum as a proton travelling at 9.55×10^{6} m/s. [4.16×10^{-14} m]

12. If an electron moves around a nucleus with a velocity of 5.87×10^{6} m/s determine its deBroglie wavelength. [1.24×10^{-10} m]

7.7 Review Assignment

1. An electron enters a magnetic field of 85.0 mT and deflects in to a circular arc with a radius of 7.8 mm. Determine the kinetic energy of the electrons in electron volts.

2. The charge-to-mass ratio for potassium ion is 2.54×10^{6} C/kg. If a potassium ion was accelerated to a speed of 4.72×10^{5} m/s and then deflected into a circular beam with a radius of 8.1 cm, determine the magnetic field causing the deflection.

Consider an incident electron with 14.2 eV of energy. It collides with an electron of an unexcited gas atom (described by the following energy levels in the diagram to the right).

Ionization ——————————— 0 eV

D ——————————— -1.5 eV

C ——————————— -8.4 eV

B ——————————— -11.4 eV

A ——————————— -14.9 eV

Ground state

3. Determine the maximum level the atom's electron could be excited to.
    -

4. Determine the number of photons of different wavelengths that could possibly be produced due to an electron at level D moving back towards ground state.

5. If the electron only exited this gas atom to energy level C, determine the
    a. kinetic energy of the incident electron left over.
    b. Is there enough energy left over to excite another gas atom? If so, to what level?

6. If the above gas atom absorbs the maximum possible energy of the incoming electron, determine all the possible wavelengths of light that could be emitted by the excited atom and indicate where their spectral lines would be observed on the spectrum ruler below.

Transition	ΔE (eV)	Wavelength (nm)	Spectral region

100 nm   200 nm   300 nm   400 nm

7. If a dark line absorption spectra for this same gas were being analyzed instead of a bright line (as above) where would the dark lines appear? Explain.

8. Describe the five main atomic models studied in this unit. Include the names of those who developed the model, strengths and weakness of the model, and a diagram. Organize in a chart.

This 44-page booklet is designed to prepare you for the Physics 30 Diploma Exam. It provides:

- a summary of each unit.
- tips and tricks to help with problems and avoid common difficulties.
- sample questions designed in the same way as actual diploma exam questions.

It is available from the Learning Resources Centre (LRC)

Product number 755869

Phone: 780-427-2767
toll-free access within Alberta,
first dial 310-0000

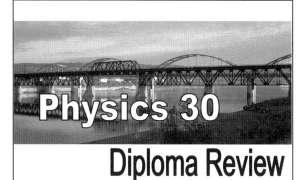

Physics 30

Diploma Review

This booklet summarizes your Physics 30 course and gives you helpful tips to prepare you to write your physics 30 diploma exam.

Tips,

Tricks

& Helpful Hints

The Physics 30 Diploma exam will be written:

Date:: _____

Time: _____

Location: _____

Introduction

An understanding of the nucleus of the atom has only been around for about one hundred years. Several discoveries lead to a better understanding of its nature. Laws such as conservation of charge, mass, energy and momentum all have an important role to play. Knowledge of the structure and behaviour of the nucleus also has implications to many realms of society; from politics to religion and more.

8.1 Summary Notes – Biological Effects of Radiation

Radioactivity

Some elements are radioactive; they spontaneously emit energy as particles: alpha, beta or gamma. Each type of radiation has enough energy to be called ionizing radiation and can damage materials, such as metals or biological cells.

📄 Notes:

_____

_____

_____

_____

_____

_____

_____

_____

_____

Type of Radiation	Symbol	Nature of particle	Penetrating ability (related to energy)
alpha	α^{2+} or $_{2}^{4}\alpha$	He nucleus ($2p^{+}$, 2n)	paper
beta	β^{-} or $_{-1}^{0}\beta$	high speed electrons	cardboard
gamma	γ or $_{0}^{0}\gamma$	high energy photons (EMR)	metal

Radiation Safety
The danger of a radioactive substance is related to the:
- type of radiation produced.
- activity of the substance. **Activity** is the amount of radiation produced in a given time. It is dependent on the stability and the amount of the radioactive substance.

Safety can be improved when working with radioactive material by,

- decreasing exposure **time**.
- increasing **distance** between people and the radioactive material.
- increasing the **shielding** used.

Example

1. Ultraviolet radiation is a type of ionizing radiation. Is it also a type of nuclear radiation? Explain.

    No. UV light is not produced through nuclear process. It is produced when electrons within an atom make a transition to a lower energy level.

Problems

1. Identify the type of nuclear radiation that requires the greatest thickness of shielding for protective purposes. [Appendix A]

2. EMR that has the ability to ionize and thus damage cells are, in order of increasing energy: ultraviolet, X-rays, and gamma rays. Identify the relationship between the ionization ability of the EMR and its frequency. [Appendix A]

Use the information below to answer question 3.

Biological damage occurs when high-energy particles cause the ionization of other atoms and molecules. If the molecules are part of a cell, then the cell may not function properly. If too many cells are damaged the body will suffer and perhaps die. Damage to DNA (the genetic code) can cause serious damage to the cell and if it reproduces before dying, it may produce more defective cells. The rate at which a tissue absorbs radiation depends upon: the type of tissue, rate of exposure, and the type of radiation.

3. Describe how a nuclear technician might reduce the hazards of working in a clean-up site that includes radioactive waste. [Appendix A]

4   The activity of a radioactive substance may be determined using a Geiger counter. Two different samples, A and B, are tested using a Geiger counter. Sample A shows a much higher activity than sample B. What can be determined regarding the danger of A relative to B? Explain. [Appendix A]

5.   Rutherford tested radioactive uranium using aluminium shields. In his Nobel Prize acceptance speech He says there were "at least two distinct types of radiation — one that is very readily absorbed … and the other of a more penetrative character." Identify the type of radiation that was more easily absorbed. [Appendix A]

Use the following information to answer question 6.

A Geiger counter may be used to detect the level of radioactivity (activity) in units of becquerels (Bq). 1 Bq = 1 emission (decay) per second. The activity does not indicate what type of radiation is occurring and, therefore, it's not the best measure of radiation danger.

Three different radioactive materials are used in an investigation. Each type of sample emits a different type of nuclear radiation. The activity is tested using a Geiger counter on the small samples and on the large samples as shown in the diagram below.

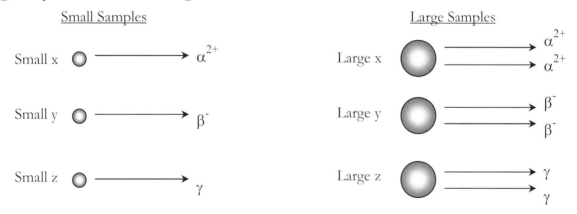

6.   Using the diagrams above, Identify the
    a.   sample(s) showing the greatest activity. [Appendix A]
    b.   sample that is probably the most dangerous. [Appendix A]
    c.   sample that is probably the least dangerous. [Appendix A]

8.2 Summary Notes – Nuclear Notation

Notes:

_____

_____

_____

_____

_____

_____

_____

_____

_____

_____

_____

_____

Protons are positively charged particles found in the nucleus of the atom.

Neutrons are neutral particles found in the nucleus of the atom.

The number of protons in the nucleus is equal to the number of electrons around the nucleus in a neutral atom.

All atoms of a given element contain the same number of protons.

Atomic number is the number of protons in the nucleus of an atom.

Atomic mass (mass number) is the total number of protons and neutrons in an atom.

Nucleons refer to the protons and neutrons in an atom's nucleus.

Isotopes are atomic nuclei that have the same number of protons but different number of neutrons.

Transmutation is the process of changing one element into another.

The nucleus of an atom is represented with the following nuclear notation:

$$^A_Z X \qquad\qquad Z = A - N$$

Where:

      X is the symbol of the element

      A is the atomic mass number (total number of protons and neutrons in the nucleus)

      Z is the atomic number (number of protons in the nucleus)

      N is the number of neutrons in the nucleus.

Examples

1. Complete the following chart.

	Isotopic notation	Name	Atomic number (Z)	Atomic mass (A)	Number of neutrons (N)
a.	$^{14}_{6}C$	carbon-14	6	14	8
b.	$^{238}_{92}U$	uranium-238	92	238	146

Problems

1. Complete the following chart. [Appendix A]

	Isotopic notation	Name	Atomic number (Z)	Atomic mass (A)	Number of neutrons (N)
a.		hydrogen-2 (deuterium)*			
b.		radon-210			
c.	$^{45}_{20}Ca$				
d.	$^{38}_{19}K$				
e.			7		7
f.			89		141
g.			12	26	
h.				144	81
i.		hydrogen-3 (tritium)*			

* common name

8.3 Summary Notes – Radioactive Decay

☐ Notes:

_____

_____

_____

_____

_____

_____

_____

_____

_____

_____

_____

_____

_____

_____

_____

_____

_____

_____

_____

_____

_____

Conservation laws apply to all nuclear process:

- Conservation of momentum
- Conservation of charge
- Conservation of nucleons (mass number)
- Conservation of mass/energy

Alpha decay

To produce an alpha particle the parent nucleus loses two protons and two neutrons (a total of four nucleons).

$$ {}_{Z}^{A}X \longrightarrow {}_{Z-2}^{A-4}Y + {}_{2}^{4}\alpha $$

Beta-negative decay

Beta particles are negative electrons emitted by the nucleus and have a much higher speed than alpha particles. The basic beta-negative decay occurring in the nucleus is:

$$ {}_{0}^{1}n \longrightarrow {}_{1}^{1}p + {}_{-1}^{0}\beta + {}_{0}^{0}\overline{\nu} $$

antineutrino

Beta-positive (positron) decay

Positrons are the antiparticle of the electron having identical mass and charge magnitude. The basic beta-positive decay occurring in the nucleus is:

$$ {}_{1}^{1}p \longrightarrow {}_{0}^{1}n + {}_{1}^{0}\beta + {}_{0}^{0}\nu $$

neutrino

Neutrinos have extremely small mass and zero charge. They were first suggested as a way to satisfy conservation laws.

Gamma decay

Gamma decay is the emission of high-energy photons from the nucleus. This often occurs after alpha or beta decay when the nucleus is left in an excited state. No change occurs to the atomic number or the mass number and therefore no transmutation occurs during gamma decay.

$$_{Z}^{A}X \longrightarrow {}_{Z}^{A}X + {}_{0}^{0}\gamma$$

Example

1. Write the decay equation when thorium-227 emits an alpha particle. Explain the decay using the law of conservation of nucleons and the law of conservation of charge.

$$_{90}^{227}Th \quad \text{-----}> \quad _{88}^{223}Ra + {}_{2}^{4}\alpha$$

Conservation of charge and conservation of nucleons must be followed:
- Conservation of nucleons: 227 nucleons on the left and a total of 227 nucleons (223 + 4) on the right.
- Conservation of charge: A total positive charge of 90 on the left and a total positive charge of 90 (88 + 2) on the right.

Problems

1. Use the conservation of nucleons and the conservation of charge to complete the following transmutation equations. [Appendix A]

   a. $_{85}^{216}At \quad \text{-----}> \quad \underline{\hspace{2cm}} + {}_{2}^{4}\alpha$

   b. $\underline{\hspace{2cm}} \quad \text{-----}> \quad _{90}^{230}Th + {}_{2}^{4}\alpha$

   c. $_{90}^{234}Th \quad \text{-----}> \quad \underline{\hspace{2cm}} + \underline{\hspace{2cm}} + {}_{0}^{0}\overline{\nu}$

   d. $\underline{\hspace{2cm}} \quad \text{-----}> \quad _{-1}^{0}\beta + {}_{25}^{55}Mn + \underline{\hspace{2cm}}$

   e. $\underline{\hspace{2cm}} \quad \text{-----}> \quad _{8}^{15}O + {}_{1}^{0}\beta + \underline{\hspace{2cm}}$

2. Write the transmutation equation of the decay of carbon-14 with the emission of a beta-negative particle. [Appendix A]

---

3.   Promethium-145 transmutates by alpha decay. Write the complete decay equation. [Appendix A]

4.   Identify the two laws used to predict the daughter product of the decay in the previous question. [Appendix A]

5.   Iodine-131 can be used to treat thyroid cancers. Radioactive iodine-131 is injected into the blood stream and collects in the thyroid glands. Its intense beta-negative radiation then destroys the cancerous cells. Write the decay equation for iodine-131. [Appendix A]

6.   The isotope dubnium-261 has a very rapid decay (high activity) as half of it decays every 65 s. It undergoes alpha decay and then its daughter product also undergoes alpha decay with the release of a gamma photon. Write the decay equation for
     a.   dubnium-261. [Appendix A]
     b.   the daughter product of dubnium-261. [Appendix A]

7.   Gamma decay by itself does not result in transmutation. It occurs when the nucleus is at too high of energy which often occurs during alpha and beta decay. Nickel-60 can release a gamma ray with an energy of 1.17 MeV.
     a.   Write the equation for Nickel-60 undergoing gamma decay. [Appendix A]
     b.   Determine the frequency of the emitted gamma ray. [2.83×10^{20} Hz]

One goal of the alchemists in the Middle Ages was to transmutate inexpensive metals into gold. This goal was never realized, and after Dalton's atomic theory was accepted, scientists thought that transmutation was impossible. Rutherford showed that transmutation was possible (making gold this way, however, is much more expensive and more impractical than mining gold).

8. Rutherford first artificially transmutated an element by bombarding nitrogen-14 with alpha particles to produce oxygen-17 and a hydrogen ion. Write the nuclear equation for Rutherford's first artificial transmutation. [Appendix A]

9. Electron capture is a decay mode for some unstable nuclei. It occurs when there isn't enough energy to emit a positron. In this type of radioactive decay, a proton in the nucleus attracts an orbiting electron. The electron collides with the proton in the nucleus thereby transmuting into a neutron and producing a neutrino. Write the decay equation for iron-55 when it captures an electron. [Appendix A]

Use the information below to answer question 10.

The Geiger-Muller Tube is a device used to detect and count radioactive decays of a substance. It is a tube filled with argon gas. When high energy particles enter the tube they ionize the argon gas. Argon ions are attracted to the central electrode creating a pulse of current in the process. This pulse is sent to a speaker and is heard as a "click"; each click is called a count representing a single decay.

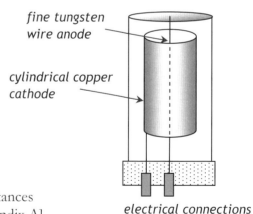

fine tungsten wire anode

cylindrical copper cathode

electrical connections to ammeter or speaker

10. Complete the decay equations for the following substances that were detected using a Geiger-Muller tube. [Appendix A]

a. $^{234}_{90}\text{Th} \quad ----> \quad ^{234}_{91}\text{Pa} \quad + \qquad\qquad +$

b. $^{55}_{24}\text{Cr} \quad ----> \quad ^{0}_{-1}\beta \quad + \qquad\qquad +$

c. $\qquad\qquad ----> \quad ^{95}_{39}\text{Y} \quad + \quad ^{0}_{1}\beta \quad +$

When a nucleus decays, its daughter nucleus is usually radioactive. Therefore, the daughter product will also decay. A series of decays then occurs.

One common decay series starts with uranium-238 and ends with the stable element lead-206. This decay series is represented on a graph of atomic number versus atomic mass below: [Appendix A]

Uranium Lead Decay Series

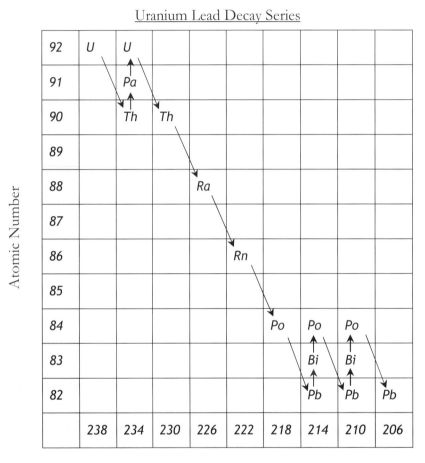

Atomic Mass

11. Use the decay series above to write the nuclear decay equation for
    a. thorium-230.

    b. uranium-234.

    c. bismuth-210.

8.4 Summary Notes – Half-Life

The nuclear **half-life** of an element is the time required for half of it to spontaneously transmutate. Mathematical analysis is used to communicate the probability of atoms out of a group will decay over a given time period.

The **activity** of an isotope is how much radiation it produces. It is a factor of half-life and sample size.

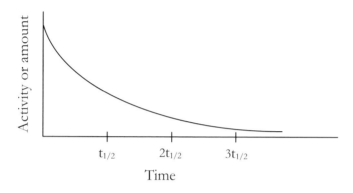

$$N = N_o \left(\frac{1}{2} \right)^n$$

Where:

N is the amount of radioactive nuclei remaining after a given time period.

N_o is the original amount of sample.

n is the number of half-lives over the time period.

The amount of a radioactive substance may be expressed in different ways: e.g., mass, number of atoms, Bq.

$$n = \frac{time}{t_{1/2}}$$

Where:

t is the time of decay.

$t_{1/2}$ is the half-life of the element.

Example

1. Phosphorous-32 undergoes beta-negative decay and has a half-life of 14.3 days. If 5.0 g of the original substance were obtained, determine the amount remaining after 24.6 days.

$t_{\frac{1}{2}} = 14.3d$ $N = N_0(\frac{1}{2})^n$

$N_0 = 5g$

$t = 24.6d$ $N = 5g \left(\frac{1}{2}\right)^{\frac{24.6d}{14.3d}}$

$N = ?$ $N = 1.517g$

A mass of 1.5 g remains after 24.6 days.

Problems

1. A 100 g sample of thorium-234 undergoes beta-negative decay with a half-life of 24.1 days. Determine the remaining amount after 241 days. [97.7 mg]

2. Three days after it was prepared, a sample of Ra-224 has a mass of 5.5 mg. Determine the original mass of the sample if its half-life is 0.778 days. [80 mg]

3. A Geiger counter may be used to detect the level of radioactivity (activity) in units of becquerels (Bq). The becquerels is a unit related to activity where one count (detection) on a Geiger counter represents a single decay. A sample of xenon-137 has a half-life of 12 days and is found to emit beta-negative particles at a rate of 240 MBq.
   a. Write the decay equation for xenon-137. [Appendix A]
   b. Determine its activity after 30 days. [42 MBq]

4. An unknown substance undergoes radioactive decay according to the graph below. [Appendix A]

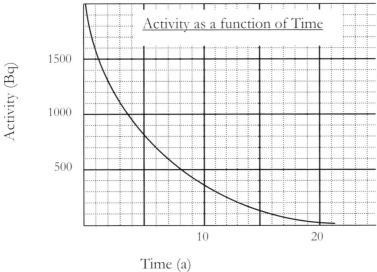

a. Determine the half-life of the substance from the graph.
b. Identify the unknown substance using the chart below.
c. Write the nuclear decay equation for the substance.

Isotope	Half-life (a)	Decay mode
$^{204}_{81}\text{Tl}$	3.78	beta-negative
$^{210}_{82}\text{Pb}$	22.3	beta-negative
$^{229}_{90}\text{Th}$	7880	alpha
$^{3}_{1}\text{H}$	12.3	beta-negative
$^{252}_{99}\text{Es}$	1.29	alpha

5. A radioactive isotope produces a decay curve as shown below. Sketch the curve representing the amount of daughter product produced (i.e., the decay product) as a function of time on the graph. [Appendix A]

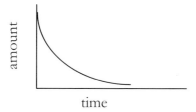

6. Artificial radio-isotopes are used to treat cancers. When cobalt-59 is bombarded with neutrons the radioactive isotope cobalt-60 is produced. Cobalt-60 has a half-life of 5.27 a and undergoes beta-negative decay while also producing gamma radiation. The gamma rays are used to kill cancerous cells. Unfortunately, healthy cells also get bombarded by the gamma rays resulting in hair loss, burns and other disorders. The first cobalt-60 treatments were made in 1951 by the Canadian physicist, Harold Johns.
   a. Write the equation for the decay of cobalt-60. [Appendix A]
   b. If a container of pure cobalt-60 is stored for 9.0 a and then found to contain 3.0 mg of cobalt-60, determine the amount of cobalt-60 initially stored. [9.8 mg]

7. Four different radioactive decay particles are sent through a magnetic field and produce paths as shown below. The particles are: gamma ray, alpha particle, beta-positive, and beta-negative. Match each decay particle with the path it would most likely take. [Appendix A]

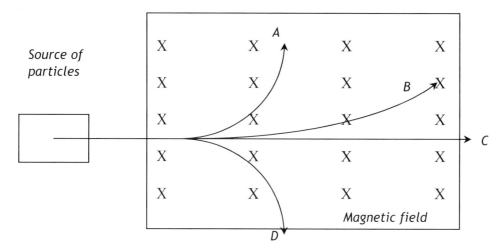

A common smoke detector design uses a small quantity (~0.4 g) of radioactive americium-241 to emit alpha particles. The alpha particles collide with air particles in the sensing chamber. The alpha particles knock electrons off the air particles giving them a positive charge which causes them to be attracted to the negative plate. The liberated electrons are attracted to the positive plate and create a current. When smoke or soot enters the chamber they attract some of the liberated electrons, thus causing a drop of current to the positive plate. The current drop is detected and signals an alarm.

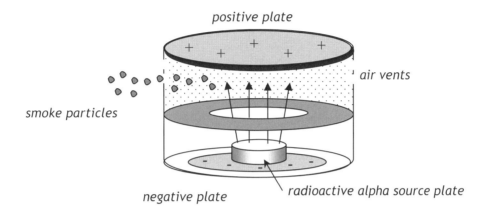

8.   Write the nuclear equation for the decay of americium-241. [Appendix A]

9.   The half-life of americium-241 is 457.699 a. A typical smoke detector contains 33.1 kBq of americium-241. Determine the amount of americium-241 remaining after 15.0 a. [32.4 kBq]

The Dental/Pharmacy building at the University of Alberta contains a low power nuclear reactor called "SLOWPOKE". One technique used at SLOWPOKE to identify unknown material is called Neutron Activation Analysis (NAA). By firing low energy neutrons (< 0.5 eV) at a substance the substance transmutes to a different isotope by adding the neutron to its nucleus. The isotope then decays and transmutes. The gamma radiation produced by the decay is analyzed and used to identify the sample.

10. Silicon microchips must be made extremely pure if they are to work effectively. A silicon microchip is analyzed for trace amounts of iron-58 using NAA. [Appendix A]
   a. Write the nuclear equation for the capture of a neutron (1.67×10^{-27} kg) by iron-58 to produce iron-59.
   b. Write the nuclear equation for the beta-negative decay of iron-59 including the emitted gamma particle.
   c. The half-life of iron-59 is 44.5 days. Determine the amount of iron-59 remaining after 26.7 days if 63 ppm were initially present. (The unit of ppm (parts per million) represents concentration.) [42 ppm]
   d. Use the chart to determine the frequency of the gamma radiation emitted by the iron-59 as it decays. [~3.20×10^{20} Hz]

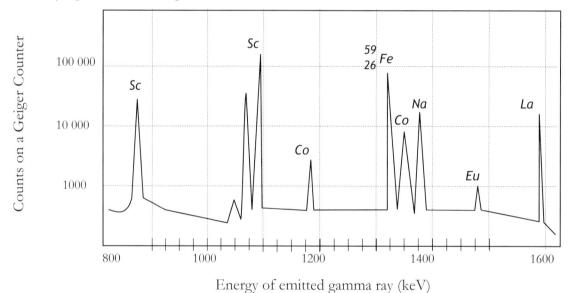

11. Polonium-214 undergoes alpha and gamma decay. Determine the percentage of a polonium-214 sample remaining after 285 μs, if it has a half-life of 164 μs. [30.0 %]

12. A graph of momentum as a function of speed for a charged particle is supplied below. Use the graph to identify the particle. [Appendix A]

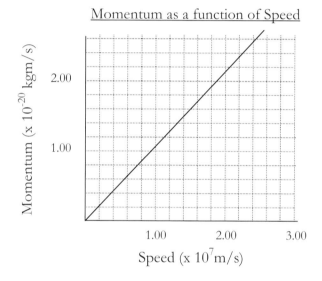

Momentum as a function of Speed

13. A neutron moving at 7.6 x 10⁴ m/s hits a stationary iron-58 atom and is captured (i.e., the neutron becomes part of the nucleus to produce iron-59). Assume a mass value of 1 u for each nucleon and use the law of conservation of momentum to determine the speed of the iron-59. [1.3 x 10³ m/s]

14. Neutrons outside a nucleus are unstable with a half-life of 10.4 minutes.
    a. Write the decay equation for an isolated neutron as it decays into a proton. [Appendix A]
    b. If a nuclear reactor produces 1000 neutrons determine the number of neutrons remaining after 2.6 minutes. [841]

Use the following information to answer question 15.

Neutrons can be difficult to detect since they have no charge and therefore are not affected by electric and magnetic fields.

Neutrons were discovered in 1932 by James Chadwick using equipment represented in the simplified diagram below. The polonium produced alpha particles. When the alpha particles collide with neutrons in beryllium, the neutrons are ejected and then collide with protons in paraffin. Since the alpha particles and protons are charged and easy to detect, the uncharged particles (i.e., neutrons) must exist.

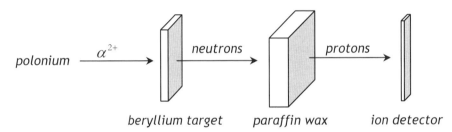

15. A 7.8 MeV alpha particle collides with a neutron in the beryllium target and transfers 40 % of its kinetic energy to the neutron. Determine the speed of the neutron after the collision. [2.4 x 10^7 m/s]

16   A radioactive substance registers 1680 counts per minute on a Geiger counter. 8.0 hours later it registers 420 counts per minute. Determine the half-life of this substance. [4.0 hours]

Use the information below to answer question 17.

The half-life of an element is unaffected by temperature, chemical or physical state; therefore isotopes decay at regular and predictable rates. This allows them to be used as timing devices.

17.   A 1.00 g sample of lead-194 undergoes beta-negative decay. After a certain time it is found that 0.25 g of lead-194 remains. The half-life for lead-194 is 11 months.
    a.   Write the nuclear decay equation for lead-194. [Appendix A]
    b.   Determine the time for this to happen. [22 months]

18.   Tin-117 is used for treatment of bone cancers and has a half-life of 14 days. A sample of tin-117 is prepared and found to register 1280 counts per minute on a Geiger counter. At a later date it was found to register 160 counts per minute. Determine the age of the tin-117. [42 days]

Use the information below to answer question 19.

Tritium has a half-life of 12.3 years and can be used to measure the age of objects up to about 100 years. Tritium is produced in the upper atmosphere by cosmic rays. It is brought to the Earth by rain. Eventually this rainwater finds its way into anything we drink.

19. An old bottle of water is found that has only 25 % the tritium content of new water. Determine the age of the water. [25 a]

Use the following information to answer question 20.

Carbon-14 is a common isotope used for radioactive dating. All living things have a certain percentage of carbon-14 composing their cell tissues. The remaining carbon is carbon-12. Neutrons are produced in the upper atmosphere by cosmic rays. These neutrons interact with nitrogen in the atmosphere to produce carbon-14.

$$^{14}_{7}N \; + \; ^{1}_{0}n \; \longrightarrow \; ^{14}_{6}C \; + \; ^{1}_{1}H$$

Carbon-14 is constantly transmuting, but the total amount remains constant in a biological organism because the supply of carbon is always being replenished through photosynthesis.
When an animal (or any carbon based life form) dies, it no longer takes in carbon-14. The percentage of carbon-14 will therefore decrease as it changes to the more stable carbon-12. Carbon-12 dating is useful for objects less than 40 000 years old.

20. Carbon-14 has a half-life of 5730 years. A 1.0 g sample of a living tree is analyzed for carbon-14 and found to emit 15.4 counts/minutes A 1.0 g sample from a wooden bowl found in an Egyptian tomb is analyzed and found to emit 7.7 counts/min.
    a. Write the nuclear equation showing the beta-negative decay of carbon-14. [Appendix A]
    b. Determine the age of the tomb. [~5700 a]

21. Fill in the blanks to properly complete the sentence.

    An isotope's activity is _____ proportional to the mass of the isotope and _____ proportional to its half-life. [Appendix A]

8.5 Summary Notes – Fission & Fusion

Fission occurs when a large nucleus is split into two daughter nuclei. It can be accomplished by colliding the large particle with a neutron. Some of the large nucleus is converted from mass into energy. (Note question 28, page 156)

□ Notes:

_____

_____

_____

_____

_____

_____

_____

_____

_____

_____

$$^{235}_{92}U \ + \ ^1_0n \ \longrightarrow \ ^{141}_{56}Ba \ + \ ^{92}_{36}Kr \ + \ 3^1_0n \ + \ 200 \ \text{MeV}$$

Fusion is the combining of small atomic nuclei to make a heavier element. Energy is released due to the binding energy per nucleon being greater than that of the original nuclei. Nuclear fusion is the reaction that powers the Sun, stars, and hydrogen bombs.

$$^2_1H \ + \ ^3_1H \ \longrightarrow \ ^4_2He \ + \ ^1_0n \ + \ 17.6 \ \text{MeV}$$

Examples

1. Uranium-235 is hit with a low energy neutron to produce barium-141 and krypton-92.
   a. Write the complete fission reaction.
   b. Explain how this reaction provides energy to the surroundings.
   a. $$^{235}_{92}U \ + \ ^1_0n \ -----> \ ^{141}_{56}Ba \ + \ ^{92}_{36}Kr \ + \ 3^1_0n$$

   b. Energy is supplied by conversion of some of the uranium's mass into energy when the heavy nucleus undergoes fission, according to $E = mc^2$.

2. Deuterium and tritium are fused together in the Sun's core producing helium.
   a. Write the complete fusion reaction.
   b. Explain how this reaction provides energy to the surroundings.
   a. $$^2_1H \ + \ ^3_1H \ -----> \ ^4_2He \ + \ ^1_0n \ + \ \text{energy}$$

   b. Energy is supplied by conversion of some of the hydrogen's mass into energy when the two light nuclei fuse together, according to $E = mc^2$.

Problems

1. Energy may be released during: a chemical reaction, phase change, fusion reaction, and fission reaction. List the four changes in order of increasing energy released. [Appendix A]

Use the information below to answer question 2.

Einstein's theory of special relativity, in 1905, showed that it was possible to convert mass in to energy ($E = mc^2$). Fermi, in 1938, discovered fission when trying to artificially transmutate uranium into a new element. The fission of uranium-235 can produce different daughter products.

2. Write the complete fission reaction when one neutron collides with a uranium-235 to produce xenon-137, another daughter product and two free neutrons. [Appendix A]

$$^{235}_{92}\text{U} \quad + \quad ^{1}_{0}\text{n} \quad \text{-----}>$$

Use the information below to answer question 3.

Both uranium-235 and plutonium-239 can undergo fission and are used to make atomic bombs. The uranium-235 is obtained from natural uranium ore while plutonium is a byproduct of some reactors such as the Canadian Candu reactors. Reactors that produce plutonium that can be used as weapons are called breeder reactors. Plutonium-239 has a half-life of 24 110 years and undergoes alpha and gamma decay.

3. The first nuclear weapon was detonated on July 16, 1945 at Trinity test site in Alamogordo, New Mexico. It used 6.2 kg of plutonium-239 with an explosive power equivalent to 20 kilotons of TNT.
    a. Write the decay equation for plutonium-239. [Appendix A]
    b. Determine the amount of plutonium-239 remaining after 10 000 years, starting with 6.2 kg. [4.7 kg]

Each of the three neutrons released during the fission of a uranium-235 nuclei are available to collide with three more U-235 nuclei. In this way a chain reaction is set up. If there is enough U-235 present, the chain reaction becomes uncontrolled. In this way, much heat energy and radiation is released. If you have at least a minimum mass of U-235 present, called critical mass, you may get a nuclear explosion.

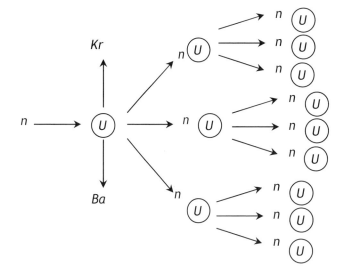

4. Determine the total energy released after 2 sets in the chain reaction if each fission releases 200 MeV of energy. [800 MeV]

5. The quote below forms the end of Pierre Currie's Nobel Prize acceptance speech in 1903; well before the development of atomic energy plants or atomic weapons.

> It can even be thought that radium could become very dangerous in criminal hands, and here the question can be raised whether mankind benefits from knowing the secrets of Nature, whether it is ready to profit from it or whether this knowledge will not be harmful for it. The example of the discoveries of Nobel is characteristic, as powerful explosives have enabled man to do wonderful work. They are also a terrible means of destruction in the hands of great criminals who are leading the peoples towards war. I am one of those who believe with Nobel that mankind will derive more good than harm from the new discoveries.

Would you agree with Currie that our knowledge of atomic energy has been put to more good than to harm? Explain. [Appendix A]

8.6 Summary Notes – Mass Defect

☐ Notes:

_____

_____

_____

_____

_____

_____

_____

_____

_____

_____

_____

_____

_____

_____

_____

_____

_____

_____

_____

_____

_____

There are four types of fundamental forces:

- Gravitational
- Weak (nuclear) Force
- Electromagnetic
- Strong Force

The strong force is the force required to overcome the electrostatic repulsion happening within the nuclei of elements. It is an attractive force and acts over a very short distance (within the nucleus). This force binds nuclei together.

- The total mass of a nucleus is less than the sum of the individual nucleon's masses. This difference, or missing mass, is called **mass defect** (Δm).
- The mass defect has an energy equivalence that may be determined using $E = mc^2$.

$$\Delta E = \Delta mc^2$$

Where:
ΔE is energy (J)
Δm is mass defect (kg)
c is the speed of light (m/s)

- The strong force comes from the mass defect energy and is responsible for holding the particles in the nucleus together.

In subatomic physics, mass may be expressed using:

- atomic mass unit or unified atomic mass unit (u): $1 \text{ u} = 1.66 \times 10^{-27}$ kg.

- the energy equivalence using units of MeV/c^2.

Examples

1. The unified atomic mass unit (u) is defined to be 1/12 that of the mass of one atom of carbon-12 where the mass of carbon-12 is defined to be exactly 12 u.

   a. Determine the average mass of a nucleon in carbon-12 in units of kg if the mass of carbon-12 is 1.993×10^{-26} kg.

   b. Convert the mass in kg to mass in units of MeV/c^2.

   $$\frac{1.993 \times 10^{-26} \, kg}{12} = 1.6608 \times 10^{-27} \, kg$$

   $$E = mc^2$$
   $$E = (1.6608 \times 10^{-27} \, kg) \, c^2$$
   $$E = 1.4947 \times 10^{-10} \, J$$

   $$mass = \frac{1.4947 \times 10^{-10} \, J}{1.6 \times 10^{-19} \, J/eV}$$
   $$mass = 934\,200\,000 \, eV$$

   a. The average mass of a nucleon in carbon-12 is 1.66×10^{-27} kg.

   b. The average mass of a nucleon in carbon-12 is 934 MeV/c^2.

2. The mass of a helium-4 nucleus is 4.0026 u. The mass of an individual proton is 1.0073 u and 1.0087 u for a neutron. Determine mass defect of the helium nucleus.
   A He nucleus made up of 2 protons and 2 neutrons:

   $$\Sigma m = 2p^+ + 2n$$
   $$\Sigma m = 2(1.0073 \, u) + 2(1.0087 \, u)$$
   $$= 4.032 \, u$$
   $$\Delta m = 4.032 \, u - 4.0026 \, u = 0.0294 \, u$$

   The mass defect is 0.0294 u.

Problems

1. Determine the mass-energy equivalence of a proton at rest in units of electron volts. [939 MeV]

---

2. Determine the maximum mass that can be created, in units of kg, from 1.025 MeV of energy. [1.82×10^{30} kg]

3. A muon is a particle that is 207X heavier than an electron and has a charge of -1. Determine the mass of a muon in units of MeV/c^2. [106 MeV/c^2]

4. The mass of a neutrino has never been measured but it is theorized that a neutrino may have a mass as high as 50 eV/c^2. Convert 50 eV/c^2 to units of kg. [8.9×10^{-35} kg]

5. Complete the chart below. [Appendix A]

	Particle	Rest Mass (kg)	Rest Mass (u)	Rest Mass (MeV/c^2)
a.	electron	9.1096×10^{-31}		
b.	proton	1.6726×10^{-27}		
c.	neutron	1.6749×10^{-27}		

- To convert to atomic mass units divide the mass in kg by 1.66×10^{-27} kg/u.
- To convert to MeV/c^2, first use $E = mc^2$ to calculate energy in joules. Then convert to energy in eV.

6. Use the following fusion reaction to determine the amount of mass that is converted to energy. [3.13×10^{-29} kg]

$$^{2}_{1}H \ + \ ^{3}_{1}H \longrightarrow \ ^{4}_{2}He \ + \ ^{1}_{0}n \ + \ 17.6 \ MeV$$

Use the information below to answer questions 7 & 8.

When a positron and electron collide they destroy each other and two gamma photons are typically produced (a.k.a. pair annihilation). Assume a positron and electron are each travelling at 8.91×10^{7} m/s when they collide head-on as shown in the diagram below.

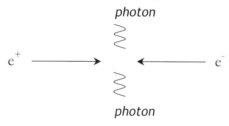

7. Assume that each photon equally shares the rest masses of the positron and electron and their kinetic energies. Determine the
    a. kinetic energy of each particle before the collision. [3.62×10^{-15} J]
    b. mass-energy equivalence of each particle before the collision. [8.20×10^{-14} J]
    c. frequency of each photon created due to the collision of the antimatter and matter. [1.29×10^{20} Hz]

8. Explain why a single photon cannot be produced from the collision. [Appendix A]

9. By experiment, using a mass spectrometer, the mass of hydrogen-2 has been determined to be 2.014 102 u. But if the individual masses of the particles that make up this hydrogen-2 atom were mathematically summed, a mass of 2.016 491 u is obtained. Determine the binding energy of the deuterium atom in eV. [2.23 MeV]

10. The mass of a helium-4 nucleus is 4.0026 u. The mass of an individual proton is 1.0073 u and 1.0087 u for a neutron. Determine the binding energy per nucleon in the helium nucleus in units of eV per nucleon. [6.86 MeV/nucleon]

As the binding energy per nucleon increases, the stability of the nucleus increases. Elements with intermediate mass numbers have the greatest binding energy per nuclear particle.

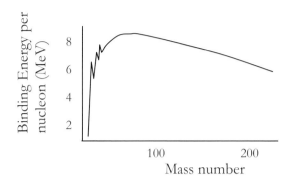

The maximum value of approximately 8.8 MeV per nucleon occurs in the vicinity of mass number 56.

11. Identify the region of the graph where elements may undergo
     a. fusion. [Appendix A]
     b. fission. [Appendix A]

12. In a process called pair production, a high-energy photon is converted into a particle and its antiparticle (e.g., an electron and a positron). This energy to mass conversion can occur according to the equation, $E = mc^2$. Explain why both charged particles must be produced and not just a single particle. [Appendix A]

Use the information below to answer question 13.

A common trait for all cultures is to observe natural phenomena and attempt to interpret them. The worldview of First Nation peoples in North America is to relate or unify apparently different phenomena. The desire to relate apparently different natural phenomena has also been an extremely important motivator in modern physics.

13. Describe the efforts of physicists in the 19th and 20th century to unify apparently different phenomena. [Appendix A]

8.7 Summary Notes – Detecting Subatomic Particles

☐ Notes:

_____

_____

_____

_____

_____

_____

_____

_____

_____

Detection chambers, such as bubble chambers, have been used to detect and analyze the nature of moving particles.

A bubble chamber is filled with a superheated liquid on the verge of boiling. When a charged particle passes through, its kinetic energy will cause the liquid to boil along its path, leaving a thin visible trail of bubbles.

Photographs of the tracks can be analyzed knowing that:

- positive and negative particles curve in opposite directions.
- lighter particles tend to curve more than heavier particles.
- all conservation laws (e.g., momentum, charge) must be obeyed.
- neutral particles don't leave tracks.

Examples

Use the information and diagram below to answer questions 1 – 3.

When bubble chambers were in common use they allowed for the analysis of many nuclear particles. A photograph was taken showing the tracks of subatomic particles through a bubble chamber inside a magnetic field.

Particles enter from here

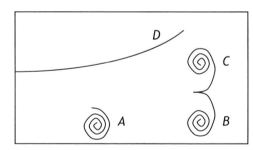

1. You and your lab partner are responsible for identifying the tracks of subatomic particles through a bubble chamber. Above is the picture you are working with and your partner has already identified the track produced by a Compton electron (A). Identify the track that is most likely a(n)
   a. electron.   Tracks A and B are probably electrons.
   b. positron.   Track C represents a positron.
   c. proton.   Track D represents a proton.

2.   Explain your choices in question 1

      Track A is produced when an electron is knocked off an atom by high energy photons. This is often called a Compton electron since it is essentially the Compton Effect occurring. Track B is a similar pattern curving in the same direction so it too should be an electron.

      Track C will be a positron; it should curve in the same direction as the proton in the magnetic field. The electron is equal in mass but is negative so it has opposite curvature.

      The proton should curve in the same direction as the positron since they both are positively charged.

3.   Identify the location where a neutral particle decayed into charged particles. Explain how you know it was a neutral particle before the decay.

      It appears as if the positron and electron were created from a neutral particle, since no track exists when they appear. Since momentum must be conserved, the positron and electron track should look the same but be opposite to each other. Charge is also shown to be conserved.

Problems

1.   Donald Glaser won the Nobel Prize in 1960 for his invention of the bubble chamber in 1952. Identify the particle(s) from the list below that should leave a track in a bubble chamber. Explain. [Appendix A]
    a.   Ultraviolet light
    b.   Gamma photon
    c.   Proton
    d.   Electron
    e.   Neutron
    f.   Positron

2.   An electron and a proton enter a bubble chamber and produce the tracks shown on the right. [Appendix A]
    a.   Identify the track most likely produced by the
       i.   electron.
       ii.   proton.
    b.   Determine the direction of the magnetic field.

Particles enter from here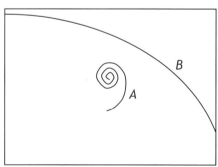

Since gamma photons are not charged particles, they do not leave tracks in a bubble chamber. Their presence is indicated, however, when they collide with an electron in the bubble medium. The electron is ejected and produces a track; this is called a Compton electron. It is easily identified and can help establish the magnetic field direction.

A photograph was taken showing the tracks of subatomic particles through a bubble chamber inside an external magnetic field. [Appendix A]

Particles enter from here

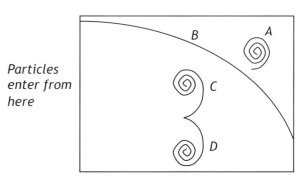

3.   Track A represents a Compton electron. Use it to determine the direction of the magnetic field in the bubble chamber.

4.   Identify the tracks (assuming electrons, protons and positrons only). Organize your answers using the chart on the right.

5.   Explain your choices in question 4.

Track	Particle
A	
B	
C	
D	

6.   Identify the location where a neutral particle decayed into charged particles. Explain how you know it was a neutral particle before the decay. [Appendix A]

A photograph was taken showing the tracks of four subatomic particles (A, B, C, and D) through a bubble chamber inside an external magnetic field. [Appendix A]

Particles enter from here

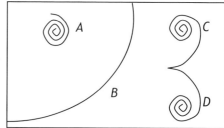

7. When an X-ray or gamma ray contacts an electron within an atom making up the superheated fluid in the bubble chamber, Compton Scattering occurs. Identify the path produced by the "Compton electron" in the diagram above.

8. The Compton electron is useful for identifying the direction of the magnetic field. Identify the direction of the magnetic field.

9. Identify the letter(s) representing negatively charged particles.

10. Identify the particles that most likely have identical mass.

Use the information below to answer question 11.

Muons (µ) are negatively charged particles produced when cosmic rays strike molecules in the upper atmosphere. They are 207 X heavier than electrons. Muons were first discovered by Carl Anderson in 1936 using a cloud chamber. A cloud chamber contains a high concentration of alcohol vapour. As charged particles travel through the chamber they ionize the air and cause alcohol droplets to form. These are seen as "tracks" in the chamber. Pictures are taken as the tracks are formed.

11. Three particles: a proton, electron, and muon enter a cloud chamber as shown in the diagram. [Appendix A]
    a. Match the particle with the track (A, B, and C) in the cloud chamber diagram. Explain.
    b. List the particles in order of increasing mass.

Particles enter from here

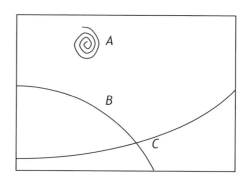

Use the information below to answer question 12.

The picture below, taken by Carl Anderson, is one of the first showing the curved track of a positron as it travels through a magnetic field in a cloud chamber. A thin lead plate is inserted into the path of the positron to slow it down.

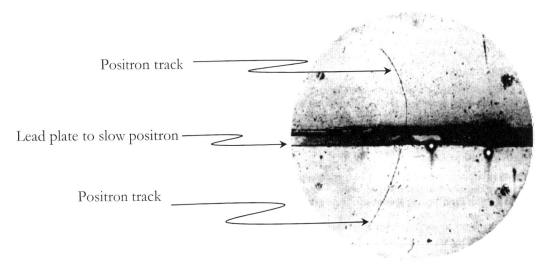

Positron track

Lead plate to slow positron

Positron track

Picture is from C.D. Anderson, *Physical Review* 43, 491 (1933)

12.   Use the diagram to identify the direction
   a.   the positron is moving.   [Appendix A]
   b.   of the magnetic field.

Use the information below to answer question 13.

Many subatomic particles are produced naturally and can be studied using cloud chambers or bubble chambers. To study other particles it is necessary to first produce them. Accelerating atoms or particles to high speeds and colliding them together is a technique used for producing subatomic particles. When this is done, parts (i.e., subatomic particles) break off and can then be studied. This technique can be used to examine the internal structure of the atom. Early particle accelerators and colliders were small and inexpensive. Large particle accelerators such as Fermilab in Chicago or CERN in France and Switzerland cost billions of dollars to build.

13.   High-energy particle accelerators are required to study subatomic particles. Explain why they must be high energy. [Appendix A]

Hundreds of subatomic particles have been detected over the last few decades. A few are listed in the table below.

Category	Name	Symbol	Antiparticle symbol	Mass (MeV/c^2)
Hadrons	proton	p	$\overline{p}$	938
	neutron	n	$\overline{n}$	939
	kaon	K^-	$\overline{K}^+$	494
		K^o	$\overline{K}^o$	498
Leptons	electron	e^-	e^+	0.511
	neutrino	$_0^0\nu$	$_0^0\overline{\nu}$	1.4×10^{-5}
	muon	μ^-	$\overline{\mu}^+$	106
	tau	τ^-	$\overline{\tau}^+$	1784

14. Various subatomic particles are sent through a bubble chamber in a magnetic field as represented in the diagram below. Use the table of particles above to identify the particles producing the tracks. Organize your answers in the chart provided. Explain. [Appendix A]

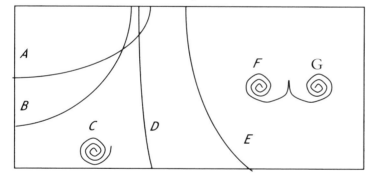

Track	Particle
A	
B	
C	
D	
E	
F	
G	

8.8 Summary Notes – The Standard Model

The Standard Model is an attempt to organize the hundreds of different subatomic particles. It reduces the hundreds of seemingly different particles to a few fundamental particles and describes the interactions (forces between them). The Standard Model postulates three classes of particles: Quarks, Leptons, and Bosons.

1. **Quarks**: relatively heavy particles that have fractional charges (i.e., less than the elementary charge). They cannot be isolated.
   e.g., Combinations of quarks make up protons and neutrons.

The existence of quarks is deduced from calculations based on scattering experiments and conservation laws.

Name (Flavour)	Charge	Mass (MeV/c^2)
Up (u)	+2/3	4
Down (d)	-1/3	10
antiUp ($\bar{u}$)	-2/3	4
antiDown ($\bar{d}$)	+1/3	10

A line is drawn over the particle symbol to represent an antiparticle. Stable matter is composed from up and down quarks (with no antiquarks).

2. **Leptons**: much lighter particles than quarks (these particles have mass but no internal structure).
   e.g., electrons and neutrinos

3. **Bosons**: particles that are exchanged between quarks and leptons to produce the fundamental forces.
   e.g., photons

Types of interactions (forces)

Interaction (force)	Definition	Range	Relative strength
strong	The force that holds the nucleus together.	nuclear sizes	Strongest
electromagnetic	The force of attraction or repulsion between charged particles.	infinite	
weak	The force that allows the transmutation of quarks; involved in radioactive decay.	nuclear sizes	
gravity	The force responsible for the attraction of two masses.	infinite	Weakest

N.B., In nuclear decay and high energy collisions, subatomic interactions obey all of the conservation laws:

- momentum
- charge
- mass-energy
- nucleon number (atomic mass)

Examples

1. Quarks that make up normal matter must be first generation quarks (no antiquarks are allowed since combinations of matter and antimatter are unstable). Use the charge on quarks to identify the three quarks that make up a
   a. proton.
   b. neutron.

$$u \quad u \quad d$$
$$+\frac{2}{3} \quad +\frac{2}{3} \quad + -\frac{1}{3} = +1$$

$$u \quad d \quad d$$
$$+\frac{2}{3} , -\frac{1}{3} , -\frac{1}{3} = 0$$

2. A neutron decays into a proton and an electron. Write the decay reaction of a neutron using
   a. nucleons.
   b. quarks.

   a. $^{1}_{0}n \longrightarrow {}^{1}_{1}p + {}^{0}_{-1}\beta + {}^{0}_{0}\bar{\nu}$

   b. $udd \longrightarrow uud + {}^{0}_{-1}\beta + {}^{0}_{0}\bar{\nu}$

3. When an electron collides with a positron, they are both annihilated and two photons are produced. Determine if the collision obeys the law of conservation of charge.

   $$e^{+} + e^{-} \longrightarrow {}^{0}_{0}\gamma + {}^{0}_{0}\gamma$$

   Yes. The net charge before the interaction is zero, which is identical to the net charge after the interaction.

Problems

1.   Fill in the blank. Protons and neutrons are made of _____. [Appendix A]

2.   Identify the fundamental force responsible for
       a. friction.
       b. planetary orbits.   [Appendix A]
       c. nuclear bonding.
       d. electrostatic attraction.

3.   Rutherford used scattering experiments to probe the internal structure of the atom in the development of his nuclear model. Explain why alpha particles would be a poor choice for probing the internal structure of a proton. [Appendix A]

4.   Determine the electrostatic force between an up quark and a down quark inside a proton when separated by a distance of 1.30×10^{-25} m. [3.03×10^{21} N]

Use the information below to answer questions 5 – 7.

Quarks were first proposed in 1964 by physicist Murray Gell-Mann as a way of trying to organize the approximately 200 known subatomic particles. He named them after a nonsense word from James Joyce's Finnegans Wake:

    "three quarks for Muster Mark"

Quarks that make up normal matter must be first generation quarks (no antiquarks are allowed since combinations of matter and antimatter are unstable).

5. Use the charge on quarks to identify the three quarks that make up a(n)
   a. proton.
   b. neutron.   [Appendix A]
   c. antiproton.

6. Free neutrons have a short half-life of 898 s and decay into a proton and a beta-negative particle. Write the decay equation using
   a. nucleons. [Appendix A]
   b. quarks. [Appendix A]

7. Write the transformation of a proton into a neutron and a beta-positive particle using
   a. nucleons. [Appendix A]
   b. quarks. [Appendix A]

Use the information below to answer questions 8 & 9.

Mesons are unstable particles made of first generation quark-antiquark pairs that are lighter than neutrons and protons. They range in mass from 140 MeV/c² to 10 GeV/c². Some mesons last long enough to be detected. The existence of mesons was first predicted in 1935 by the Japanese physicist, Yukawa Hideki. Two common types of mesons are the pi mesons (aka pions) and the K meson (aka kaons).

8. Use the charge values on quarks to identify the two quarks that make up a positive pion (π^+). [Appendix A]

9. A neutral pion is its own antiparticle. Use the charge values on quarks to identify the two possible quark combinations that make up a neutral pion (π°). [Appendix A]

10. The large cyclotron at TRIUMF in Vancouver, BC produces mesons for research. Mesons are thought to be the exchange particles between nucleons to create the strong nuclear force. This is part of the theory of quantum chromodynamics (QCD). Write the decay equation for a positive pion (π^+) that decays into a positron. [Appendix A]

Use the information below to answer questions 11 – 14.

First generation quarks make up normal matter (no antiquarks are allowed since combinations of matter and antimatter are unstable). Second and third generation particles are short lived and decay into first generation particles. Only the first seem necessary for the natural world. It is not understood why three generations exist. Each quark has a corresponding antiquark, equal in magnitude but opposite in sign. A line is drawn over the particle symbol to represent an antiparticle.

Generation	Name/Flavour	Charge	Mass (MeV/c²)	Name/Flavour	Charge	Mass (MeV/c²)
I	up (u)	+2/3	4	down (d)	-1/3	10
II	charm (c)	+2/3	1500	strange (s)	-1/3	150
III	top (t)	+2/3	174000	bottom (b)	-1/3	4500

11. A five quark combination called the pentaquark or theta-plus has been hypothesized to exist. It is a combination of two ups, two downs, and one antistrange quark. Determine the net charge on a pentaquark. [Appendix A]

12. Would the theta-plus be a stable particle? Explain. [Appendix A]

13. K mesons are often called kaons for short. A kaon contains a quark antiquark pair where one of the quarks or antiquarks must be a strange quark flavour. Identify the quarks that make up a neutral kaon (κ^0). [Appendix A]

14. Two charm quarks and a strange quark give a total charge of +1. Could a proton be composed of these quarks? Explain. [Appendix A]

15. None of the following reactions can occur because they violate one or more conservation laws. Identify the conservation law(s) violated for each reaction. [Appendix A]

    a. μ^+ ------> e^- + $_0^0\gamma$

    b. $_1^1p$ -------> π^+ + π^o

    c. $_1^1p$ + $_0^1n$ -------> $_1^1p$ + π^o

    d. $_1^1p$ -----> e^- + $_0^0\gamma$

16. Any possible product may be produced in a nuclear reaction as long as all conservation laws are followed. Determine if the following collision between a high-speed proton and antiproton obey the conservation of
    a. charge. [Appendix A]
    b. nucleon number. [Appendix A]

    $_1^1p$ + $_{-1}^{1}\overline{p}$ --------> e^+ + e^-

17. Use conservation laws to determine if it is possible for a neutron to decay into a proton and a beta-negative particle. [Appendix A]

18. A proton contains three quarks and has a mass of 938 MeV while an upsilon meson is a particle consisting of two quarks (bottom, antibottom) and has a much larger mass of 9460 MeV. Explain what the Standard Model has to say regarding the mass disparity. [Appendix A]

Use the information below to answer question 19.

The structure of the atom was determined by Rutherford using scattering experiments by directing alpha particles at atoms. Quarks were also discovered using scattering experiments by Richard Taylor and others in 1970 at Stanford University. Dr. Taylor's experiment involved directing a beam of high-energy electrons at protons (hydrogen gas). Dr. Taylor is a physicist originally from Medicine Hat Alberta. He was awarded a Nobel Prize in 1990 for his part in the discovery. If a nucleon was a solid billiard ball type of object a certain scattering pattern should be observed.

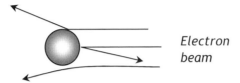

Electron beam

Upon closer inspection, however, a more complex scattering pattern was observed indicating that the proton was not a solid sphere, but was composed of three smaller objects, called quarks, each with their own fractional charge.

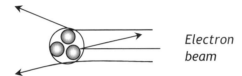

Electron beam

Three objects and their fractional charges that made up the nucleus affected the scattering pattern. This is called deep inelastic scattering. Eventually other quarks were proposed and discovered.

19.   Explain why high-energy electrons are required to probe the nucleus (to reveal its structure) rather than low energy electrons or alpha particles. [Appendix A]

8.9 Extensions

1. Describe how the proton was discovered. [Appendix A]

2. Explain briefly what the weak nuclear force is responsible for. [Appendix A]

3. If the activity of a radioactive sample of is 28 Bq and 8.0 h later its activity is 18 Bq, determine the half-life of the sample. [13 h]

4. Identify the location of Canada's neutrino detector. Briefly describe its design. [Appendix A]

5. Carbon-14 has a half-life of 5730 years. A 1.0 g sample of a living tree is analyzed for carbon-14 and found to emit 15.4 counts/minutes A 1.0 g sample from a wooden artifact found in an ancient Babylon burial site is analyzed and found to emit 9.3 counts/min.
    a. Write the nuclear equation showing the beta-negative decay of carbon-14. [Appendix A]
    b. Determine the age of the burial site. [~4000 a]

6. Potassium-40 undergoes positron decay with a half-life of 1.277×10^9 years and is often used to determine the age of rocks (e.g., when volcanic rocks cooled). Potassium-40 dating works well for rocks that are between 100 000 and 4.3 billion years old. A 200 g sample of a potassium based rock has 98.23 % of its original potassium remaining. Determine the age of the rock. [3.290×10^7 a]

7. In 1997, Hobson and Wassenaar from Saskatoon used radioactive tritium, having a half-life of 12.3 years, to track the migratory patterns of monarch butterflies as they travelled across North America. If the tritium initially registers 1280 counts per minute on a Geiger counter and later registers 1241 counts per minute, determine the time between measurements. [6.59 months]

Use the information below to answer question 8.

While gluons are the exchange particle between quarks, pions are responsible for the strong interactions between neutrons and protons within a nucleus. Pions (positive pion is made from an up and antidown quark) are continually transferring between nucleons changing them from neutrons to protons and back.

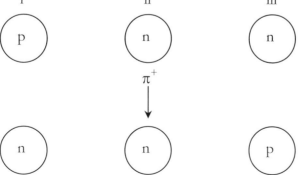

8. Explain how charge and mass-energy are conserved during the exchange of the pion. [Appendix A]

9. Carrier particles were introduced as an attempt to explain action (force) at a distance. Particles can be exchanged to cause repulsion or attraction between leptons and hadrons. Identify the force carrier(s) that cannot be isolated. [Appendix A]

8.10 Review

1. Identify the incorrect notation for an isotope from the list below.
   a. $^{234}_{92}$U
   b. $^{234}_{90}$Th
   c. $^{176}_{72}$Ta
   d. $^{210}_{86}$Rn

2. A neutron decays to produce a beta-negative particle and a
   a. proton and antineutrino
   b. proton and neutrino
   c. proton and electron
   d. alpha particle and antineutrino

3. Under the Standard Model, identify the particle that is considered to be an elementary particle.
   a. proton
   b. neutron
   c. electron
   d. alpha particle

4. Identify the particle from the list below that does not contain quarks.
   a. proton
   b. neutron
   c. electron
   d. alpha particle

5. Bubble chambers are a technology whereby scientists can
   a. blow large bubbles
   b. picture quarks
   c. identify particle tracks
   d. observe neutrinos

6. Complete the chart [Appendix A]

	Isotopic notation	Name	Atomic number (Z)	Atomic mass (A)	Number of neutrons (n)
a.	$^{234}_{92}U$				
b.	$^{234}_{90}Th$				
c.		carbon-12			
d.			8		8

7. Write the nuclear reaction for the decay of each of the following radioactive elements. Use the Lead decay series found on page 318. [Appendix A]
   a. uranium-238
   b. polonium-218
   c. lead-210
   d. lead-214

8. Identify the mass of a gamma ray. [Appendix A]

9. Can deuterium or hydrogen undergo alpha decay? Explain. [Appendix A]

10. 140 mg of tungsten-188 (a.k.a. wolfram-188) undergoes beta-negative decay with a half-life of 65 d.
    a. Write the nuclear decay equation for the wolfram-188. [Appendix A]
    b. Determine the remaining mass after 74 d. [64 mg]

11. 100 mg of a given radioactive isotope, x, has a half-life of 1.0 hr. It then decays into another element called y. Plot the amount of original sample has a function of time (its decay curve). [Appendix A]

12. Germanium-68 has a half-life of 250 days. Determine the fraction of a sample of germanium-68 remaining after 4.2 years. [0.014]

13. Geiger counters detect radiation. Each time they detect an alpha particle, beta particle or gamma radiation they show a "count". A radioactive substance registers 1280 counts per minute on a Geiger counter. 6.0 h later it registers 320 counts per minute. Determine the half-life of the substance. [3.0 h]

A photograph was taken showing the tracks of three subatomic particles (A, B, and C) through a bubble chamber inside an external magnetic field directed into the page. [Appendix A]

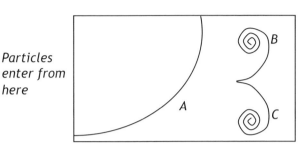

Particles enter from here

14. Identify the letter(s) representing negatively charged particles.

15. Write the transformation of a proton into a neutron when an electron is captured, in terms of
     a. nucleons. [Appendix A]
     b. quarks. [Appendix A]

8.11 Review Assignment

1. In the early days of the study of radioactivity the dangers were not well known. Pierre Curie discussed some of the dangers in his speech accepting the Nobel Prize in 1903:

    If one leaves a wooden or cardboard box containing a small glass ampulla with several centigrams of a radium salt in one's pocket for a few hours, one will feel absolutely nothing. But 15 days afterwards a redness will appear on the epidermis, and then a sore which will be very difficult to heal.

Pierre Curie did limited testing on himself; much later others did extensive animal testing to better determine the risks and benefits of radiation. Considering the beneficial aspects radiation has had in medicine, is animal testing justified?

2. Complete the following chart.

	Isotopic notation	Name	Atomic number (Z)	Atomic mass (A)	Number of neutrons (n)
a.		europium-167			
b.	$^{34}_{16}S$				
c.				239	145
d.			100		157

3. Write the decay equation when tungsten-187 emits a beta-negative particle.

4. A high energy gamma ray beam is collided with the nucleus of an atom to create an electron and positron pair.
   a. Explain why, using conservation laws, a positron must be created when an electron is created.
   b. Calculate the minimum energy, in units of electron volts, required to produce an electron and a positron.

5. The classical forces of gravity and electromagnetism cannot account for the stability of the nucleus. The force of repulsion due to the closeness of the protons is far greater than the gravitational attraction between the nucleons and the latter could not hold the nucleus together, yet the nucleus exists, so there must be a new force between the nucleons that is strong enough to overcome the coulombic, or electrostatic repulsion. Explain what the strong force is responsible for.

6. An isotope emits an electron and an anti-neutrino during radioactive decay. The electron moves east with a momentum of 9.28×10^{-26} kg·m/s, and the anti-neutrino moves north with a momentum of 7.47×10^{-27} kg·m/s as shown in the diagram. Determine the momentum of the recoiling nucleus.

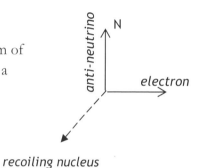

recoiling nucleus

7. An experiment is done to identify a radioactive isotope using its half-life. The following data is collected.

Counts	Time (a)
2000	0
799	10
320	20
128	30
51.1	40

   a. Graph the data.
   b. Determine the half-life of the substance from the graph.

8. Tritium can be used to measure the age of objects up to about 100 years. Its half-life is 12.3 years. Tritium is produced in the upper atmosphere by cosmic rays. It is trapped in water molecules and brought to the Earth by rain. A bottle of pop has been sitting on the shelf for at least a few years and has only 20 % the tritium content of new pop. Determine the age of the pop on the shelves.

9. A photograph was taken showing the tracks of subatomic particles through a bubble chamber inside a magnetic field. Particle track A represents an electron produced via the Compton Effect.

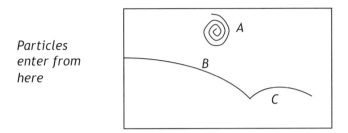

Particles enter from here

    a. Determine the direction of the magnetic field.
    b. Identify the charge on the particle that created track B and Track C.

10. High energy gamma rays can be used to create an electron and a positron. A high energy green laser beam is collided with high energy electrons to create the electron and positron pair.
    a. Explain why, using conservation laws, a positron must be created when an electron is created.
    b. Calculate the minimum energy, in units of electron volts, required to produce an electron and a positron.

Use the information below to answer questions 11 & 12.

The Standard Model explains mass using the idea of a Higgs Boson. When particles move through a special field, called Higgs field, they may create waves that produce the property we call mass. The waves produced can also be thought of as a particle, since modern physics makes no fundamental distinction. Therefore, the Higgs boson is the particle that is responsible for the mass of any particle.

When photons move through the Higgs field their properties do not create waves and therefore they have no mass. Other particles, such as an electron, have properties that create waves in the Higgs field and therefore create mass.

The Large Hadron Collider at CERN was completed in 2010 and may be capable of detecting the Higg's boson. The LHC will be the most powerful particle accelerator at about 7 TeV with a circumference of 27 km.

11. What conclusions did CERN reach about the Higgs particle using the Large Hadron Collider in 2011?

12. Billions of dollars are required to build high-energy particle accelerators necessary to do modern research into the nature of the atom. Can this be justified considering all the other important needs requiring funding? Explain.

Appendix A

1.1

1. a. ~3.8, 2
   b. ~3.87, 3

2. a. 6   b. 3   c. 5
   d. Not applicable – counting number

3. a. 0.004 10 d
   b. 7.25 cm
   c. 5.00 g
   d. 8.65×10^4 km
   e. 1.85×10^7 km
   f. 8.43×10^4 cm^2
   g. 0.000 409 g
   h. 3.00×10^8 m/s

4. a. 4.9×10^{12} mm
   b. 23 400 000 L
   c. 0.000 0356 cm
   d. 9.5×10^{-7} m

5. a. 4.30 m
   b. 140 cm
   c. 0.800 m
   d. 4100 g
   e. 0.076 kg
   f. 335 g
   g. 650 mL
   h. 0.0550 L
   i. 120 s
   j. 557 ms

6. a. 0.13
   b. 6.2×10^{-4}

1.2

1.

b.	$y = knx + 5$	kn	5
c.	$y = \dfrac{x}{2a}$	$\dfrac{1}{2a}$	0
d.	$y = -2Bx + \dfrac{A}{2B}$	$-2B$	$\dfrac{A}{2B}$

2. e. The 100 N/m from graph should be a more reliable number than the arithmetic mean of 84 N/m. For three reasons:
   1. The zero offset error is eliminated (line does not go through zero, thus eliminating a consistent error present in the data)
   2. Random errors are reduced by obtaining a weighted average when drawing a best-fit line.
   3. Stray data points are easier to identify and eliminated.

3.

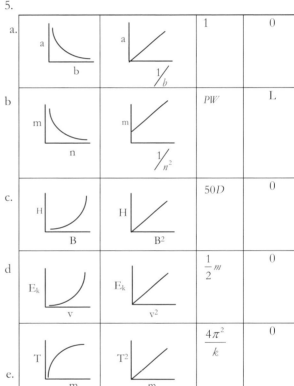

$E_k = \dfrac{1}{2}mv^2$	v	E_k
$T = 2\pi\sqrt{\dfrac{m}{k}}$	m	T
$F_c = \dfrac{mv^2}{r}$	r	F_c
$F_g = \dfrac{Gm_1m_2}{r^2}$	r	F_g

5.

a.	a vs b	a vs $1/b$	1	0
b	m vs n	m vs $1/n^2$	PW	L
c.	H vs B	H vs B^2	$50D$	0
d	E_k vs v	E_k vs v^2	$\dfrac{1}{2}m$	0
e.	T vs m	T^2 vs m	$\dfrac{4\pi^2}{k}$	0

1.3

3.

4. ii

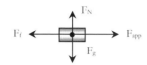

1.4

3.

4.

0		10 right	← ▭ →
0		5 right	← ▭ →
	15 left		← ▭
5 left	25 left		← ▭ →

7. a.

c.

1.5

1. a. 6.4 m   c. 31°
   b. 5.3 cm   d. 44°

2.

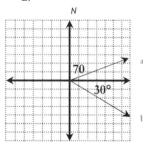

3.

Vector	Bearing	Cardinal reference	Cardinal reference
A	40°	40° E of N	50° N of E
B	160°	70° S of E	20° E of S
C	330°	60° N of W	30° W of N

6. Order is irrelevant.

9. a.   b.

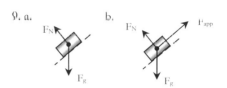

14.

a. velocity components   c. free-body diagrams

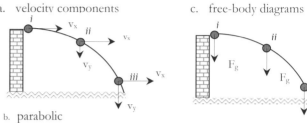

b. parabolic

1.6

1

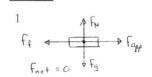

2. 200 N, 0

6. According to the Law of Conservation of Energy the ball will have 20 J of kinetic energy as it hits the ground.

7.

Height (m)	Kinetic energy (J)	Gravitational Potential energy (J)	Total Mechanical energy (J)
1.00	0	10	10
0.75	2.5	7.5	10
0.50	5.0	5.0	10
0.25	7.5	2.5	10
0	10	0	10

10.

Number of complete swings	Gravitational potential energy (J)
0	10
1	8.0
2	6.4
3	5.1

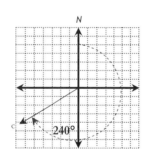

1.7

1. a. iii   b. ii   c. i

2.1

10.
a. velocity

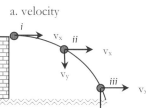

b. momentum components

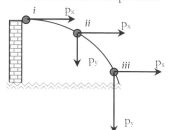

2.2

4. south

10. a. They have the same impulse.
    b. The first car uses a smaller force to stop over a longer time.

12. The soft mat allows the vaulter to slow down gradually thus reducing the forces acting on the vaulter as described by the equation Ft = mΔv. This equation shows that as the time of impact increases the force of impact decreases.

13. As the car stops the occupant's inertia carries them forward. The air bag brings the occupant to rest over a longer period of time (slow down gradually), thus decreasing the force on the person. This relationship between force and time is shown by the equation Ft = mΔv as the time of the deceleration increases, the force will decrease.

16. a. F = mΔv/t

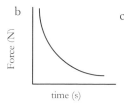

b
c.
Force (N)
time (s)

17

1.00	0.85	-4.4	4.08	8.48	0.066
1.00	0.44	-4.4	2.938	7.34	0.057

b. The impulse is less on a soft surface than on a hard surface. This is because the collision time is larger with softer objects.

2.3

7. a. They each experienced the same force magnitude.
   b. They each experience the same magnitude of impulse.
   c. The smaller vehicle (car) experienced the larger acceleration.

2.5

3. No. As much as possible must be lost without violating the Law of Conservation of Momentum.

4. b. The kinetic energy after the collision is less than the kinetic energy before the collision; therefore the collision was inelastic.

5 a. The momentum is conserved. They had equal and opposite momenta.
   b. Since as much kinetic energy as possible was lost the collision is completely inelastic.

6. b. The initial kinetic energy does not equal the final kinetic energy; therefore it is inelastic.

9.

before (m/s)	after (m/s)	before (g•m/s)	after (g•m/s)
0.444	0.371	87.91	73.46
0.449	0.230	88.00	45.08

The collision was not elastic because 52 % of the kinetic energy was lost during the collision.

2.6

1. No. The problem referred to volume, not mass.

2.7

1. b   2. b   3. a   4. b   5. d

7. Ft = mΔv The stretchy cord increases the amount of time it takes to come to a stop, decreasing the magnitude of force acting upon the body in bringing it to a stop.

8.
   a. momentum
   b. inertia
   c. momentum, momentum, momentum
   d. impulse

10. Ft = mΔv. The smaller force acting over a longer time can yield a greater impulse compared to a larger force acting over a shorter time frame.

---

1. The hair must have the opposite charge of the togue according to the law of conservation of charge.

2. a. Rabbit fur-Teflon
   b. Styrofoam becomes negative which charges the electroscope negative. Since the glass is positive it will cause the negatively charged leaves of the electroscope to collapse when brought near-by.

3. The concern is that the friction between two different fabrics, the car seat and the clothes you are wearing may produce static electricity and ignite the propane fumes.

4. According to the law of electric charge, electrons will repel each other. In a conductor the distance between them will be maximized and the electrons will spread evenly on the surface of the conductor. In an insulator the charges will not be free to flow so the charge will remain localized at the area of contact.

5.

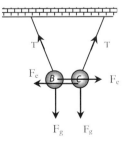

6.

7. The positively charged ruler induces a charge separation in the neutral pith ball. The negative charges in the pith ball are closer to the ruler than the positive so there is a net force of attraction.

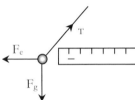

8. a. B must be positive because of the repulsion with A. Therefore, C could be negative or neutral.

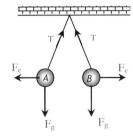

9. a.

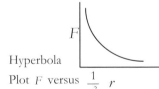

b. The charged balloon induces a charge separation in the ceiling; the mobile electrons are attracted to a positively charged balloon. This results in a net force of attraction.

10.

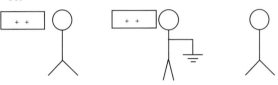

4. a. repulsive

7. Neither. They each exert equal forces on each other according to Newton's third law.

8.

-1.60×10^{-19}	1.76×10^{11}
$+1.60 \times 10^{-19}$	9.58×10^{7}
0	0
$+1.60 \times 10^{-19}$	1.76×10^{11}
$+3.20 \times 10^{-19}$	4.82×10^{7}

9. The alpha particle would provide the strongest electrostatic force because it has the largest charge.

14. a.
$$F_e = \frac{kq_1q_2}{r^2}$$
b.

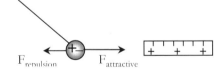

c. Hyperbola
d. Plot F versus $\frac{1}{r^2}$ r
e. $slope = kq_1q_2$ or kq^2
f. y-intercept = 0

15. a. The charge on object A is positive and negative on object B.

17. negative

18. a. The charge on objects B and C is negative.

1.

a.

← |E| P

b.

P —— |E| →

c.

← |E|₂ P —— |E|₁ →

d.

← |E|₂ P
← |E|₁

e.

← |E|₂ P — |E|₁ →

f.

← |E|₂ P
← |E|₁

4. a. $|E| = \frac{kq}{r^2}$ b. |E| graph

c. Hyperbola

d. Plot $|E|$ versus $\frac{1}{r^2}$

e. $slope = kq$

f. y-intercept = 0

5. a. A, B, E, C, D
   b. Both are positive

6.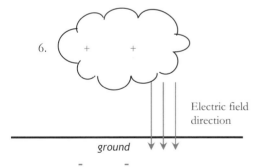

Electric field direction

ground

10. north

13.

a.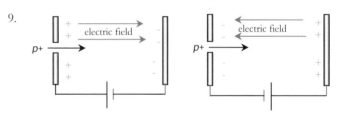

b.

c.

d.

e.

f.

8.

	Energy (J)	Energy (eV)
a.	1.68 x 10⁻¹⁸	10.5
b.	5.42 x 10⁻¹⁹	3.39
c.	8.80 x 10⁻¹⁹	5.50

9.

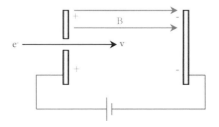

13. 5000 V. By definition an electron accelerating across a potential difference of 1 V obtains 1 eV of kinetic energy.

14. a. 600 V   b. 600 eV

19.

22. 500 V
   By definition an electron accelerating across a
   potential difference of 1 V obtains 1 eV of kinetic
   energy.

23. The stopping voltage must be 3.6 MV

24. force, parallel

26.

Kinetic energy (eV)	Electrical potential energy (eV)
0	100
25	75
50	50
75	25
100	0

27. According to the Law of Conservation of Energy,
   the energy lost is 10 eV. Thus the voltage is 10 V.

30. The neutron's speed is unchanged because it is not
   a charged particle.

31. positive, negative, electric, 1, 2, parabolic

34. b   35. d   36. d   37. a   38. c

3.5

1.
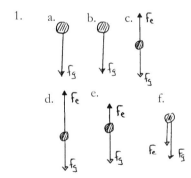

   2. downwards

   10. Quantized means discrete (distinct) quantities; not
      continually varying from one value to the next.

   11. a. 1   b. 3   c. 2 and 4

   12. a.
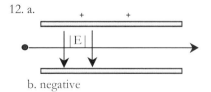
      b. negative

15.

16. a. positive
   b. to the left
   c.

3.6

1. Do not seek shelter under or near a tree or other
   tall object.
   Do not be in an open field (do not be the tallest
   object around).
   Seek shelter in a car or house.
   Do not touch plumbing inside a house.

6.

$$k = \frac{1}{4\pi\varepsilon_0}$$

3.7

1. d   2. b   3. c   4. b   5. a

6. The neutral can has an induced charge separation. The
   electrostatic force between the separated charges
   causes the can to accelerate toward the negatively
   charged comb.

7. b.

8. Atomic and subatomic masses can generally be treated
   as negligible. For charged droplets where there are
   many molecules involved the weight can not be
   disregarded.

1.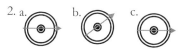

2. a.   b.   c.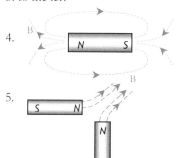

3. to the left

4.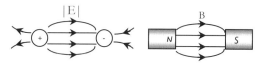

5.

6.

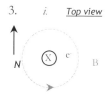

7.

| charge | attraction and repulsion | infinite |
| moving charges | attraction and repulsion | infinite |

8.

| Small positive charge |
| Compass needle |

1. To the right

2. right to left in front of the wire

3.   i.   *Top view*   ii.   *Side view*

The magnetic field is directed to the east.

4. Up the wire in both cases

5. Into the page of the paper (X).

6. The direction of the magnetic field south of the wire is towards the west.

7.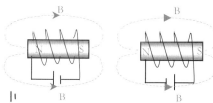

8.

9.

10.

11.

Location	Prediction	Observation
A	left	left
B	right	right
C	left	left
D	left	left

14. Cause disruption to electrical devices due to strong magnetic fields.

15. High temperatures allow the domains to randomize.

16. The carbon holds the domains in place so they remain ordered.

3. a. Parabolic trajectory to the top of the page.
   b. Circular arc out of the page.

10. Particle c would experience the greatest magnetic force since it is travelling perpendicular to the magnetic field.

11. circular, perpendicular, magnetic

12. forced into the page.

13. A is south and B is north. Since the positive charges are initially moving upwards (due to the electric field) the right hand rule may be used with the thumb pointing the direction of initial motion and the palm representing the force causing them to be directed out of the page. This orientation of the thumb and palm leaves the fingers (representing the magnetic field) to be pointing to the left.

17. zero

18. a.   b.   c.

19.

F_e

H^+

F_m

25.

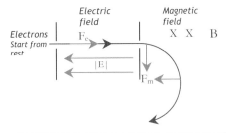

Electric field

Magnetic field

Electrons Start from rest

F_e

$|E|$

X X B

F_m

27.

i.	positive
ii.	to the right
i.	up towards the top plate
ii.	top plate is positive, bottom is negative
iii.	into the page inside the wire loop
iv.	The positive terminal on the left, negative on the right
i.	to the centre of the turn
ii.	into the page

28. a. to the right
    b. C
    c. out of the page

29. propane

30. pentane

32. b   33. b   34. a

35. A magnetic south is northern Canada

36. You should walk 17.3° to the west of where your compass points.

37. The compass will not be reliable; it is not to be trusted.

38. The solar radiation could damage equipment and people.

39. Greater cancer rates as people are exposed to more cosmic rays.

41. As the charged particles enter the Earth's magnetic field, they experience a magnetic deflecting force. It is this force that causes them to spiral towards the Earth's poles.

4.4

1.

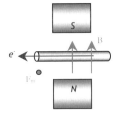

2.

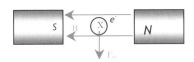

3.

7.

F_m

F_g

13.

F_m B

A F_m

14. Counter clockwise.

15. A looped wire allows the wire to rotate and therefore stay inside the magnetic field.

16. The commutator allows the current to change direction so that the armature continues to spin in the same direction.

17. down

4.5

1. Electron flow is to the

a.
top of the page

b.
left of the page

c.
left of the page

d.
top of the page

2. Wire P has a maximum current directed **into** the page. Wire Q will have **no** current since it is moving parallel to the field.

5.

8. As current moves through a conductor it always produces some heat.

9. a. from right to left
   b. from right to left

12. b. The kinetic energy starts at zero at point A and continues to increase until it reaches the bottom of the tube.
The gravitational potential energy starts at a maximum and decreases as the magnet falls.
If the bottom of the tube is used as a reference point, then according to the Law of Conservation of Energy, the initial gravitational potential energy is equal to the kinetic energy at the bottom of the tube.
c. The kinetic energy starts at zero at point A and increases until it reaches point B. At point B the magnet is falling at constant velocity and therefore with a constant kinetic energy.
The gravitational potential energy starts at a maximum and decreases as the magnet falls.

d.   The only force acting on the non-magnet is the force due to gravity.

When a magnet moves by a conductor it induces a current in the conductor. The current then produces its own magnetic field which opposes the motion of the original magnetic field.

4.6

1. attract

2.
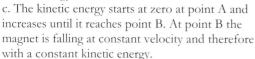

3. South

4.

5. Towards C

6. Area B

4.7

1. a   2. d   3. b

4.
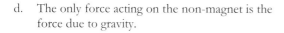

5. a.   b.

6. A – none (neutral) B- none (not crossing any field lines) C – Forced out of the page

9.

10. a. from left to right   b. from left to right

12. The changing electric field produces a changing magnetic field in the primary coil which then produces a changing electric field leading to a changing magnetic field in the secondary coil. This allows electric charge in the wire to be influenced by an induced voltage that will cause a reading to register in the secondary coils voltmeter.

5.1

1. Violet, Indigo, Blue, Green, Yellow, Orange, Red

2. Ultraviolet, since it has the most energy it can cause the most damage.

3. The magnetic field oscillates up-down.

4. accelerating, magnetic, 3.0×10^8 m/s

5.

Type of field(s)
Gravitational Electrical
Gravitational Electrical Magnetic
Gravitational Changing electrical Changing magnetic

6. 4 H

11. b. The beam's colour is red

15.

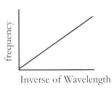

16. a.

b. The speed of EMR

15. One doesn't have to have access to the standard bar to determine the length of a metre. The metal bar will change over time

1. The angle of incidence is 35.0°.

2.

θ₁ (degrees)	θ₂ (degrees)	θ₃ (degrees)
30	30	60
40	20	70
50	10	80

3. The bending of a wave as it passes from one medium into another medium.

8. Throw below where you see the fish since light refracts as it leaves the water as shown in the diagram

16. As the index of refraction increases, the speed of light decreases relative to the speed of light in a vacuum.

17. a. decreases   b. decreases   c. same

23. Total internal reflection will occur

26. 14.6 %

1. a.

Characteristics	Dimensions
inverted	d_i = 17.6 cm
larger	h_i = -5.6 cm
real	

b.

Characteristics	Dimensions
upright	d_i = -5.8 cm
larger	h_i = 5.6 cm
virtual	

c.

Characteristics	Dimensions
upright	d_i = -4.1 cm
smaller	h_i = 1.7 cm
virtual	

2.

Characteristics	Dimensions
inverted	d_i = 14.0 cm
smaller	h_i = -4.1 cm
real	

3. real, virtual

6. a. Since the object is beyond the focal point the image is real, smaller & inverted.
   b. The brain must invert the image so we can see it right side up.

7. real, smaller, inverted

8. No. the object is located at the lens' focal point. This means the light rays will not converge to form an image.

9. virtual, upright, smaller

10. The student would observe a smaller virtual image of the object while looking through the lens but could not take a picture of it as the light diverges rather than converges onto the location of the film.

12. Converging/Convex lens

13. The refractive index of the water and the lens and cornea are so similar that light does not bend enough to focus on the back of the eye.

15

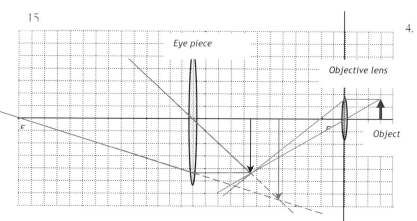

Eye piece

Objective lens

F

F

Object

5.5

1. a.

Characteristics	Dimensions
inverted	$d_i = 10.6$ m
smaller	$h_i = -4.0$ m
real	

b.

Characteristics	Dimensions
inverted	$d_i = 12.0$ m
larger	$h_i = -4.0$ m
real	

c.

Characteristics	Dimensions
upright	$d_i = -3.0$ m
smaller	$h_i = +1.2$ m
virtual	

2.

Characteristics	Dimensions
inverted	$d_i = 24.2$ cm
larger	$h_i = -4.0$ cm
real	

3.

	Graphically	Algebraically
d_i	31 cm	30 cm
h_i	-11 cm	-10 cm
M	2.0 X	2.0 X

Characteristics
inverted
larger
real

4.

	Graphically	Algebraically
d_i	-2.1 cm	-1.8 cm
h_i	1.0 cm	1.2 cm
M	0.50 X	0.61 X

Characteristics
upright
smaller
virtual

7. a, b. It's a convex mirror, producing a virtual image.

8. 57.6 m

11. No. When the object is at the focal point the rays do not combine to form an image of the object

12. Convex mirror

5.6

1. violet - largest, red - smallest

2. The spreading out of light into its spectral colours

3. a.   ii
   b.   i
   c.   iii

5. a. Each wavelength has its own unique refractive index so they will be separated from each other when they refract.
   b. A high refractive index will help ensure that all light will reflect internally so it can better be directed out the top of the diamond

6. Hold a polarizer in front and rotate it. If the laptop light is polarized you should see the light change intensity as you rotate the polarizer through 180°.

8. The transverse wave nature of light allows it to be polarized; longitudinal waves cannot be polarized.

9. Since each wavelength of light has its own refractive index, each wavelength will focus at a slightly different point as the light undergoes dispersion.

5.7

3. infra-red

9. b. violet

12. a. refraction   b. diffraction

15. c. A third order image cannot be produced.

16. Gradually scientists started thinking of light as a wave rather than a particle

5.8

1. Radio waves reflect off the ionosphere. The ionosphere is created by the Sun. At night the ionosphere is higher than during the day allowing for radiowaves to travel further.

3 b. infra-red

5. It has its risks and benefits: privacy and safety issues must be considered.

6. It has its risks and benefits: privacy and safety issues must be considered.

9. The oxygen, nitrogen and dust particles in the air scatter blue wavelengths of light.

5.9

1. c   2. c   3. d   4. d   5. a

8. VIBGYOR (High frequency to low)

13. a. upright, larger, virtual   b. concave

14. a. upright, larger, virtual.

15. b. IR

6.1

6.

	Energy (J)	Energy (eV)
a.	1.80×10^{-18}	11.3
b.	4.52×10^{-19}	2.83
c.	3.20×10^{-19}	2.00
d.	8.96×10^{-19}	5.60

9.

red	green	violet
690	540	380
4.35×10^{14}	5.56×10^{14}	7.89×10^{14}
2.88×10^{-19}	3.69×10^{-19}	5.23×10^{-19}
1.80	2.30	3.27

14. a. Q   b. A   c. Q   d. Q   e. A

15. Reject the theory
     Modify the theory
     Redo experiment to double check the data

4. UV

5. UV

7. a. work function
   b. threshold frequency
   c. Planck's constant

12. The slopes are identical - all are Planck's constant

14. electrons

15. Only two points need to be plotted to get the expected straight line: the work function is the y-intercept and the threshold frequency is the x-intercept.

17.

	Work Function	Threshold Wavelength	Threshold Frequency
a.	8.00	249	1.21
b.	7.21	276	1.09
c.	5.77	345	0.870

18. Uranium has the smallest work function and therefore will require the least energy to eject an electron. This leaves more energy remaining for kinetic energy.

20. increase, greater

21.

25. The electron's stopping voltage is 3.1 V

26. a. ammeter   b. voltmeter

28. a. The flow of electric charge in a photoelectric cell.
    b. An electron ejected out of a metal (photoelectric metal) by an incoming photon that has enough energy to knock it out of its position.

29. The photoelectric effect can be better explained using the concept of light being a particle rather than light being a wave. A wave could release electrons by heating the metal, but not instantaneously; a collision between particles could be an instantaneous release if the energy of the particle is greater than the work required to release the electron.

30. It only deals with surface electrons as compared to those electrons located nearer to the nucleus of the photoelectric element.

32.

21. The photoelectric effect ejects one electron per incoming photon. The Compton Effect ejects one electron plus a lower energy X-ray. (Other comparisons may be done here).

22.

Scattered X-ray	Scattered Electron
2.40	1.12
2.40	2.40

24. Out of the page.

1.

1. d   2. c   3. b   4. d   5. c

7. UV

9. UV

10.

Graph	Interpretation
slope	Planck's constant
y-intercept	Work function
x-intercept	Threshold frequency

11. a. increases   b. decreases

7.1

5.

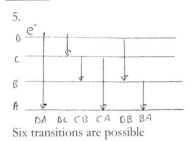

8. The alpha particles are knocking off electrons.

9. Maxwell's theory of electromagnetism predicts the failure of the planetary model because an <u>accelerating charge</u> should emit energy as EMR. If the electron is emitting energy, it should gradually undergo orbital decay and the atomic structure should collapse.

7.2

5.

Six transitions are possible

7. d. Visible

9.

	Transition	ΔE (eV)	λ (m)	Spectral region
a.	C-A	4.86	2.56×10^{-7}	UV
b.	C-B	0.22	5.65×10^{-6}	IR
c.	B-A	4.64	2.68×10^{-7}	UV

10. The energy that the gas atoms can emit to produce a bright line spectra are identical to the energies that can be absorbed to produce the dark line spectra because of the quantized energy levels.

11. An energy difference of 0.22 eV occurs for the transition from n = B to n = C.

12. Photons will be absorbed if they are the exact amount of energy – no more and no less. This is like coins in a vending machine. Electrons can transfer energy to an atom as long as they have enough energy; they keep the extra energy. This is like getting change at a store after a purchase.

13. Yes. Photons are emitted at all the wavelengths. However, there are fewer photons at the locations of the dark lines.

7.3

3. No. It would not be possible to diffract the student. The wavelength is too small.

7.4

2. C

3. Four complete wavelengths surround the nucleus.

4. probability

5. Atom "a" has the higher energy since it shows a wavelength with the greater frequency.

6. Destructive interference occurs between the allowed energy levels. Therefore, the wave cannot exist between orbits. This explains why electrons are allowed only certain orbits – constructive interference occurs at these certain orbits.

9. Depending on the circumstances or the experiment observed a photon must be thought of as being a particle or must be treated as a wave. This is also true for electrons. When electrons are sent one at a time through double slits, an interference pattern is produced.

10. Only certain proportions of a wave are allowed to produce standing waves. When the electron acts as a waves surrounding a nucleus it sets up a standing wave of only certain allowed proportions.

7.6

1. d   2. a   3. c   4. c   5. c

8. d. UV

10.

a.	C-A	4.78	260	UV
b.	C-B	0.14	8879	IR
c.	B-A	4.64	268	UV

8.1

1. Gamma radiation

2. As frequency increases, the ionization ability of the EMR increases.

3. The technician should
   i. limit the <u>time</u> working around the site.
   ii. wear protective <u>shielding</u> such as lead lined clothing.
   iii. maintain maximum possible <u>distance</u> from the waste. Using a shovel to pick up the waste would help

4. While more particles are being emitted in sample A, not enough information is supplied to properly asses the danger. The type of radiation is also an important factor to determine possible risks.

5. alpha radiation

6. a. all the large samples
   b. large z
   c. small x

8.2

1.

	Isotopic notation	Name	(Z)	(A)	(n)
a.	$^{2}_{1}H$	hydrogen-2	1	2	1
b.	$^{210}_{86}Rn$	radon-210	86	210	124
c.	$^{45}_{20}Ca$	calcium-45	20	45	25
d.	$^{38}_{19}K$	potassium-38	19	38	19
e.	$^{14}_{7}N$	nitrogen-14	7	14	7
f.	$^{230}_{89}Ac$	actinium-230	89	230	141
g.	$^{26}_{12}Mg$	magnesium-26	12	26	14
h.	$^{144}_{63}Eu$	europium-144	63	144	81
i.	$^{3}_{1}H$	hydrogen-3	1	3	2

0.3

1. a. $^{212}_{83}Bi$ b. $^{234}_{92}U$ c. $^{234}_{91}Pa, ^{0}_{-1}\beta$

   d. $^{55}_{24}Cr, ^{0-}_{0}\nu$ e. $^{15}_{9}F, ^{0}_{1}\beta + ^{0}_{0}\nu$

2. $^{14}_{6}C \dashrightarrow ^{14}_{7}N + ^{0}_{-1}\beta + ^{0-}_{0}\nu$

3. $^{145}_{61}Pm \dashrightarrow ^{141}_{59}Pr + ^{4}_{2}\alpha$

   prometheus-145   protactinium-141

4. Law of conservation of nucleons and the law of conservation of charge are used to predict the daughter product.

5. $^{131}_{53}I \dashrightarrow ^{131}_{54}Xe + ^{0}_{-1}\beta + ^{0-}_{0}\nu$

6. a. $^{261}_{105}Db \dashrightarrow ^{257}_{103}Lr + ^{4}_{2}\alpha$

   b. $^{257}_{103}Lr \dashrightarrow ^{253}_{101}Md + ^{4}_{2}\alpha + ^{0}_{0}\gamma$

7. $^{60}_{28}Ni \dashrightarrow ^{60}_{28}Ni + \gamma$

8. $^{14}_{7}N + ^{4}_{2}\alpha \dashrightarrow ^{17}_{8}O + ^{1}_{1}H^{+}$

9. $^{55}_{26}Fe + ^{0}_{-1}e \dashrightarrow ^{55}_{25}Mn + ^{0}_{0}\nu$

10. a. $^{0}_{-1}\beta + ^{0-}_{0}\nu$

    b. $^{0}_{-1}\beta + ^{55}_{25}Mn + ^{0-}_{0}\nu$

    c. $^{95}_{40}Zr \dashrightarrow + ^{0}_{0}\nu$

11. a. $^{230}_{90}Th \dashrightarrow ^{226}_{88}Ra + ^{4}_{2}\alpha$

    b. $^{234}_{92}U \dashrightarrow ^{230}_{90}Th + ^{4}_{2}\alpha$

    c. $^{210}_{83}Bi \dashrightarrow ^{210}_{84}Po + ^{0}_{-1}\beta + ^{0-}_{0}\nu$

3. a. $^{137}_{54}Xe \longrightarrow ^{137}_{55}Cs + ^{0}_{-1}\beta + ^{0}_{0}\overline{v}$

4. $^{204}_{81}Tl \longrightarrow ^{204}_{82}Pb + ^{0}_{-1}\beta + ^{0}_{0}\overline{v}$

5.

----- Daughter product

6. a. $^{60}_{27}Co \longrightarrow ^{60}_{28}Ni + ^{0}_{-1}\beta + ^{0}_{0}\gamma + ^{0}_{0}\overline{v}$

7. A   positron
   B   alpha particle
   C   gamma ray
   D   electron

8. $^{241}_{95}Am \longrightarrow ^{237}_{93}Np + ^{4}_{2}\alpha$

10. a. $^{58}_{26}Fe + ^{1}_{0}n \longrightarrow ^{59}_{26}Fe$

   b. $^{59}_{26}Fe \longrightarrow ^{59}_{27}Co + ^{0}_{-1}\beta + ^{0}_{0}\gamma + ^{0}_{0}\overline{v}$

12. proton

14. a. $^{1}_{0}n \longrightarrow ^{1}_{1}p + ^{0}_{-1}\beta + ^{0}_{0}\overline{v}$

17. a. $^{194}_{82}Pb \longrightarrow ^{194}_{83}Bi + ^{0}_{-1}\beta + ^{0}_{0}\overline{v}$

20. a. $^{14}_{6}C \longrightarrow ^{14}_{7}N + ^{0}_{-1}\beta + ^{0}_{0}\overline{v}$

21. directly, inversely

1. The general order is: phase change, chemical reaction, fission, and fusion (comparing equal masses).

2. $^{137}_{54}Xe + ^{97}_{38}Sr + 2^{1}_{0}n$

3. a. $^{239}_{94}Pu \longrightarrow ^{235}_{92}U + ^{4}_{2}\alpha + \gamma$

5. It may be a matter of opinion, but one response may be: While atomic energy has been used to kill many people, it is certain that nuclear medicine has saved many lives. The risk and benefits of nuclear power plants has always been highly debated.

5.

0.000 549	0.512
1.01	941
1.01	942

8. A single particle cannot be produced because the law of conservation of <u>momentum</u> would be violated.

11.

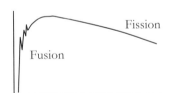

12. While the law of conservation of <u>momentum</u> could allow for the production of only one particle, the law of conservation of <u>charge</u> shows that if a charged particle is created an oppositely charged particle must also be created to conserve charge.

13. Orsted showed that magnetism and electricity are related (electromagnetism). Maxwell then unified electromagnetism with visible light and the entire EMR spectrum. Einstein's special theory of relativity related mass and energy showing that they were different manifestations of the same thing. The Grand Unification Theory is an attempt to relate gravity to the other physical phenomena. Einstein spent many years in this endevour.

1. Only particles c, d and f will produce a track in a bubble chamber since they are electrically charged.

2. a. A is electron's track, B is the proton's track. Small particles will tend to curve more than larger particles.
   b. Using a hand rule it is determined that the magnetic field is out of the page.

3. Using a hand rule it can be determined that the magnetic field is directed out of the page.

4 & 5. Since an <u>electron</u> is light, it should have a tight spiral. Since it is negative it should spiral in the same direction as the identified Compton electron.
The <u>positron</u> should curve in a tight spiral in the opposite direction as the electron. The electron and positron appear suddenly are most likely the result of pair production from a gamma ray that cannot be seen on a bubble chamber picture.
The <u>proton</u> should curve in the same direction as the positron since they both are positively charged. Since it is much larger, it has greater momentum and is likely to curve less

Track	Particle
A	electron
B	proton
C	electron
D	positron

6. It appears as if the positron and electron were created from a neutral particle, since no track exists when they appear. Since momentum must be conserved, the positron and electron track should look the same but be opposite each other. The two particles produced must have opposite charges to obey the law of conservation of charge.

7. Path A is created by an electron as a result of the Compton Effect.

8. Using the track produced by the Compton electron and a hand rule it can be determined that the magnetic field must be directed into the page.

9. A must be a Compton electron. D must be an electron created through pair production with a positron.

10. The tracks A, C and D appear to have similar but opposite curvature. Therefore they probably represent particles that have identical mass but opposite charge (e.g., electron and positron).

11. a. Track C curves the least and therefore probably represents the heaviest particle – the proton. Track A curves the most and therefore should represent the electron. Track B indicates a negative curvature but a mass greater than an electron and less than a proton. Therefore it must be the muon.
    b. A, B, C.

12. a. When the curvature is greater, the positron must be moving slower. Therefore, the positron moves from the bottom of the picture to the top.
    b. Using the third right hand rule the magnetic field is into the page

13. Particles with more energy are moving faster. As particles collide at greater speeds, more types of particles are produced; that atoms break into more pieces (especially to overcome the extremely strong forces inside the nucleus) allowing for a better understating of how the atom is put together.

14. Track C appears to be a Compton electron – it curves lots and does not appear to be associated with any other tracks.
    Tracks F and G have a curvature much like the Compton electron. Because of the symmetry between F and G they should have identical mass and opposite charge. Therefore F is an electron and G is a positron. They may be produced by a high-energy photon at the point their tracks appear (pair production).
    Particles A and B must be negatively charged since they curve in the same direction as the Compton electron. Since their curvature is much less than an electron's curvature they are heavier. The two negative particles that are heavier than an electron in order are: muon (A) and a kaon (B).
    Tracks D and E curve opposite the electron and therefore are positively charged. Track D curves less, therefore it is probably the heavier particle. The two positive particles in order of mass are: tau (D) and the proton (E).

14.

A	muon
B	kaon
C	electron
D	anti tau
E	proton
F	electron
G	positron

8.8

1. quarks

2. a. electromagnetic   b. gravitational
   c. strong nuclear   d. electromagnetic

3. Since they are so massive compared to an electron it is harder to get them travelling at a high enough velocity to overcome the electrostatic repulsive forces between them and the nucleus they are trying to collide with.

5. a. proton (uud)
   b. neutron (udd)
   c. antiproton (two anti-ups and one anti-down)

6. a. $^1_0n \ \text{------>} \ ^1_1p + ^0_{-1}\beta + ^0_0\bar{v}$

   b. dud ------> uud $+ ^0_{-1}\beta + ^0_0\bar{v}$

7. a. $^1_1p \ \text{------>} \ ^1_0n + ^0_1\beta + ^0_0v$

   b. uud ------> udd $+ ^0_1\beta + ^0_0v$

8.
   $$u \quad \bar{d}$$
   $$+\tfrac{2}{3} + \tfrac{+1}{3} = +1 \quad \therefore \quad \pi^+ \text{ is } u\bar{d}$$

9.
   $$u \quad \bar{u}$$
   $$+\tfrac{2}{3} - \tfrac{2}{3} = 0 \quad \text{or}$$

   $$d \quad \bar{d}$$
   $$-\tfrac{1}{3} + \tfrac{+1}{3} = 0 \quad \therefore \quad \pi^0 \text{ is } u\bar{u} \text{ or } d\bar{d}$$

10. $\pi^+ \ \text{------>} \ ^0_1\beta + ^0_0v$

11. +1

12. No. Matter-anitmatter combinations are not stable.

13. A neutral kaon may be composed of a strange and antidown quark or an antistrange and down Quark.

   $$S \quad \bar{d}$$
   $$-\tfrac{1}{3} + \tfrac{+1}{3} = 0$$

   $$\bar{S} \quad d$$
   $$+\tfrac{1}{3} + -\tfrac{1}{3} = 0$$

14. No. While the charges could be made to add appropriately, only first generation quark combinations are stable. Protons must be stable.

15.
   a.   Charge
   b.   Nucleons
   c.   Nucleons
   d.   Charge and Nucleons

16. The conservation of charge is obeyed, but the conservation of nucleon number is not.

17. $^1_0n \ \text{------>} \ ^1_1p + ^0_{-1}\beta + ^0_0\bar{v}$

   The decay follows the conservation of charge and nucleon number. Therefore, according to these two conservation laws the decay should be possible.

18. Standard Model cannot explain the mass problem, though a mass/energy conversion may be occurring. The Higgs boson may play a role.

19. The high energy is required in order to get past the atom's surrounding electrons and overcome any repulsive forces. An alpha particle is too big to easily give a high speed and its positive charge is repelled by the nucleus' positive charge making it difficult to hit the nucleus with enough energy.

8.9

1. The idea of the proton was proposed by many such as Rutherford as a means of balancing negative electrons.

2. beta-negative decay

4. Sudbury. It uses large amounts of heavy water buried 2 km underground.

5. a. $^{14}_6 C \ \text{-------->} \ ^{14}_7 N + ^0_{-1}\beta + ^0_0\bar{v}$

8. The net charge between the two nucleons continues to be +1 before, during and after the exchange.
   Energy may be converted into mass to create the pion for the exchange. The pion is created from energy within the proton and then can then be converted back to energy when it is received by the neutron.

9. Gluons and graviton (not yet detected).

$$^{188}_{74}W \longrightarrow \ ^{188}_{75}Re \ + \ ^{0}_{1}\beta \ + \ ^{0}_{0}\overline{V}$$

1. c   2. a   3. c   4. c   5. c

6.

	Isotopic notation	Name	(Z)	(A)	(n)
a.	$^{234}_{92}U$	uranium-234	92	234	142
b.	$^{234}_{90}Th$	thorium-234	90	234	144
c.	$^{12}_{6}C$	carbon-12	6	12	6
d.	$^{16}_{8}O$	oxygen-16	8	16	8

7. a) $^{238}_{92}U \longrightarrow \ ^{234}_{90}Th \ + \ ^{4}_{2}\alpha$

b) $^{218}_{84}Po \longrightarrow \ ^{214}_{82}Pb \ + \ ^{4}_{2}\alpha$

c) $^{210}_{82}Pb \longrightarrow \ ^{210}_{83}Bi \ + \ ^{0}_{1}\beta \ + \ ^{0}_{0}\overline{V}$

d) $^{214}_{82}Pb \longrightarrow \ ^{214}_{83}Bi \ + \ ^{0}_{1}\beta \ + \ ^{0}_{0}\overline{V}$

8. A gamma photon is considered pure energy (as is all EMR) and therefore will have no mass. However, it can have mass equivalence according to Einstein's $E = mc^2$.

9. Deuterium & hydrogen cannot undergo an alpha decay. To emit an alpha particle would not follow the law of conservation of nucleons.

10. a.

$$^{188}_{74}W \longrightarrow \ ^{188}_{75}Re \ + \ ^{0}_{1}\beta \ + \ ^{0}_{0}\overline{V}$$

11.

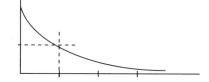

14. A must be a proton. B must be a positron created through pair production with an electron C.

15. a. $^{1}_{1}p$ + e^- -------> $^{1}_{0}n$

b.   uud   + e^- ------->   udd

Appendix B – Equations

Kinematics

$$\vec{v} = \frac{\vec{d}}{t} \qquad \vec{d} = \left(\frac{\vec{v}_f + \vec{v}_i}{2}\right)t$$

$$\vec{a} = \frac{\vec{v}_f - \vec{v}_i}{t} \qquad \vec{v}_f^2 = \vec{v}_i^2 + 2\vec{a}\vec{d}$$

$$\vec{d} = \vec{v}_i t + \tfrac{1}{2}\vec{a}t^2 \quad v = \frac{2\pi r}{T} \quad a_c = \frac{v^2}{r}$$

Dynamics

$$\vec{a} = \frac{\vec{F}_{net}}{m} \qquad \vec{g} = \frac{\vec{F}_g}{m}$$

$$\vec{F}_f = \mu \vec{F}_N \qquad a_c = \frac{4\pi^2 r}{T^2}$$

$$\vec{F} = -k\vec{x} \qquad F_g = \frac{Gm_1 m_2}{r^2} \qquad g = \frac{Gm_1}{r^2}$$

Momentum & Energy

$$\vec{p} = m\vec{v} \qquad \vec{F}\Delta t = m\Delta\vec{v}$$

$$E_p = mgh \qquad E_k = \frac{1}{2}mv^2 \qquad W = Fd$$

$$\text{P} = \frac{\text{W}}{\text{t}} \qquad E_p = \frac{1}{2}kx^2 \qquad W = \Delta E$$

$$W = Fd\cos\theta$$

Waves & Light

$$T = \frac{1}{f} \qquad T = 2\pi\sqrt{\frac{m}{k}} \qquad T = 2\pi\sqrt{\frac{\ell}{g}}$$

$$v = f\lambda \qquad f = f_s\left(\frac{v}{v \pm v_s}\right) \qquad \frac{1}{f} = \frac{1}{d_o} + \frac{1}{d_i}$$

$$\lambda = \frac{dx}{n\ell} \qquad \lambda = \frac{d\sin\theta}{n} \qquad m = \frac{h_i}{h_o} = \frac{-d_i}{d_o}$$

$$\frac{\sin\theta_1}{\sin\theta_2} = \frac{n_2}{n_1} = \frac{v_1}{v_2} = \frac{\lambda_1}{\lambda_2}$$

Quantum & Nuclear Physics

$$\Delta E = \Delta mc^2 \qquad p = \frac{h}{\lambda} \qquad E = pc$$

$$\Delta\lambda = \frac{h}{mc}\left(1 - \cos\theta\right)$$

Atomic Physics

$$E = hf \qquad E = \frac{hc}{\lambda}$$

$$W = hf_o \qquad E_{k_{max}} = qV_{stop}$$

$$N = N_o \left(\tfrac{1}{2}\right)^n$$

Electricity & Magnetism

$$F_e = \frac{kq_1 q_2}{r^2} \qquad \vec{E} = \frac{\vec{F}_e}{q} \qquad |E| = \frac{kq_1}{r^2}$$

$$\Delta V = \frac{\Delta E}{q} \qquad |E| = \frac{\Delta V}{\Delta d} \qquad F_m = I\ell_\perp B$$

$$F_m = qv_\perp B \qquad I = \frac{q}{t}$$

Appendix C – Data

Constants

Earth's surface Gravitational Acceleration	$g = 9.81$ m/s^2 or 9.81 N/kg
Universal Gravitational Constant	$G = 6.67$ x 10^{-11} N•m^2/kg^2
Speed of Light in Vacuum	$c = 3.00$ x 10^8 m/s
Elementary Charge	$e = 1.60$ x 10^{-19} C
Coulomb's Constant	$k = 8.99$ x 10^9 N•m^2/C^2
Electron Volt	$1\ eV = 1.60$ x 10^{-19} J
Planck's Constant	$h = 6.63$ x 10^{-34} J•s or 4.14 x 10^{-15} eV•s
Atomic Mass Unit	$u = 1.66$ x 10^{-27} kg

Metric Prefixes

tera	T	10^{12}	centi	c	10^{-2}
giga	G	10^{9}	milli	m	10^{-3}
mega	M	10^{6}	micro	μ	10^{-6}
kilo	k	10^{3}	nano	n	10^{-9}

Trigonometry & Geometry

$$\sin \theta = \frac{opposite}{hypotenuse}$$

$$\cos \theta = \frac{adjacent}{hypotenuse}$$

$$\tan \theta = \frac{opposite}{adjacent} = \frac{\sin \theta}{\cos \theta}$$

$$\frac{a}{\sin A} = \frac{b}{\sin B} = \frac{c}{\sin C}$$

$$c^2 = a^2 + b^2$$

$$c^2 = a^2 + b^2 - 2ab \cos C$$

$$slope = m = \frac{\Delta y}{\Delta x}$$

Area

$rectangle = lw$

$triangle = \frac{1}{2}bh$

$circle = \pi r^2$

Circumference

$circle = 2\pi r$

Particles

	Charge	Mass
Alpha	$+2e$	6.65 x 10^{-27} kg
Electron	$-1e$	9.11 x 10^{-31} kg
Proton	$+1e$	1.67 x 10^{-27} kg
Neutron	0	1.67 x 10^{-27} kg

First Generation Fermions

	Charge	Mass
Electron	$-1e$	0.511 MeV/c^2
Positron	$+1e$	0.511 MeV/c^2
antineutrino	0	<50 MeV/c^2
neutrino	0	<50 MeV/c^2
Up quark	$+\frac{2}{3}e$	~ 5 MeV/c^2
antiUp quark	$-\frac{2}{3}e$	~ 5 MeV/c^2
Down quark	$-\frac{1}{3}e$	~ 10 MeV/c^2
antiDown quark	$+\frac{1}{3}e$	~ 10 MeV/c^2

Indices of Refraction (n)

Air	1.00
Diamond	2.42
Water	1.33
Ice	1.31
Crown glass	1.52
Ethanol	1.36
Quartz	1.54
Flint glass	1.60
Vacuum	1.00

Appendix D - Physics Principles

The following are the main physics principles studied in Physics 30.

0 Uniform Motion ($F_{net} = 0$)

1 Accelerated motion ($F_{net} \neq 0$)

2 Uniform circular motion (F_{net} is radial inward)

3 Work-energy theorem

4 Conservation of momentum

5 Conservation of energy

6 Conservation of mass-energy

7 Conservation of charge

8 Conservation of nucleons

9 Wave-particle duality

These principles are to be used as a starting point or framework for questions that ask for an explanation and for questions where a mathematical relationship is to be derived.